MISCELLANIES

Oliver Goldsmith.

MISCELLANIES

BY

AUSTIN DOBSON

*Ipsâ varietate tentamus efficere, ut alia
aliis, quædam fortasse omnibus placean*
PLINY TO PATERNUS

NEW YORK

DODD, MEAD AND COMPANY

1898

Republished, 1970
Scholarly Press, 22929 Industrial Drive East
St. Clair Shores, Michigan 48080

Standard Book Number 403-00250-8
Library of Congress Catalog Card Number: 75-108473

CONTENTS.

——————◆——————

MISCELLANIES.

————•————

GOLDSMITH'S POEMS AND PLAYS.

THIRTY years of taking-in; fifteen years
of giving-out; — that, in brief, is Oliver
Goldsmith's story. When, in 1758, his failure
to pass at Surgeons' Hall finally threw him on
letters for a living, the thirty years were finished,
and the fifteen years had been begun. What
was to come he knew not; but, from his bare-
walled lodging in Green-Arbour-Court, he could
at least look back upon a sufficiently diversified
past. He had been an idle, orchard-robbing
schoolboy; a tuneful but intractable sizar of
Trinity; a lounging, loitering, fair-haunting,
flute-playing Irish " buckeen." He had knocked
at the doors of both Law and Divinity, and
crossed the threshold of neither. He had
set out for London and stopped at Dublin; he
had started for America and arrived at Cork.
He had been many things: a medical student,
a strolling musician, an apothecary, a corrector

of the press, an usher at a Peckham " academy."
Judged by ordinary standards, he had wantonly
wasted his time. And yet, as things fell out, it
is doubtful whether his parti-coloured experiences were not of more service to him than any
he could have obtained if his progress had been
less erratic. Had he fulfilled the modest expectations of his family, he would probably have
remained a simple curate in Westmeath, eking
out his " forty pounds a year " by farming a field
or two, migrating contentedly at the fitting season from the " blue bed to the brown," and (it
may be) subsisting vaguely as a local poet upon
the tradition of some youthful couplets to a
pretty cousin, who had married a richer man.
As it was, if he could not be said to have " seen
life steadily, and seen it whole," he had, at all
events, inspected it pretty closely in parts ; and,
at a time when he was most impressible, had preserved the impress of many things, which, in his
turn, he was to re-impress upon his writings.
" No man " — says one of his biographers [1] —
" ever put so much of himself into his books as
Goldsmith." To his last hour he was drawing
upon the thoughts and reviving the memories of
that " unhallowed time" when, to all appearance, he was hopelessly squandering his oppor-

[1] Forster's *Life*, Bk. ii., ch. vi.

tunities. To do as Goldsmith did would
scarcely enable a man to write a " Vicar of
Wakefield " or a " Deserted Village," certainly his practice cannot be preached with
safety " to those that eddy round and round."
But viewing his entire career, it is difficult not
to see how one part seems to have been an indispensable preparation for the other, and to
marvel once more (with the philosopher Square)
at " the eternal Fitness of Things."

The events of Goldsmith's life have been
too often narrated to need repetition, and we
shall not resort to the well-worn device of repeating them in order to say so. But the progress of time, advancing some things and effacing
others, lends a fresh aspect even to masterpieces ; for which reason it is always possible to
speak of a writer's work. In this instance we
shall restrict ourselves to Goldsmith's Poems
and Plays. And, with regard to both, what
strikes one first is the extreme tardiness of that
late blossoming upon which Johnson commented.
When a man succeeds as Goldsmith succeeded,
friends and critics speedily discover that he had
shown signs of excellence even from his boyish
years. But setting aside those half-mythical
ballads for the Dublin street-singers, and some

doubtful verses for Jane Contarine, there is no definite evidence that, from a doggerel couplet in his childhood to an epigram not much better than doggerel composed when he was five and twenty, he had written a line of verse of the slightest importance ; and even five years later, although he refers to himself in a private letter as a " poet," it must have been solely upon the strength of the unpublished fragment of " The Traveller," which, in the interval, he had sent to his brother Henry from abroad. It is even more remarkable that — although so skilful a corre- spondent must have been fully sensible of his gifts — until under the pressure of circum- stances he drifted into literature, the craft of letters seems never to have been his ambition. He thinks of turning lawyer, physician, clergy- man, — anything but author ; and when at last he engages in that profession, it is to free himself from a scholastic slavery which he seems to have always regarded with peculiar bitterness, yet to which, after a first unsatisfactory trial of what was to be his true vocation, he unhesitatingly returned. If he went back anew to the pen, it was only to enable him to escape from it more effectually, and he was prepared to go as far as Coromandel. But Literature, " *toute entière à sa proie attachée,*" refused to relinquish him ; and, although he continued to make spasmodic efforts to extricate himself from the toils, detained him to the day of his death.

If there is no evidence that he had written much when he entered upon what has been called his second period, he had not the less formed his opinions on many literary questions. Much of the matter of the " Polite Learning " is plainly manufactured *ad hoc;* but in its references to authorship and criticism, there is an individual note which is absent elsewhere ; and when he speaks of the tyranny of publishers, the petty standards of criticism, and the forlorn and precarious existence of the hapless writer for bread, he is evidently reproducing a condition of things with which he had become familiar during his brief bondage on the " Monthly Review." As to his personal views on poetry in particular, it is easy to collect them from this and later utterances. Against blank verse he objects from the first, as suited only to the sublimest themes, — which is a polite way of shelving it altogether ; while in favour of rhyme he alleges — perhaps borrowing his illustration from Montaigne — that the very restriction stimulates the fancy, as a fountain plays highest when the aperture is diminished. Blank verse, too (he asserts), imports into poetry a " disgusting solemnity of

manner" which is fatal to "agreeable trifling,"
—an objection intimately connected with the
feeling which afterwards made him the champion
on the stage of character and humour. Among
the poets who were his contemporaries and immediate predecessors, his likes and dislikes were
strong. He fretted at the fashion which Gray's
"Elegy" set in poetry; he considered it a fine
poem, but "overloaded with epithet," and he
deplored the remoteness and want of emotion
which distinguished the Pindaric Odes. Yet
from many indications in his own writings he
seems to have genuinely appreciated the work
of Collins. Churchill, and Churchill's satire, he
detested. With Young he had some personal
acquaintance, and had evidently read his "Night
Thoughts" with attention. Of the poets of the
last age, he admired Dryden, Pope, and Gay,
but more than any of these, if imitation is to be
regarded as the surest proof of sympathy, Prior,
Addison, and Swift. By his inclinations and his
training, indeed, he belonged to this school.
But he was in advance of it in thinking that
poetry, however didactic after the fashion of his
own day, should be simple in its utterance and
directed at the many rather than at the few.
This is what he meant when, from the critical
elevation of Griffiths' back parlour, he recom-

mended Gray to take the advice of Isocrates,
and " study the people." If, with these ideas, he
had been able to divest himself of the "warbling
groves" and " finny deeps" of the Popesque
vocabulary (of much of the more "mechanic
art" of that supreme artificer he *did* successfully
divest himself), it would have needed but little
to make him a prominent pioneer of the new
school which was coming with Cowper. As it
is, his poetical attitude is a little that intermediate one of Longfellow's maiden, —

> "Standing, with reluctant feet,
>   Where the brook and river meet."

Most of his minor and earlier pieces are
imitative. In " A New Simile," and " The
Logicians Refuted" (if that be his) Swift is his
acknowledged model ; in " The Double Transformation" it is Prior, modified by certain
theories personal to himself. He was evidently
well acquainted with collections such as the
" Ménagiana," and with the French minor poets
of the eighteenth century, many of which latter
were among his books at his death. These he
had carefully studied, probably during his continental wanderings, and from them he derives,
like Prior, something of his grace and metrical
buoyancy. The " Elegy on the Death of a

Mad Dog," and "Madam Blaize," are both
more or less constructed on the old French
popular song of the hero of Pavia, Jacques de
Chabannes, Seigneur de la Palice (sometimes
Galisse), with, in the case of the former, a tag
from an epigram by Voltaire, the original of
which is in the Greek Anthology, though Voltaire simply "conveyed" his version from an
anonymous French predecessor. Similarly the
lively stanzas "To Iris in Bow Street," the
lines to Myra, the quatrain called "A South
American Ode," and that "On a Beautiful
Youth struck blind with Lightning," are all
confessed or unconfessed translations. If Goldsmith had lived to collect his own works, it is
possible that he would have announced the
source of his inspiration in these instances as
well as in one or two other cases, — the epitaph
on Ned Purdon, for example, — where it has
been reserved to his editors to discover his obligations. On the other hand, he might have
contended, with perfect justice, that whatever
the source of his ideas, he had made them his
own when he got them ; and certainly in lilt
and lightness, the lines "To Iris" are infinitely
superior to those of La Monnoye on which they
are based. But even a fervent admirer may
admit that, dwelling as he did in this very vitre-

ous palace of Gallic adaptation, one does not
expect to find him throwing stones at Prior
for borrowing from the French, or commenting
solemnly in the Life of Parnell upon the heinous-
ness of plagiarism. " It was the fashion," he
says, " with the wits of the last age, to conceal
the places from whence they took their hints
or their subjects. A trifling acknowledgment
would have made that lawful prize which may
now be considered as plunder." He might judiciously have added to this latter sentence the
quotation which he struck out of the second
issue of the " Polite Learning," — " *Haud
inexpertus loquor.*"

Of his longer pieces, " The Traveller " was
apparently suggested to him by Addison's " Letter from Italy to Lord Halifax," a poem to
which, in his preliminary notes to the " Beauties
of English Poesy," he gives significant praise.
" There is in it," he says, " a strain of political
thinking that was, at that time, new in our
country." He obviously intended that " The
Traveller " should be admired for the same reason ; and both in that poem and its successor,
" The Deserted Village," he lays stress upon the
political import of his work. The one, we are told,
is to illustrate the position that the happiness of
the subject is independent of the goodness of the

sovereign ; the other, to deplore the increase of luxury, and the miseries of depopulation. But, as a crowd of commentators have pointed out, it is hazardous for a poet to meddle with " political thinking," however much, under George the Second, it may have been needful to proclaim a serious purpose. If Goldsmith had depended solely upon the professedly didactic part of his attempt, his work would be as dead as " Freedom," or " Sympathy," or any other of Dodsley's forgotten *quartos.* Fortunately he did more than this. Sensibly or insensibly, he suffused his work with that philanthropy which is " not learned by the royal road of tracts and platform speeches and monthly magazines," but by personal commerce with poverty and sorrow ; and he made his appeal to that clinging love of country, of old association, of " home-bred happiness," of innocent pleasure, which, with Englishmen, is never made in vain. Employing the couplet of Pope and Johnson, he has added to his measure a suavity that belonged to neither ; but the beauty of his humanity and the tender melancholy of his wistful retrospect hold us more strongly and securely than the studious finish of his style.

" *Vingt fois sur le métier remettez votre ouvrage,*" said the arch-critic whose name, according to Keats, the school of Pope displayed upon their "decrepit standard." Even in "The Traveller" and "The Deserted Village," there are indications of over-labour; but in a poem which comes between them — the once famous "Edwin and Angelina" — Goldsmith certainly carried out Boileau's maxim to the full. The first privately printed version differs considerably from that in the first edition of the "Vicar;" this again is altered in the fourth; and there are other variations in the piece as printed in the "Poems for Young Ladies." "As to my 'Hermit,'" said the poet complacently, "that poem, Cradock, cannot be amended," — and undoubtedly it has been skilfully wrought. But it is impossible to look upon it now with the unpurged eyes of those upon whom the "Reliques of Ancient Poetry" had but recently dawned, still less to endorse the verdict of Sir John Hawkins that "it is one of the finest poems of the lyric kind that our language has to boast of." Its over-soft prettiness is too much that of the chromo-lithograph, or the Parian bust (the porcelain, not the marble), and its "beautiful simplicity" is in parts perilously close upon that inanity which Johnson, whose sturdy good sense not even friendship could silence, declared to be the characteristic of much of Percy's collection. It is instructive as a study of poetical progress to contrast it with a ballad of our own day in the same measure, — the " Talking Oak " of Tennyson.

The remaining poems of Goldsmith, excluding the " Captivity," and the admittedly occasional " Threnodia Augustalis," are not open to the charge of fictitious simplicity, or of that hyper-elaboration which, in the words of the poet just mentioned, makes for the " ripe and rotten." The gallery of kit-cats in " Retaliation," and the delightful *bonhomie* of " The Haunch of Veni-son," need no commendation.   In kindly humour and not unkindly satire Goldsmith was at his best, and the imperishable portraits of Burke and Garrick and Reynolds, and the inimitable dinner at which Lord Clare's pasty was *not*, are as well known as any of the stock passages of " The Deserted Village " or " The Traveller " though they have never been babbled " *in extremis vicis* " by successive generations of schoolboys.   It is usually said, probably with truth, that in these poems and the delightful " Letter to Mrs. Bun-bury," Goldsmith's metre was suggested by the cantering anapests of the " New Bath Guide," and it is to be observed that " Little Comedy's " invitation is to the same favourite tune.   But it is also the fact that a line of the once popular lyric of " Ally Croaker," —

"Too dull for a wit, too grave for a joker," —

has a kind of echo in the —

"Too nice for a statesman, too proud for a wit" —

of Burke's portrait in "Retaliation." What is
still more remarkable is that Gray's "Sketch of
his own Character," the resemblance of which
to Goldsmith has been pointed out by his editors,
begins, —

"Too poor for a bribe, and too proud to importune."

Whether Goldsmith was thinking of Anstey or
"Ally Croaker," it is at least worthy of passing
notice that an Irish song of no particular literary
merit should have succeeded in haunting the
two foremost poets of their day.

Poetry brought Goldsmith fame, but money
only indirectly. Those Saturnian days of the
subscription-edition, when Pope and Gay and
Prior counted their gains by thousands, were
over and gone. He had arrived, it has been
truly said, too late for the Patron, and too early
for the Public. Of his lighter pieces, the best
were posthumous; the rest were either paid for at
hack prices or not at all. For "The Deserted
Village" Griffin gave him a hundred guineas, a
sum so unexampled as to have prompted the
pleasant legend that he returned it. For "The
Traveller" the only payment that can be defi-

nitely traced is £21. " I cannot afford to court the draggle-tail muses," he said laughingly to Lord Lisburn ; " they would let me starve ; but by my other labours I can make shift to eat, and drink, and have good clothes." It was in his " other labours " that his poems helped him. The booksellers, who would not or could not remunerate him adequately for delayed production and minute revision, were willing enough to secure the sanction of his name for humbler journey-work. If he was ill-paid for " The Traveller," he was not ill-paid for the " Beauties of English Poesy " or the " History of Animated Nature."

Yet notwithstanding his ready pen, and his skill as a compiler, his life was a treadmill. " While you are nibbling about elegant phrases, I am obliged to write half a volume," he told his friend Cradock ; and it was but natural that he should desire to escape into walks where he might accomplish something " for his own hand," by which, at the same time, he might exist. Fiction he had already essayed. Nearly two years before " The Traveller " appeared, he had written a story about the length of " Joseph Andrews," for which he had received little more than a third of the sum paid by Andrew Millar to Fielding for his burlesque of Richardson's " Pamela." But obscure circumstances delayed

the publication of the " Vicar of Wakefield " for
four years, and when at last it was issued, its
first burst of success — a success, as far as can
be ascertained, productive of no further profit
to its author — was followed by a long period
during which the sales were languid and uncertain. There remained the stage, with its two-
fold allurement of fame and fortune, both payable
at sight, added to which it was always possible
that a popular play, in those days when plays
were bought to read, might find a brisk market
in pamphlet form. The prospect was a tempting
one, and it is scarcely surprising that Goldsmith,
weary of the " dry drudgery at the desk's dead
wood," and conscious of better things within
him, should engage in that most tantalising of
all enterprises, the pursuit of dramatic success.

For acting and actors he had always shown a
decided partiality.[1] Vague stories, based, in all
probability, upon the references to strolling

[1] This is not inconsistent with the splenetic utterances
in the letters to Daniel Hodson, first made public in the
" Great Writers " life of Goldsmith, where he speaks
of the stage as "an abominable resource which neither
became a man of honour, nor a man of sense." Those
letters were written when the production of " The
Good-Natur'd Man" had supplied him with abundant
practical evidence of the vexations and difficulties of
theatrical ambition.

players in his writings, hinted that he himself had once worn the comic sock as " Scrub " in " The Beaux' Stratagem ; " and it is clear that soon after he arrived in England, he had completed a tragedy, for he read it in manuscript to a friend. That he had been besides an acute and observant playgoer is plain from his excellent account in " The Bee " of Mademoiselle Clairon, whom he had seen at Paris, and from his sensible notes in the same periodical on " gestic lore " as exhibited on the English stage. In his " Polite Learning in Europe," he had followed up Ralph's " Case of Authors by Profession," by protesting against the despotism of managers, and the unenlightened but economical policy of producing only the works of deceased playwrights ; and he was equally opposed to the growing tendency on the part of the public — a tendency dating from Richardson and the French *comédie larmoyante* — to substitute sham sensibility and superficial refinement for that humourous delineation of manners which, with all their errors of morality and taste, had been the chief aim of Congreve and his contemporaries. To the fact that what was now known as " genteel comedy " had almost wholly supplanted this elder and better manner, must be attributed his deferred entry upon a field so obviously adapted

to his gifts.   But when, in 1766, the "Clandes-
tine Marriage" of Garrick and Colman, with its
evergreen "Lord Ogleby," seemed to herald a
return to the side of laughter as opposed to that
of tears, he took heart of grace, and, calling to
mind something of the old inconsiderate benevolence which had been the Goldsmith family-
failing, set about his first comedy, "The Good-
Natur'd Man."

Even without experiment, no one could have
known better than Goldsmith upon what a sea
of troubles he had embarked.   Those obstacles
which, more than thirty years before, had been
so graphically described in Fielding's "Pas-
quin," — which Goldsmith himself had indicated
with equal accuracy in his earliest book, — still
lay in the way of all dramatic purpose, and he
was to avoid none of them.   When he submitted
his completed work to Garrick, the all-powerful
actor, who liked neither piece nor author, blew
hot and cold so long that Goldsmith at last, in
despair, transferred it to Colman.   But, as if
fate was inexorable, Colman, after accepting it
effusively, also grew dilatory, and ultimately
entered into a tacit league with Garrick not to
produce it at Covent Garden until his former
rival had brought out at Drury Lane a comedy
by Goldsmith's countryman, Hugh Kelly, a sen-

timentalist of the first water. Upon the heels
of the enthusiastic reception which Garrick's
administrative tact secured for the superfine en-
tanglements of " False Delicacy," came limping
"The Good-Natur'd Man" of Goldsmith, wet-
blanketed beforehand by a sombre prologue
from Johnson. No first appearance could have
been less favourable. Until it was finally saved
in the fourth act by the excellent art of Shuter
as " Croaker," its fate hung trembling in the
balance, and even then one of its scenes — not
afterwards reckoned the worst — had to be withdrawn in deference to the delicate scruples of an
audience which could not suffer such inferior
beings as bailiffs to come between the wind and
its gentility. Yet, in spite of all these disad-
vantages, "The Good-Natur'd Man" obtained
a hearing, besides bringing its author about five
hundred pounds, a sum far larger than anything
he had ever made by poetry or fiction.

That the superior success of " False Delicacy," with its mincing morality and jumble of
inadequate motives, was wholly temporary and
accidental is evident from the fact that, to use a
felicitous phrase, it has now to be disinterred in
order to be discussed. But, notwithstanding
one's instinctive sympathy for Goldsmith in his
struggles with the managers, it is not equally

clear that everything considered, " The Good-
Natur'd Man " was unfairly treated by the public. Because Kelly's play was praised too much,
it by no means follows that Goldsmith's play was
praised too little. With all the advantage of its
author's reputation, it has never since passed
into the *répertoire*, and, if it had something of
the freshness of a first effort, it had also its in-
experience. The chief character, Honeywood,
— the weak and amiable "good-natur'd man," —
never stands very firmly on his feet, and the first
actor of the part, Garrick's promising young
rival, Powell, failed, or disdained to make it a
stage success. On the other hand, " Croaker,"
an admitted elaboration of Johnson's sketch of
" Suspirius " in the *Rambler*, is a first-rate comic
creation, and the charlatan " Lofty," a sort of
" Beau-Tibbs-above-Stairs," is almost as good.
But, as Garrick's keen eye saw, to have a second male figure of greater importance than the
central personage was a serious error of judgment, added to which neither " Miss Richland "
nor " Mrs. Croaker " ever establishes any hold
upon the audience. Last of all, the plot, such
as it is, cannot be described as either particularly
ingenious or particularly novel. In another
way the merit of the piece is, however, incontestable. It is written with all the perspicuous

grace of Goldsmith's easy pen, and, in the
absence of stage-craft, sparkles with neat and
effective epigrams. One of these may be mentioned as illustrating the writer's curious (perhaps unconscious) habit of repeating ideas which
had pleased him. He had quoted in his "Polite
Learning" the exquisitely rhythmical close of
Sir William Temple's prose essay on "Poetry,"
and in "The Bee" it still seems to haunt him.
In "The Good-Natur'd Man" he has absorbed
it altogether, for he places it, without inverted
commas, in the lips of Croaker.[1]

But if its lack of constructive power and its
errors of conception make it impossible to regard "The Good-Natur'd Man" as a substantial
gain to humourous drama, it was undoubtedly a
formidable attack upon that "mawkish drab of
spurious breed," Sentimental Comedy, and its
success was amply sufficient to justify a second
trial. That Goldsmith did not forthwith make
this renewed effort must be attributed partly to
the recollection of his difficulties in getting his
first play produced, partly to the fact that, his dramatic gains exhausted, he was almost immediately
involved in a sequence of laborious taskwork.

---

[1] In the same way he annexes, both in "The Hermit"
and "The Citizen of the World," a quotation from
Young.

Still, he had never abandoned his ambition to re-
store humour and character to the stage ; and as
time went on, the sense of his past discouragements grew fainter, while the success of "The
Deserted Village" increased his importance as
an author. Sentimentalism, in the meantime,
had still a majority. Kelly, it is true, was now
no longer to be feared. His sudden good fortune had swept him into the ranks of the party-
writers, with the result that the damning of his
next play, "A Word to the Wise," had been
exaggerated into a political necessity. But the
school which he represented had been recruited
by a much abler man, Richard Cumberland, and
it was probably the favourable reception of
Cumberland's "West Indian" that stimulated
Goldsmith into striking one more blow for legitimate comedy. At all events, in the autumn of
the year in which "The West Indian" was produced, he is hard at work in the lanes at Hen-
don and Edgware, "studying jests with a most
tragical countenance" for a successor to "The
Good-Natur'd Man."

To the modern spectator of "She Stoops to
Conquer," with its unflagging humour and bustling action, it must seem almost inconceivable
that its stage qualities can ever have been questioned. Yet questioned they undoubtedly were,

and Goldsmith was spared none of his former
humiliations. Even from the outset, all was
against him. His difference with Garrick had
long been adjusted, and the Drury Lane manager would now probably have accepted a new
play from his pen, especially as that astute observer had already detected signs of a reaction
in the public taste. But Goldsmith was morally
bound to Colman and Covent Garden; and
Colman, in whose hands he placed his manuscript, proved even more disheartening and un-
manageable than Garrick had been in the past.
Before he had come to his decision, the close of
1772 had arrived. Early in the following year,
under the irritation of suspense and suggested
amendments combined, Goldsmith hastily transferred his proposal to Garrick; but, by Johnson's advice, as hastily withdrew it. Only by
the express interposition of Johnson was Colman at last induced to make a distinct promise
to bring out the play at a specific date. To believe in it, he could not be persuaded, and his
contagious anticipations of its failure passed insensibly to the actors, who, one after another,
shuffled out of their parts. Even over the epi-
logue there were vexatious disputes, and when
at last, in March, 1773, " She Stoops to Conquer " was performed, its leading actor had pre-

viously held no more exalted position than that
of ground-harlequin, while one of its most prominent characters had simply been a post-boy in
"The Good-Natur'd Man." But once fairly
upon the boards neither lukewarm actors nor an
adverse manager had any further influence over
it, and the doubts of every one vanished in the
uninterrupted applause of the audience. When,
a few days later, it was printed with a brief and
grateful dedication to its best friend, Johnson,
the world already knew with certainty that a
fresh masterpiece had been added to the roll of
English Dramatic Literature, and that " genteel
comedy " had received a decisive blow.

The effect of this blow, it must be admitted,
had been aided not a little by the appearance,
only a week or two earlier, of Foote's clever
puppet-show of " The Handsome Housemaid ;
or, Piety in Pattens," which was openly directed at Kelly and his following. But ridicule
by itself, without some sample of a worthier
substitute, could not have sufficed to displace a
persistent fashion. This timely antidote " She
Stoops to Conquer," in the most unmistakable
way, afforded. From end to end of the piece
there is not a sickly or a maudlin word. Even
Sheridan, writing " The Rivals " two years later,
thought it politic to insert " Faulkland " and

" Julia " for the benefit of the sentimentalists.
Goldsmith made no such concession, and his
wholesome, hearty merriment put to flight the
Comedy of Tears, — even as the Coquecigrues
vanished before the large-lunged laugh of Pan-
tagruel. If, as Johnson feared, the plot bor-
dered slightly upon farce — and of what good
comedy may this not be said ? — at least it can
be urged that its most farcical incident, the mis-
taking of a gentleman's house for an inn, had
really happened, since it had happened to the
writer himself. But the superfine objections of
Walpole and his friends are now ancient history,
— history so ancient that it is scarcely credited,
while Goldsmith's manly assertion (after Fielding) of the author's right " to stoop among the
low to copy nature," has been ratified by successive generations of novelists and playwrights.
What is beyond dispute is the healthy atmosphere, the skilful setting, the lasting freshness
and fidelity to human nature of the persons of
his drama. Not content with the finished portraits of the Hardcastles (a Vicar and Mrs.
Primrose promoted to the squirearchy), — not
content with the incomparable and unapproach-
able Tony, the author has managed to make
attractive what is too often insipid, his heroines
and their lovers. Miss Hardcastle and Miss

Neville are not only charming young women, but charming characters, while Marlow and Hastings are much more than stage young men. And let it be remembered — It cannot be too often remembered — that in returning to those Farquhars and Vanbrughs "of the last age," who differed so widely from the Kellys and Cumberlands of his own, Goldsmith has brought back no taint of their baser part. Depending solely for its avowed intention to "make an audience merry," upon the simple development of its humourous incident, his play (wonderful to relate!) attains its end without resorting to impure suggestion or equivocal intrigue. Indeed, there is but one married woman in the piece, and she traverses it without a stain upon her character.

"She Stoops to Conquer" is Goldsmith's last dramatic work, for the trifling sketch of "The Grumbler" had never more than a grateful purpose. When, only a year later, the little funeral procession from 2, Brick Court laid him in his unknown grave in the Temple burying-ground, the new comedy of which he had written so hopefully to Garrick was still non-existent. Would it have been better than its last fortunate predecessor? — would those early reserves of memory and experience have still proved inexhaustible ? The question cannot be answered. Through debt, and drudgery, and depression, the writer's genius had still advanced, and these might yet have proved powerless to check his progress.   But at least it was given to him to end upon his best, and not to outlive it.   For, in that critical sense which estimates the value of a work by its excellence at all points, it can scarcely be contested that "She Stoops to Conquer" is his best production.   In spite of their beauty and humanity, the lasting quality of "The Traveller" and "The Deserted Village" is seriously prejudiced by his half-way attitude between the poetry of convention and the poetry of nature — between the gradus epithet of Pope and the direct vocabulary of Wordsworth. With the "Vicar of Wakefield" again, immortal though it be, it is less his art that holds us than his charm, his humour, and his tenderness, which tempt us to forget his inconsistency and his errors of haste.   In "She Stoops to Conquer," neither defect of art nor defect of nature forbids us to give unqualified admiration to a work which lapse of time has shown to be still unrivalled in its kind.

ANGELO'S "REMINISCENCES."

IN the year 175— (it is not possible to fix the date more precisely), there was what would now be called a public assault of arms at one of the great hotels of pre-revolutionary Paris. Among the amateurs who took part in it — for there were amateurs as well as professionals — was a foreign *protégé* of the Duke de Nivernais, that amiable and courteous nobleman who subsequently visited this country at the close of the Seven Years' War, in the character of Ambassador Extraordinary and Plenipotentiary from His Most Christian Majesty, Louis XV. The stranger, who was in the prime of life, was of graceful figure and address, and his name had been no sooner announced than an English lady, then visiting the French capital, and possessed of great vivacity and considerable personal attractions, stepped forward and presented him with a bunch of roses. He received it with becoming gallantry, fastened it carefully on his left breast, and forthwith declared that he would defend it against all comers. What is more, he kept his promise. He afterwards " fenced with several of the first masters, not one of whom," says the narrator of the story, " could disturb a single leaf of the *bouquet*." The lady was the celebrated Mrs. Margaret Woffington, then in the height of her fame as a beauty and an actress ; the gentleman was an Italian, travelling for his pleasure. He was the son of a well-to-do merchant at Leghorn, and and he was called Dominico Angelo Malevolti Tremamondo.

Shortly after the foregoing incident, Signor Dominico Angelo Malevolti Tremamondo ("I love" — says Goldsmith of Miss Carolina Wilelmina Amelia Skeggs — "to give the whole name!") transported his foil and his good looks to this country. In addition to his proficiency as a fencer, he was "a master of equitation," having been a pupil of the then famous scientific horseman, Teillagory[1] the elder. These were accomplishments which speedily procured for him both popularity and patrons in London. He became in a few months *écuyer* to Henry Herbert, tenth Earl of Pembroke, who was not only an accomplished cavalier himself, but was then, or was soon to be, lieutenant-colonel of Elliot's Light Horse, a crack dragoon regiment, which,

[1] Here and elsewhere we correct Angelo's spelling.

by the way, numbered among its corporals the
future Astley of the Westminster Bridge Road
Amphitheatre.   Lord Pembroke had private
manèges both in the neighbourhood of his house
in Whitehall Gardens (part of the present No.
7), and at his family seat of Wilton, near Salisbury.   At first his *écuyer* confined himself to
teaching riding ; but a chance encounter at the
Thatched House Tavern with Dr. Keys, a well-
known Irish fencer, in which he vanquished his
antagonist, determined his choice of the calling of
a *maître d'armes.*   His first pupil was the Duke
of Devonshire.   Later he was engaged by the
Princess of Wales to instruct the young princes
in horsemanship and the use of the small sword,
for which purposes premises were provided
in Leicester Fields, within two doors from
Hogarth's dwelling in the east corner.   Before
many years were over, Dominico Angelo — for
he seems to have discarded first one and then
the other of his last two names — set up a riding
school of his own in Soho.   But previously to
all this, and apparently not long after his arrival
in London, he had fallen in love with, and taken
to wife, the daughter of an English naval officer.
Judging from the picture of her which Reynolds painted in 1766, the bride (who was a
minor) must have been as handsome as her

husband.   The marriage took place in February,
1755, at St. George's, Hanover Square, the
register of which duly records the union, by
license of the Archbishop of Canterbury, of
Domenico Angelo Malevolti, bachelor, and
Elizabeth Johnson, spinster.   The pair had a
son, the Henry Angelo from whose disorgan-
ised and gossiping " Reminiscences "[1] most of
the foregoing particulars are derived.

Harry Angelo, so he was called, is not explicit
as to the date of his birth, which probably took
place at the end of 1755 or the beginning of
1756.   It seems at first to have been intended
that he should enter the Navy ; and, as a matter
of fact, he was actually enrolled by Captain
Augustus Hervey (Lady Hervey's second son)
on the books of the *Dragon* man-of war in the
capacity of midshipman, thereby becoming entitled, at an extremely tender age, to some
twenty-five guineas prize money.   After a short
period under Dr. Rose of Chiswick, the translator of Sallust, he went to Eton, where his father
taught fencing ; and at Eton he remained for
some years.   Two of his school-fellows were
Nathan   and Carrington Garrick, the actor's

[1] " Reminiscences of Henry Angelo, with Memoirs of
his late Father and Friends," 2 vols., London : Colburn
and Bentley, 1830.

nephews ; and young Angelo had pleasant memories of their uncle's visits to Eton, where, being a friend of the elder Angelo, he would regale
all three boys sumptuously at the Christopher
inn, and amuse them with quips and recitations.[1]
Harry Angelo had even the good fortune, while
at Eton, to be taken to that solemn tom-
foolery, the Stratford Jubilee of 1769, in which
his father doubled the part of Mark Antony
with that of director of fireworks. Another
occasional visitor to the school, magnificently
frogged and braided after the fashion of his
kind, was the Italian quack Dominicetti, also a
family friend, who treated the boys royally.
But perhaps the most interesting memories of
young Angelo's Eton days are those which
recall a holiday spent at Amesbury with his
father and mother, as the guest of the Duke
and Duchess of Queensberry. In his old age
he could clearly picture the tall, thin figure of
the taciturn Duke, in high leather gaiters,
short-skirted frock, and gold-laced hat ; and he

---

[1] Apparently Garrick often did this. Once, at Hampton, he read Chaucer's " Cock and Fox " to the boys after
supper, and then, having recited Goldsmith's " Hermit,"
fell asleep in his arm-chair. Thereupon Mrs. Garrick,
taking off her lace apron, fondly placed it over his face,
and motioned her young friends away to bed.

well remembered the Duchess, then nearly
eighty, but still energetic and garrulous, in a
Quaker-coloured silk and black hood. He also
remembered that he was allowed (like Gay
before him) to fish for carp in the Amesbury
water.

When he was entering his seventeenth year,
Harry Angelo was sent to Paris to learn French.
He was placed *en pension* in the Rue Poupé
with a M. Boileau, a half-starved *maître de
langue*, who, since he is seriously likened by his
pupil to the Apothecary in " Romeo and Juliet."
must really have resembled the typical Frenchman as depicted by Smollett and Rowlandson.
Boileau was a conscientious teacher, but a miserable caterer; and young Angelo, after nar-
rowly escaping collapse from starvation and close
confinement, was eventually removed from his
care. He passed, in the first instance, to a M.
Liviez, whose wife was English, and (notwithstanding an undeniable squint) of a shape suffi-
cently elegant to have served as the model for
Roubillac's figure of Eloquence on the Argyll
tomb at Westminster Abbey. M. Liviez had
been a dancer, and ballet-master at a London
theatre. At this date he was a *bon vivant*, who
collected prints. He was also subject to fits of
hypochondria (probably caused by over-eating),

when he would imagine himself Apollo, and
fiddle feverishly to the nine Muses, typified for
the nonce by a hemicycle of chairs. As both he
and his wife preferred to speak English, they
made no pretence to teach their lodger French ;
but, from the point of commissariat, the change
from the Rue Poupé to the Rue Battois was
" removal from Purgatory to Paradise." While
Angelo was in Paris, Garrick sent him an introduction to Préville, whom Sterne describes as
" Mercury himself," and who was, indeed, in
some respects Garrick's rival. Préville knew
Foote ; and when Foote came to the French
capital, he invited Angelo to a supper, at which
Préville was present. Foote, binding Angelo
to secrecy, delighted the company by mimick-
ing their common acquaintance, the great Ros-
cius ; and Préville in his turn imitated the leading
French comedians. All this was not very favourable to proficiency in the French language,
which Angelo would probably have learned
better in M. Boileau's garret. On the other
hand, under Motet, then the champion *pareur*
of the Continent, he became an expert swords-
man — able, and only too willing, to take part
in the encounters which, in the Paris of the day,
were as common as street rows in London.
But apart from swallowing the button and some

inches of a foil when fencing with Lord Masse-
reene in the Prison of the Abbaye (where that
nobleman was unhappily in durance for debt),
he seems to have enjoyed an exceptional immun-
ity from accidents of all kinds.

He returned to London in 1775. His home
at this time was at Carlisle House,[1] in King's
Square Court (now Carlisle Street), Soho. It
was a spacious old Caroline mansion of red
brick, which had belonged to the Howard family,
and had been bought by Dominico Angelo from
Lord Delaval, brother of Foote's patron, the
Sir Francis to whom he dedicated his comedy
of " Taste." There were lofty rooms with enriched ceilings ; there was a marble-floored hall ;
there was a grand decorated staircase painted by
Salvator's pupil, Henry Cook. In this building,
at the beginning of 1763, its new owner had
opened his fencing school, and subsequently, in
the garden at the back, had erected stables and
a *manège*, which extended to Wardour Street.
Between pupils, resident and otherwise, and
troops of friends, Carlisle House must always

---

[1] Not to be confounded with Carlisle House on the
other side of Soho Square, which was occupied from 1760
to 1778 by the enterprising Mrs. Teresa Cornelys, whose
ballroom was in Sutton Street, on the site of the present
Roman Catholic Church of St. Patrick.

have been well filled and animated. Garrick,
who was accustomed to consult the elder Angelo
on matters of costume and stage machinery, was
often a visitor, and presented his adviser with a
magnificent silver goblet (long preserved by the
Angelos as an heirloom), which held three bottles
of Burgundy. Richard Brinsley Sheridan and
his father were also friends, and it was from
Dominico Angelo that the younger man, as a
boy at Harrow, acquired that use of the small
sword which was to stand him in such good
stead in his later duel with Captain Mathews.
Wilkes, again, resplendent in his favourite scarlet and gold, not seldom looked in on his way
from his Westminster or Kensington houses ;
and Foote, the Chevalier D'Éon, and General
Paoli were constant guests. Horne Tooke,
who lived hard by in Dean Street, was another
intimate ; and, when he was not discussing contemporary politics with Wilkes and Tom Sheridan, would sometimes enliven the company by
singing a parody on " God save the King," which
was not entirely to the loyal taste of the elder
Angelo. Bach of the harpsichord,[1] with Abel of

---

[1] This was John Christian Bach, Bach's son, familiarly
known as "English Bach." Angelo calls him Sebastian,
but John Sebastian Bach died in 1750. Bach and Abel
jointly conducted Mrs. Cornelys' concerts.

the *viol-da-gamba*, were next-door neighbours and free of the house ; Bartolozzi the engraver, and his inseparable Cipriani, were on an almost equally favoured footing. Another *habitué* was Gainsborough, whose passion for music is historical, and from whom any one could extract a sketch in return for a song or a tune. The walls of Abel's room were covered by drawings acquired in this manner, and pinned loosely to the paper-hangings, — drawings which afterwards fetched their price at Langford's in the Piazza. Besides these, came Philip de Loutherbourg, whom Dominico Angelo had introduced to Garrick as scene painter for Drury Lane ; and Canaletto, whom he had known at Venice ; and Zoffany ; and George Stubbs, the author of the "Anatomy of the Horse," who carried on his studies in the Carlisle House Riding School, no doubt taking for model, among others, that famous white charger Monarch, of which the presentment survives to posterity, under King William III. of immortal memory, in West's "Battle of the Boyne." [1] "All the celebrated horse painters of the last, and some of the veterans of the present age," says the author of the

[1] The "Battle of the Boyne" was engraved by John Hall, Raimbach's master. See *post*, "An English Engraver in Paris."

" Reminiscences," "were constant visitors at
our table or at the *manége*."   Lastly, an enthusiastic, though scarcely artistic, amateur of the
Carlisle Street stud was the corpulent " Hero
of Culloden," — otherwise " Billy the Butcher."
If not the greatest, he was certainly the heaviest
prince in Christendom, since he rode some four-
and-twenty stone, and, as a boy, Harry Angelo
well remembered the significant sidelong dip of
the carriage when His Royal Highness poised
his ponderous body on the step.

An establishment upon the scale and traditions of Carlisle House (and there was also a
"cake-house" or country-box at Acton, for which
Zoffany painted decorations) could only have
been maintained at considerable expense.   But
in this respect Dominico Angelo seems to have
been unusually fortunate, even for a foreigner.
Within a short period after his arrival in England
his income, according to his son, was over two
thousand a year; and this sum, in the height
of his prosperity, was nearly doubled.   After
Harry Angelo's account of his life in Paris, his
records, always disconnected, grow looser in
chronology; added to which, it is never quite
easy to distinguish his personal recollections
from the mere floating hearsay of a retentive
but capricious memory.   One of his earliest

experiences, however, on returning to England, must have been his attendance, in December, 1775, at the trial, in the Old Bailey, of Mrs. Margaret Caroline Rudd, for complicity in the forgery for which the Brothers Perreau were subsequently hanged.[1] His description of this fair-haired siren suggests a humbler Becky Sharp or Valérie Marneffe, and there can be little doubt that, as he implies, she owed her undeserved acquittal to the " irresistible power of fascination " which captivated Boswell, and interested even his "illustrious Friend." Another incident at which Angelo assisted shortly afterwards, and which it is also possible to place precisely, was the riot that, in February, 1776, accompanied the attempt to produce at Drury Lane Parson Bate's unpopular opera of " The Blackamoor wash'd White." Angelo was one of a boxful of the author's supporters, who were forced to retire under the furious cannonade of " apples, oranges, and other such missiles," to which they were exposed. But a still more important theatrical event was his presence on

---

[1] One wonders whether Thackeray was thinking of this *cause célèbre* in " Denis Duval," where there is a Miss *Rudge* and a Farmer *Perreau.* Angelo, it may be added, was present at the hanging at Tyburn of M. de la Motte, an actual character in the same book.

that historic June 10, 1776, when Garrick bade
farewell to the stage.   He and his mother were
in Mrs. Garrick's box, and the two ladies continued sobbing so long after they had quitted
the house as to prompt the ironic comment
of the elder Angelo that they could not have
grieved more at the great man's funeral itself.
Harry Angelo was also a spectator of the progress to Tyburn, in the following February, of
the unfortunate Dr. Dodd, to whom, and to the
horrors of " Execution Day " in general, he de-
votes some of the latter pages of his first volume.
" His [Dodd's] corpse-like appearance produced
an awful picture of human woe.   Tens of thousands of hats, which formed a black mass, as
the coach advanced were taken off simultane-
ously, and so many tragic faces exhibited a
spectacle the effect of which is beyond the
power of words to describe.   Thus the procession travelled onwards through the multitude,
whose silence added to the awfulness of the
scene."   Two years later Angelo witnessed the
execution of another clergyman, James Hack-
man, who was hanged for shooting Lord Sandwich's mistress, Miss Martha Reay.   The
murder — it will be remembered — took place
in the Piazza at Covent Garden, as the lady was
leaving the theatre, and Angelo, according to his

own account, had only quitted it himself a few minutes before. He afterwards saw the body of the hapless criminal under dissection at Surgeons' Hall, — a gruesome testimony to the truth of Hogarth's final plate in the " Four Stages of Cruelty."

The above, the Gordon riots of '80, and the burning in '92 of Wyatt's Pantheon, are some of the few things in Angelo's first volume which it is practicable to date with certainty. The second volume is scarcely more than a sequence of headed paragraphs, roughly parcelled into sections, and difficult to sample. Like his father (who died at Eton in 1802), he became a " master of the sword," and like him, again, he lived upon terms of quasi-familiarity with many titled practitioners of that art, — being, indeed, upon one occasion the guest of the Duke of Sussex at the extremely select Neapolitan Club, an honour which — as the Prince of Wales was also present — seems to have been afterwards regarded as too good to be believed. Like Dominico Angelo, also, he had an extensive acquaintance with the artists and actors of his day. He had himself learned drawing at Eton under the Prince's master, Alexander Cozens, the apostle of " blottesque," and had studied a little with Bartolozzi and Cipriani. He had even

ventured upon a few caricatures, in particular
one of Lady Queensberry's black *protégé*, Sou-
bise ; and he was intimate with Thomas Rowlandson, whom he had known from boyhood, and
followed to his grave in April, 1827. When
Rowlandson was on his continental travels, Angelo was living in Paris, and he possessed many
of the drawings which his friend executed at
this time. In London they were frequently
companions at Vauxhall and other places of
amusement, where Rowlandson's busy pencil
found its field of activity ; and together they
often heard the chimes at midnight in the house
at Beaufort Buildings inhabited by Rowlandson's fat Mæcenas, the banker Mitchel, one of
whose favourite guests was Peter Pindar. Angelo gives a good many anecdotes which have
been utilised by Rowlandson's biographers ; but
perhaps the least hackneyed record of their
alliance is contained in the pages which describe
their joint visit to Portsmouth to see the French
prizes after Lord Howe's victory of the 1st
June, 1794. Angelo got down first. and went
on board the largest French vessel, the *Sans
Pareil* (80 guns). He gives a graphic account of
the appalling devastation, — the decks ploughed
up by the round shot, the masts gone by the
board, the miserable boyish crew, the hogshead

of spirits to keep up their courage in action, the jumble of dead and dying in the 'tween decks, and above all, the terrible, sickening stench. On Howe's vessel, the *Queen Charlotte,* on the contrary, there was scarcely a trace of battle, though another ship, the *Brunswick,* had suffered to a considerable extent. Rowlandson joined Angelo at Portsmouth, and they witnessed together the landing of the prisoners. Afterwards they visited Forton, where, upon leaving one of the sick wards, Rowlandson made a ghastly study of a dying " Mounseer " sitting up in bed to write his will, a priest with a crucifix at his side. By this time Angelo had had enough of the horrors of war, and he returned to town, leaving Rowlandson to go on to Southampton to make — so he says — sketches of Lord Moira's embarkation for La Vendée. Here, however, the writer's recollection must have failed him, for Lord Moira's fruitless expedition was nearly a year old. What Rowlandson no doubt saw was his Lordship's departure for Ostend to join the Duke of York. Angelo speaks highly of the — for Rowlandson — unusual finish and spirit of these drawings, with their boatloads of soldiers and studies of shipping. They were purchased by Fores of Piccadilly, but do not appear to have been reproduced. There is,

however, at South Kensington a sketch by
Rowlandson of the French prizes coming into
Portsmouth, which must have been made at
this date.

Another associate of Angelo, and also of
Rowlandson, was John (or more familiarly,
Jack) Bannister, the actor. Bannister and
Rowlandson had been students together at the
Royal Academy, and had combined in wor-
rying, by mimicry and caricature, gruff Richard
Wilson, who had succeeded Frank Hayman
as librarian. In the subsequent pranks of this
practical joking age, Angelo, who had known
them both from boyhood, often made a third ;
and he was present upon an occasion which was
as unfeignedly pathetic as Garrick's famous farewell, — the farewell of Bannister to the stage.
Many of the anecdotes contained in the entertainment which preceded this leave-taking —
namely, " Bannister's Budget," — were included
by permission in the " Reminiscences ; " and
Angelo, who had learned elocution from Tom
Sheridan, and was an excellent amateur actor,
more than once played for Bannister's benefits,
notably at the Italian Opera House in 1792 as
Mrs. Cole in Foote's " Minor," and in 1800
before the Royal Family at Windsor as Papillon
in " The Liar," also by Foote. On this latter

occasion the bill records that Mr. H. Angelo,
" by particular desire," obliged with " A Solo
Duet ; or, Ballad Singers in Cranbourn Alley."
These were by no means his only dramatic essays.
At the pretty little private theatre which, in
1788, that emphatically lively nobleman, Richard, seventh Earl of Barrymore, erected at War-
grave-on-Thames, he was a frequent performer.
His first, or one of his first parts, was that
of Dick in Vanbrugh's " Confederacy," when
Barrymore played Brass ; and a later and
favourite impersonation was Worsdale's *rôle* of
Lady Pentweazel in Foote's " Taste." Angelo is
careful, however, to explain that the exigencies
of his professional engagements did not permit
him to go to the full length of the Wargrave Court
of Comus — some of whose revels must have
closely resembled that " blind hookey " by which
the footman in " The Newcomes " described
the doings of Lord Farintosh. As he seems,
nevertheless, to have accompanied Barrymore
to low spouting clubs like Jacob's Well ; to have
driven with him at night through the long straggling street of Colnbrook, while his sportive
Lordship was industriously " fanning the day-
lights," i.e. breaking the windows to right and
left with his whip ; and to have serenaded Mrs.
Fitzherbert in his company at Brighton, — he

had certainly sufficient opportunities for studying the "caprices and eccentricities" of this illustrious and erratic specimen of what the late Mortimer Collins was wont to describe as the "strong generation." Besides acting at Wargrave, he had also often joined in the private theatricals at Brandenburgh House, then the Hammersmith home of Lord Berkeley's sister, that Margravine of Anspach whose comedy of "The Sleep-Walker" Walpole had printed at the Strawberry Hill Press. Lastly, he was a member of the short-lived Pic-Nic Society inaugurated by Lady Buckinghamshire, an association which combined balls and private plays with suppers on the principle of the line in Goldsmith's "Retaliation", —

"Each guest brought his dish, and the feast was united."

Lady Buckinghamshire, a large personage, with a good digestion and an unlimited appetite for pleasure, was one of the three card-loving leaders of fashion satirised so mercilessly by Gillray as "Faro's Daughters," — her fellow-sinners being Lady Archer and Mrs. Concannon. But whatever may have happened over the green tables at St. James's Square, "gaming" — says Angelo — "formed no part of the plan of the Pic-Nics." Not the less, they had their ele-

ment of chance. It was the practice to draw
lots for furnishing the supper, an arrangement
which, if it sometimes permitted the drawers
to escape with a pound cake or a bag of China
oranges, as often imposed upon them the enforced provision of a dozen of champagne or a
three-guinea Perigord pie.

It would take a lengthy article to exhaust the
budget of these chaotic memories, even if one
made rigid selection of those incidents only in
which the writer affirms that he was personally
concerned. Not a few of the stories, however,
are common property, and are told as well elsewhere. For instance, Angelo repeats the anecdote of Goldsmith's " Croaker," Shuter, who,
following — for his " Cries of London " — a particularly musical vendor of silver eels, found to
his vexation that on this particular occasion the
man was unaccountably mute. Questioning him
at length, the poor fellow explained, with a burst
of tears, that his *vife* had died that day, and that
he could not cry. This is related in Taylor's
" Records," and no doubt in a dozen places
besides. Similarly, the anecdote of Hayman
the painter, and the Marquis of Granby, both
gouty, having a bout with the gloves previous
to a sitting, is to be found in the " Somerset
House Gazette " of " Ephraim Hardcastle "

(W. H. Pyne) ; and it has been suggested, we
know not upon what authority, that Pyne had a
good deal to do with Angelo's chronicles. Be
this as it may, there are plenty of anecdotes
which are so obviously connected with the narrator that, even if all the make-weights be discarded, a residue remains which is far too large
to be dealt with here. We shall confine ourselves to the few pages which refer to Byron,
whom Angelo seems to have known well.
Byron, who had been one of Angelo's pupils at
Harrow, had interested himself in establishing
Angelo as a fencing master at Cambridge, where
he entertained him and Theodore Hook at dinner, seeing them off himself afterwards by the
London stage, duly fortified with stirrup cups
of the famous St. John's College beer. When
later Byron left Cambridge for town, Angelo
seems to have taken great pains to find a book
which his noble friend wanted in order to decide
a wager, and his eventual success increased the
favour in which he stood. He was subsequently in the habit of giving Byron lessons at
the Albany in the broadsword, — a fearsome
exercise which was chosen in view of the pupil's
tendency to flesh, and for which he elaborately
handicapped himself with furs and flannels. Of
these relations between Angelo and Byron at

this date a memento is still said to survive at Mr. John Murray's in Albemarle Street. It is a screen made by Angelo for his patron. On one side are all the eminent pugilists from Broughton to Jackson ; on the other the great actors from Betterton to Kean. When Byron left the country in 1816 the screen was sold with his effects, and so passed into the pious hands of its present possessor.

Reference has already been made to what Mr. Egerton Castle accurately describes as Angelo's " graceful ease " in eluding dates, and it should be added that he gives very few particulars respecting his personal history or his professional establishments. At first, it may be assumed, he taught fencing at his father's school in Carlisle Street. Later on, the *salle d'armes* which he mentions oftenest is that formerly belonging to the Frenchman Redas in the Opera House buildings at the corner of the Haymarket, almost facing the Orange Coffee House, then the chosen resort of foreigners of all sorts. When the Opera was burned down in 1789, these rooms were destroyed, and Angelo apparently transferred his quarters to Bond Street. Under the heading " My Own Boastings," he gives a list of his titled and aristocratic pupils to the year 1817, and it is certainly an imposing one. " In the year of [Edmund] Kean's benefit" [1825?] he strained his thigh when fencing with the actor, and was thenceforth obliged "to bid adieu to the practical exertions of the science." His last years seem to have been passed in retirement at a village near Bath, and from his description of his means as "a small annuity" it must be presumed that he was poor. He had been married, and he speaks of two of his sons to whom the Duke of York had given commissions in the army; but that is all he says on the subject. Beside the two volumes of "Reminiscences," he compiled another miscellany of memories entitled "Angelo's Pic-Nic," to which George Cruikshank contributed a characteristic frontispiece. He also published a translation in smaller form of his father's "École des Armes," a magnificent subscription folio which had first appeared in 1763.[1] The translation was by Rowlandson, and the book so produced was afterwards inserted under the head *Escrime* in the "Encyclopédie" of Diderot and D'Alembert. Rowlandson also etched twenty-four

[1] Dominico Angelo, Lord Pembroke, and the Chevalier D'Éon stood as models for the illustrations to this book, which were designed by Gwynn the painter. They were engraved by Grignion, Ryland, and Raimbach's master, Hall.

plates for Angelo on the use of the Hungarian and Highland broadsword, which were put forth in 1798–9 by T. Egerton of the Military Library near Whitehall, the adventurous publisher who subsequently issued the first three novels of Jane Austen.

THE LATEST LIFE OF STEELE.

ONE of the things that most pleased Lord Macaulay in connection with his famous article in the *Edinburgh* on Miss Aikin's " Life of Addison," was the confirmation of a minor statement which he had risked upon internal evidence. He had asserted confidently that Addison could never have spoken of Steele in the " Old Whig " as " Little Dickey ; " and by a stroke of good fortune, a few days after his article appeared, he found the evidence he required. At a bookstall in Holborn he happened upon Chetwood's " History of the Stage," and promptly discovered that " Little Dickey " was the nickname of Henry Norris, a diminutive actor who had made his first appearance as " Dicky " in Farquhar's " Constant Couple." Norris — it may be added — must have been a familiar figure to both Addison and Steele, because, besides taking a female part in " The Funeral," he had played Mr. Tipkin in " The Tender Husband," which contained " many applauded strokes " from Addison's hand ; and,

only three years before Addison wrote the " Old
Whig," had also acted in Addison's own comedy
of " The Drummer." But the anecdote, with
its tardy exposure of a time-honoured blunder,
aptly illustrates the main function of the modern
biographer who deals with the great men of the
last century. Rightly or wrongly — no doubt
rightly as regards their leading characteristics —
a certain conception of them has passed into
currency, and it is no longer practicable to alter
it materially. A " new view," if sufficiently ingenious or paradoxical, may appear to hold its
own for a moment, but, as a rule, it lasts no
longer. Swift, Addison, Pope, Steele, Fielding, Goldsmith, Johnson, remain essentially
what the common consent of the past has left
them, and the utmost that latter-day industry can
effect lies in the rectification of minute facts, and
the tracing out of neglected threads of inquiry.
Especially may it concern itself with that literary
nettoyage à sec which has for its object the atten-
uation, and, if possible, the entire dispersing, of
doubtful or discreditable tradition.

Of this method of biography, the " Life of
Steele,"[1] by Mr. George A. Aitken is a favourable, and even typical, example. That Mr.

[1] *The Life of Richard Steele.* By George A. Aitken,
2 vols., London : Isbister, 1889.

Aitken is an enthusiast is plain ; but he is also
an enthusiast of exceptional patience, acuteness,
and tenacity of purpose. He manifestly set out
determined to know all that could possibly be
known about Steele, and for some five years
(to judge by his first advertisements) he laboured
unweariedly at his task. The mere authorities
referred to in his notes constitute an ample literature of the period, while the consultation of
registers, the rummaging of records, and the
general disturbance of contemporary pamphlets
and documents which his inquiries must obviously have entailed, are fairly enough to take
one's breath away. That in these days of hasty
research and hastier publication such a train of
investigation should have been undertaken at all,
is remarkable ; that so prolonged and arduous
an effort should have been selected as the
diploma-work of a young and previously untried
writer, is more remarkable still. It would have
been discouraging in the last degree if so much
industry and perseverance had been barren of
result, and it is satisfactory to find that Mr.
Aitken has been fortunate enough to add considerably to the existing material respecting
Steele. In the pages that follow it is proposed,
not so much to recapitulate Steele's story, as to
emphasise, in their order, some of the more im-

portant discoveries which are due to his latest biographer.

Richard Steele, as we know already, was born at Dublin in March, 1672 (N. S.), being thus about six weeks older than Addison, who first saw the light in the following May. Beyond some vague references in the *Tatler*, nothing definite has hitherto been ascertained about his parents, although his father (also Richard Steele) was reported to have been a lawyer. But Mr. Aitken's investigations establish the fact that one Richard Steele, of Mountain (Monkstown), an attorney, was married in 1670 to a widow named Elinor Symes. These were Steele's father and mother. Steele himself tells us (*Tatler*, No. 181) that the former died when he was "not quite five years of age," and his mother, apparently, did not long survive her husband. The boy fell into the charge of his uncle, Henry Gascoigne, secretary to the first and second Dukes of Ormond. Gascoigne, concerning whom Mr. Aitken has recovered many particulars, had married a sister of one of Steele's parents. Through Ormond's influence his nephew was placed, in November, 1684, upon the foundation at the Charterhouse. Two years later he was joined there by Addison. It was then the reign of Dr. Thomas Walker, after-

wards " the ingenious T. W." of the *Spectator*,
but nothing has been recovered as to Steele's
school-days. In November, 1689, he was elected
to Christ Church, Oxford, with the usual exhibition of a boy on the Charterhouse foundation,
and he matriculated in March, 1690, — Addison,
then a demy at Magdalen, having preceded him.
Letters already printed by Mr. Wills and others
show that Steele tried hard for a studentship
at Christ Church ; but eventually he became a
post-master at Merton, his college-tutor being
Dr. Welbore Ellis, to whom he subsequently
refers in the preface to the " Christian Hero."
Of his intercourse with Addison at Smithfield
and Oxford no record has come to light, and it
is therefore still open to the essayist to piece the
imperfections of this period by fictitious scores
with the apple-woman or imaginary musings on
the Merton terraces. But, in any such excur-
sions in search of the picturesque, the fact that
Steele was older instead of younger than Addison cannot safely be disregarded.

Why Richard Steele quitted the University to
become a " gentleman of the army " still remains
obscure. His University career, if not brilliant,
had been respectable, and he left Merton with
the love of " the whole Society." Perhaps, like
his compatriot Goldsmith, he preferred a red coat

to a black one.   At all events, in 1694, his restless Irish spirit prompted him to enlist as a cadet
in the second troop of Horse Guards, then commanded by his uncle's patron, James Butler,
second Duke of Ormond.   When he thus
" mounted a war-horse, with a great sword in
his hand, and planted himself behind King William the Third against Lewis the Fourteenth "
he lost (he says) " the succession to a very good
estate in the county of Wexford in Ireland ; "
for which, failing further particulars, we may
perhaps provisionally read " castle in Spain."
His next appearance was among the crowd of
minstrels who, in black-framed *folio*, mourned
Queen Mary's death.   Already he had written
verse, and had even burned an entire comedy at
college.   The chief interest, however, of " The
Procession," which was the particular name of
this particular " melodious tear," was its diplomatic dedication to John, Lord Cutts, himself a
versifier, and what was more important, also the
newly appointed colonel of the Coldstream
Guards.   Cutts speedily sought out his anonymous panegyrist, took him into his household,
and eventually offered him a standard in his
regiment.   There is evidence, in the shape of
transcripts from the Blenheim MSS., that Steele
was acting as Cutts' secretary *circa* 1696-7 (a

circumstance of which, by the way, there is
confirmation in Carleton's " Memoirs "[1]) ; and
it has hitherto been supposed that by his employ-
er's interest — for Cutts gave him little but patronage — he became a captain in Lucas's Fusileers. Here, however, Mr. Aitken's cautious
method discloses an unsuspected error. Steele
is spoken of as a captain as early as 1700, and
" Lord Lucas's Regiment of Foot " (not speci-
fically " Fusileers ") was only raised in February,
1702. If, therefore, before this date Steele had
any right to the title of captain, it must have
been as captain in the Coldstream Guards.
Unfortunately, all efforts to trace him in the
records of that regiment have hitherto proved
unsuccessful. Neither as captain nor as ensign
could its historian, General MacKinnon, though
naturally watchful on the point, find any mention
of his name.

By 1700 the former post-master of Merton
had become a seasoned man about town, a recognised wit, and an habitual frequenter of Will's.
" Dick Steel is yours," writes Congreve to a

---

[1] " At the time appointed " (says Carleton, writing at
the date of the Assassination Plot of 1696) " I waited on
his lordship [Lord Cutts], where I met Mr. Steel (now
Sir Richard, and at that time his secretary), who immediately introduced me." (" Memoirs," 1728, ch. iii.)

friend early in the year. Already, too, there
are indications that he had begun to feel the
" want of pence which vexes public men."
From this, however, as well as his part in the
coffee-house crusade against Dryden's " Quack
Maurus," Blackmore, we must pass to Mr.
Aitken's next rectification. That Steele fought
a duel is already known. That it was forced
upon him, that he endeavoured in every honourable way to evade it, and that finally, by misadventure, he all but killed his man, have been
often circumstantially related. But the date of
the occurrence has always been a mystery.
Calling Luttrell and the *Flying-Post* to his
aid, Mr. Aitken has ascertained that the place
was Hyde Park, the time June 16, 1700, and
the other principal an Irishman, named Kelly.
Luttrell's description of Steele as " Capt. Steele,
of the Lord Cutts regiment," is confirmatory
of the assumption that he was a captain in the
Guards. Whether this was his only " affair of
honour," or whether there were others, is
doubtful ; but it is not improbable that the repentant spirit engendered by this event, for his
adversary's life long hung trembling in the balance, is closely connected with the publication,
if not the preparation, of the " Christian Hero,"
which made its appearance a few months later.

Upon the scheme of this curious and by no means uninstructive manual, once so nearly forgotten as to be described as a poem, it is not necessary to linger now. But it may be noted that it was dated from the Tower Guard, where it was written, and that the governor of the Tower was the Lord Lucas in whose regiment Steele became an officer.

The year of which the first months witnessed the publication of the " Christian Hero " witnessed in its close the production of Steele's first play, and, inconsequently enough, the one was the cause of the other. It was an almost inevitable result of the book that many of the author's former associates were alienated from him, while others, not nicely sensitive to the distinction drawn in Boileau's *ami de la vertu plutôt que vertueux*, maliciously contrasted his precepts with his practice. Finding himself "slighted" (he says) "instead of being encouraged, for his declarations as to religion," it became " incumbent upon him to enliven his character, for which reason he writ the comedy called ' The Funeral,' in which (though full of incidents that move laughter) Virtue and Vice appear just as they ought to do." In other words, Steele endeavoured to swell that tide of reformation which Collier had set flowing by his

5

" Short View of the Immorality and Profane-
ness of the English Stage," and he followed up
his first effort of 1701 by the " Lying Lover"
(1703) and the " Tender Husband" (1705), the
second of which was avowedly written " in
the severity Collier required." His connection
with the purification of the contemporary drama,
however, would lead us too far from the special
subject of this paper, — the revised facts of his
biography. Among these, the order of the plays
as given above is an important item. Owing
to some traditional misconception, the " Lying
Lover," which was a rather over-emphatic pro-
test against duelling, was believed by all the
older writers to be the last of Steele's early dramatic efforts. As a natural consequence, its
being " damned for its piety " was made responsible for the author's long abstinence from the
task of theatrical regeneration. Unfortunately
for logic, the facts which, in this instance, Mr.
Aitken has extended rather than discovered, are
diametrically opposed to any such convenient
arrangement. The " Tender Husband," and
not the " Lying Lover," was the last of Steele's
first three plays, — that is to say, the moralised
Collier mixture was succeeded by a strong infu-
sion of Molière, while, so far from leaving off
writing for the stage, there is abundant evidence

that, but for other cares and more absorbing
occupations, Steele would speedily have proceeded to "enliven his character" with a fresh
comedy. Indeed, in a very instructive suit
against Christopher Rich of Drury Lane, which
Mr. Aitken has exhumed from the Chancery
Pleadings in the Record Office, mention is made
of what may well have been the performance in
question. It was to have treated a subject
essayed both by Gay and Mrs. Centlivre, the
" Election of Gotham."

The Chancery suit above referred to, which
arose out of the profits of the " Tender Husband," began in 1707. Early in 1702 Steele
had become a captain in Lucas's, and between
that date and 1704 must have spent a considerable portion of his time at Landguard Fort, doing garrison duty with his company. He lodged,
according to report, in a farmhouse at Walton.
Mr. Aitken prints from various sources several
new letters which belong to this period, together with some account of another in the
long series of lawsuits about money with which
Steele's biography begins to be plentifully be-
sprinkled. In an autograph now in the Mor-
rison collection, we find him certifying with
Addison to the unimpeachable character of one
" Margery Maplesden, late Sutler at the Tilt-

yard Guard," and we get passing glances of him
at the Kit Cat Club and elsewhere.   Perhaps
we are right, too, in placing about this date the
account of his search for the "philosopher's
stone."   The details of this episode in his career
rest mainly upon the narrative of Mrs. De la
Rivière Manley, the author of that " cornucopia
of scandal," the " New Atalantis ; " but there is
little doubt that there was ground for the story,
since Steele himself, in later life, printed, without contradiction, a reference to it in *Town
Talk*, and it is besides connected with the
next of Mr. Aitken's discoveries.   According to
" Rivella," an empiric, who found the sanguine
Steele " a bubble to his mind," engaged him in
the pursuit of the *magnum arcanum*.   Furnaces
were built without delay, and Steele's available
resources began to vanish rapidly.   In these
transactions Mrs. Manley's husband played
an ambiguous part, and, if we are to believe
her, she herself impersonated the *Dea ex
machina*, and warned Steele that he was being
duped.   It was not too soon.   He only just
saved his last negotiable property, his commission, and had to go into hiding.   " Fortune,"
Mrs. Manley continues, " did more for him in
his adversity than would have lain in her way
in prosperity ; she threw him to seek for refuge

in a house where was a lady with very large possessions ; he married her, she settled all upon him, and died soon after."

This — and to some extent it is a corroboration of the story — was Steele's first wife, who until now has been little more than a shifting shadow in his biography. Her actual personality still remains veiled ; but Mr. Aitken with infinite pains has ascertained her name, and a number of facts about her family. She was a West Indian widow called Margaret Stretch, who had inherited an estate in Barbados of £850 a year from her brother, Major Ford. Steele married her in the spring of 1705, and buried her two years later. There is some indication that her death was caused by a fright given her (when *enceinte*) by Steele's only sister, who was insane ; but upon this point nothing definite can be affirmed. Looking to the circumstances in which (as narrated by Mrs. Manley) the acquaintanceship began, it is not improbable that the personal charms of the lady had less to do with the marriage than the *beaux yeux de sa cassette.* In any case Steele can scarcely escape the imputation which usually attaches to the union of a needy bachelor with a wealthy widow, and, as will presently be seen, he was not long inconsolable.

Whether, even at the time of the marriage, the Barbados estate was really productive of much ready money may be doubted. But in August, 1706, Steele was appointed Gentleman Waiter to Queen Anne's consort, Prince George of Denmark, and a few weeks after his wife's death, through the recommendation of Arthur Mainwaring, one of the members of the Kit Cat Club, Harley, then a Secretary of State, gave him the post of Gazetteer with an increased salary of £300 a year. "The writer of the ' Gazette ' now," says Hearne in May, 1707, " is Captain Steel, who is the author of several romantic things, and is accounted an ingenious man." As " Captain Steele " he continued for many years to be known, but it is assumed that he left the army before his second marriage, which now followed. To his first wife's funeral had come as mourner a lady of about nine and twenty, the daughter of a deceased gentleman of Wales, and the Miss Mary Scurlock who has since become historical as the " Prue " of the well-known Steele letters in the British Museum. That she was an heiress, and, as Mrs. Manley says, a " cried-up beauty," was known, though in the absence of definite pictorial assurance of the latter fact, it has hitherto been difficult to see her with the admiring eyes of the enthusiastic writer who signs himself her "most obsequious obedient husband." But while unable to add greatly to our knowledge of her character, Mr. Aitken has succeeded in discovering and copying her portrait by Kneller, a portrait which sufficiently justifies her husband's raptures. In Sir Godfrey's "animated canvas," she is shown as a very beautiful brunette, in a cinnamon satin dress, with a high, almost too high, forehead, and dark, brilliant eyes. Steele's phrase " little wife " must have been a " dear diminutive," for she is not especially *petite*, but rather what Fielding's Mrs. James would style " a very fine person of a woman," and she has an arch, humourous expression which suggests the wit with which she is credited. From the absence of a ring it has been conjectured that the portrait was taken before marriage. But Kneller was much more likely to have painted Mrs. Steele than Miss Scurlock, and the simple explanation may be either that rings were neglected or that the hands were painted in from a model. As in the case of Mrs. Stretch, Mr. Aitken has collected a mass of information about Mrs. Steele's relations. His good luck has also helped him to one veritable find. In her letter to her mother announcing her engagement, Miss Scurlock refers scornfully to a certain " wretched impudence, H. O.," who had recently written to her.   This was manifestly a rejected but still importunate suitor, although the precise measure of his implied iniquity remained unrevealed.   From documents now first printed by Mr. Aitken, it seems that his name was Henry Owen of Glassalt, Carmarthenshire, and that he was an embarrassed widower of (in the circuitous language of the law) " thirty, thirty-five, or forty years of age at the most " — that is to say, he was over forty. Miss Scurlock had known him as a neighbour from childhood, and for four or five years past, at Bath, at London, and at other places, he, being a needy man with an entailed estate, had been besieging her with his addresses.   Only two years before her engagement to Steele, finding her obdurate, he had trumped up a suit against her for breach of contract of marriage, which apparently was not successful.   The " Libel " and " Answer," which Mr. Aitken prints from the records of the Consistorial Court of London, are more curious than edifying, and tend to show that Owen was rather a cur.   But the whole story is useful indirectly as suggesting that Miss Scurlock's constitutional prudery was not the only reason why she surrounded Steele's worship of her with so

much mystery. Abhorrence of "public doings" in "changing the name of lover for husband" was certainly superficially justifiable in
the circumstances. A gentleman who had
brought a suit against her in 1704 for breach of
contract, and was still pestering her in August,
1707, with his unpalatable attentions, was quite
capable of putting awkward obstacles in the
way of that other ardent wooer from Lord
Sunderland's office in Whitehall, who, in order
to pay his court to "the beautifullest object in
the world," was confessedly neglecting the
"Gazette" and the latest news from Ostend.

According to the license the marriage was to
have taken place at St. Margaret's, Westminster; but the registers of that church, as well as
those of St. James's, Piccadilly, and St. Martin's-
in-the-Fields, have been fruitlessly searched for
the record, and it is clear that, for some days,
the ceremony was kept a secret, pending the
arrival from Wales of Mrs. Scurlock's consent.
It probably took place on the 9th of September,
1707, the day after the license was granted. In
the previous month of August, Steele had rented
a house, now no longer standing, in Bury Street,
close to the turning out of Jermyn Street. This
was a quarter of the town described by contemporary advertisements as in close proximity "to

St. James's Church, Chapel, Park, Palace, Coffee and Chocolate Houses " — in other words, it was in the very heart of the *beau monde ;* and here Steele, moreover, would be within easy distance of the Court, and the Cockpit at Whitehall. He appears to have begun his establishment upon the lavish footing of a gentleman whose expectations are larger than his means, and whose wife's dignity demands, if not " the gilt coach and dappled Flanders mares " of Pope's Pamela, at least a chariot, a lady's-maid, and an adequate equipment of cinnamon satin. On paper his yearly income from all sources, Mrs. Scurlock's allowance not included, was about £1250. But by far the largest portion of this was derived from the Barbados property, which, besides being encumbered by legacies, seems to have made irregular returns. His salary as Gazetteer was also subject to " deductions," and as with the modest pay of a captain in Lucas's he had dabbled in alchemy, he was probably considerably in debt. The prospect was not a cheerful one, either for him or for " Prue," as he soon begins to call his more circumspect better-half, and the signs of trouble are speedily present. Always irrepressibly sanguine, and generally without ready money, he is constantly turning some pecuniary corner or

other, not without anticipations and borrowings
that bring their inevitable train of actions and
bailiffs. All this has to be gently tempered to
the apprehensive " Prue," who, to her other
luxuries, contrives to add a confidante, described
as Mrs. (probably here it means Miss) Binns.
Meanwhile her husband, bustling to and fro,
now detained in his passage by a friend (and a
" pint of wine "), — now, it is to be feared,
attentively " shadowed " by the watchful
" shoulder-dabbers," — scribbles off, from re-
mote " blind taverns " and other casual coigns
of vantage, a string of notes and notelets designed to keep his " Absolute Governess " at
Bury Street minutely acquainted with his doings.
Through all of these the " dusky strand " of the
" West Indian business " — in other words, the
protracted negotiation for the sale of the Barbados property — winds languidly and inextricably.

Steele's letters to his wife, accessible in the
reprints by Nichols of 1787 and 1809, are, however, too well known to need description, and
although Mr. Aitken has collated them with the
originals, he does not profess to have made any
material addition to their riches. As they progress, they record more than one of the various
attempts at advancement with which their writer,
egged on by his ambition and his embarrass-

ments, is perpetually preoccupied. To-day it is
a gentleman-ushership that seems within his
reach, to-morrow he is hoping to be Under-
Secretary, *vice* Addison promoted to Ireland.
Then the strange disquieting figure of Swift appears upon the scene, not, as it seems, to exercise its usual power of fascination over " Prue,"
by whom — Swift declares later — Steele is
governed " most abominably, as bad as Marlborough." With April, 1709, comes the establishment of the *Tatler*, and we enter upon
thrice-gleaned ground. The period covered by
" Mr. Bickerstaff's Lucubrations " and their
successor, the *Spectator*, lighted as it is by stray
side-rays from the wonderful " Journal to
Stella," offers few opportunities for fresh illumi-
nation. Mr. Aitken's account of the inception
of the two papers, and of their several imitators,
is copious and careful, but beyond printing from
the Blenheim MSS. some interesting accounts
of Tonson, bearing upon the sale of the collected
editions, and, from the British Museum, an
assignment to Buckley the bookseller of a share
in the *Spectator*, he adds nothing that is abso-
lutely new to what has already been collected
by Drake, Percy, Chalmers, Nichols, and other
writers. With respect to the unexplained ces-
sation of the *Tatler*, he apparently inclines to

the view that it was in some sort the result of
an understanding with Harley, by which Steele,
having been deprived of his Gazetteership as a
caution, was allowed to retain, *quamdiu se bene
gesserit*, his recently acquired appointment as
Commissioner of Stamps. But it is not probable
that we shall ever know much more of a transaction concerning which Addison was uncon-
sulted, and Swift uninformed. With all his
customary openness, Steele could, if he pleased,
keep his own counsel, and he seems to have
done so on this occasion.

Nor are we really any wiser as to the reasons
for the termination of the *Spectator* in December,
1712, except that we know it to have been pre-
meditated, since the *Guardian* was projected
before the *Spectator* ceased to appear. From
the Berkeley letters among Lord Egmont's
MSS., we learn that Steele was once more
dallying with his first love, the stage ; and from
the same source that, either early in February or
late in January, the death of his mother-in-law
had put him in possession of £500 per annum.
To this improvement in his affairs is doubtless
traceable that increased spirit of independence
which precipitated what all lovers of letters
must regard as his disastrous plunge into politics.
Whatever the origin of the *Guardian*, and how-

ever sincere its opening protests of neutrality, the situation was far too strained for one who, having a journal at his command, had been from his youth a partisan of the Revolution, and had already made rash entry into party quarrels. Before May, 1713, he was involved in bitter hostilities with Swift, arising out of a Tory attack on the Nottinghams for their desertion to the Whigs. A few weeks later found him insisting upon the demolition, under the Treaty of Utrecht, of the harbour and fortifications of Dunkirk, which demolition, it was shrewdly suspected, the Ministry were intending to forego. In June he had resigned his Commissionership of Stamps, and in August he was elected member for the borough of Stockbridge. Almost concurrently he issued a pamphlet entitled "The Importance of Dunkirk consider'd." Swift, henceforth hanging always upon his traces, retorted with one of his cleverest pamphlets, "The Importance of the *Guardian* considered," and the "underspur-leathers" of the Tory press began also to ply their pens against Steele, who by this time had dropped the *Guardian* for a professedly political organ, the *Englishman*. Shortly afterwards he issued "The Crisis," a pamphlet on the Hanoverian succession, which Swift followed by his masterly "Publick Spirit of the Whigs."

No sooner had Steele taken his seat in the House in February than he found that in the eyes of those in power he was a marked man. He was at once impeached for seditious utterances in "The Crisis," and, though he seems to have made an able defence, was expelled. Then, after a few doubtful months, Queen Anne died, his party came into power, and his troubles as a politician were at an end. In his best pamphlet, his "Apology for Himself and his Writings," he has given an account of this part of his career.

That career, as far as literature is concerned, may be said to close with the publication of the "Apology," in October, 1714. Not many months afterwards, on presenting an address, he was knighted by King George. During the rest of his life, which was prolonged to September, 1729, when he died at Carmarthen, he continued to publish various periodicals and tracts, none of which is of great importance. In December, 1718, Lady Steele died, and four years later her husband produced a fourth comedy, that "Conscious Lovers" which honest Parson Adams declared to be (in parts) "almost solemn enough for a sermon," but which is nevertheless, perhaps by reason of Cibber's collaboration, one of the best constructed of his plays. Part of Mr. Aitken's second volume is occu-

pied by Steele's connection, as patentee and
manager, with Drury Lane Theatre, concerning which he has brought together much curious
and hitherto unpublished information. Other
points upon which new light is thrown are
the publication of " The Ladies Library," the
establishment of the " Censorium," Steele's
application for the Mastership of the Charterhouse, Mr. John Rollos and his mechanical
hoop-petticoat, the failure of Steele's once famous contrivance, the Fish-Pool, his connection
with the Dyers, etc. But it would be impossible to schedule in detail the numerous instances in which Mr. Aitken has been able
either to supplement the existing material or to
supersede it by new. A careful and exhaustive
bibliography is not the least of his achievements.

As regards Steele's character, Mr. Aitken's
inquiries further enforce the conclusion that
in any estimate of it, considerable allowance
must be made for the influence of that miserable
and malicious contemporary gossip, of which, as
Fielding says, the " only basis is lying." For
much of this, Steele's ill-starred excursion into
faction is obviously responsible. " Scandal between Whig and Tory," said the ingenuous and
experienced author of the " New Atalantis,"
" goes for nothing," and apart from her specific

recantation in the dedication to " Lucius," this
sentiment alone should suffice to discredit her,
at all events in the absence of anything like
corroborative evidence. The attacks of Dennis
and the rest are as worthless. We know that
Steele was not "descended from a trooper's
horse," and we know that he was not "born at
Carrickfergus" (whatever social disqualification
that particular accident may entail). Why
should we listen to the circulators of these or
other stories — those of Savage, for example?
With respect to Swift, the most dangerous because the most powerful detractor, it is clear,
from the way in which he speaks of Steele and
Steele's abilities *before* the strife of party had
estranged them, that, if they had never quarrelled,
he would have ranked him only a little lower than
Addison.[1]   And if Steele has suffered from scandal and misrepresentation, he has also suffered
from his own admissions. The perfect frankness
and freedom of his letters has been accepted
too literally. Charming and unique as they are,

---

[1] Swift's extraordinary pertinacity of hatred to Steele
cannot wholly be explained by his sense of Steele's in-
gratitude.   Steele had wounded him hopelessly in his
most vulnerable part — he had laughed at his pretensions
to political omnipotency, and he had (as Swift thought)
also challenged his Christianity.

they leave upon many, who do not sufficiently
bear in mind their extremely familiar character,
an ill-defined impression that he was over-uxorious,
over-sentimental. But a man is not necessarily
this for a few extravagant *billets-doux*, or many
irreproachable persons who now, in the time-
honoured words of Mr. Micawber, "walk erect
before their fellow-men," would incur the like
condemnation. Again, it is, to all appearance,
chiefly due to the careless candour of some half-
dozen of these documents that Steele has been
branded as a drunkard. The fact is that, in an
age when to take too much wine was no disgrace, he was neither better nor worse than his
contemporaries ; and there is besides definite
evidence that he was easily overcome — far more
easily than Addison. As regards his money
difficulties, they cannot be denied. But they
were the difficulties of improvidence and not of
profligacy, of a man who, with Fielding's joy of
life and Goldsmith's "knack of hoping," always
rated an uncertain income at its highest and not
at its average amount, and who, moreover, paid
his debts before he died. For the rest, upon
the question of his general personality, it will
suffice to cite one unimpeachable witness, whose
testimony has only of late years come to light.
Berkeley, who wrote for the *Guardian,* and

visited Steele much at Bloomsbury (where he saw nothing of Savage's bailiffs in livery), speaks expressly, in a letter to Sir John Perceval, of his love and consideration for his wife, of the generosity and benevolence of his temper, of his cheerfulness, his wit, and his good sense. He should hold it, he says, a sufficient recompense for writing the "Treatise on Human Knowledge" that it gained him "some share in the friendship of so worthy a man." The praise of Berkeley — Berkeley, to whom Pope gives "every virtue under heaven," and who is certainly one of the noblest figures of the century — outweighs whole cartloads of Grub-street scandal and skip-kennel pamphleteers.

With Steele's standing as a man of letters we are on surer ground, since his own works speak for him without the distortions of tradition. To the character of poet he made no pretence, nor could he, although — witness the Horatian lines to Marlborough, which Mr. Aitken now dates 1709 — he possessed the eighteenth-century faculty of easy octosyllabics. Of his plays it has been said that they resemble essays rather than dramas, a judgment which sets one wondering what would have been the critic's opinion if Steele had never written the *Spectator*, and the *Tatler*. It is perhaps more to the point

that their perception of strongly marked humourous character is far more obvious than their
stage-craft, and that their shortcomings in this
latter respect are heightened by Steele's debata-
ble endeavours not (as Cowper says) " to let
down the pulpit to the level of the stage," but
to lift the stage to a level with the pulpit.　As
a political writer, his honesty and enthusiasm
were not sufficient to secure him permanent
success in a line where they are not always
thrice-armed that have their quarrel just; and
it is no discredit to him that he was unable to
contend against the deadly irony of Swift.　It is
as an essayist that he will be best remembered.
In the past, it has been too much the practice
to regard him as the humbler associate of Addison.　We now know that he deserves a much
higher place; that Addison, in fact, was quite
as much indebted to Steele's inventive gifts as
Steele could possibly have been indebted to
Addison's sublimating spirit.　It may be that he
was a more negligent writer than Addison; it
may be that he was inferior as a literary artist;
but the genuineness of his feelings frequently
carries him farther.　Not a few of his lay sermons on anger, pride, flattery, magnanimity, and
so forth, are unrivalled in their kind.　He ral-
lied the follies of society with unfailing tact and

good-humour; he rebuked its vices with admirable courage and dignity; and he wrote of
women and children as, in his day, no writer
had hitherto dared to do. As the first painter
of domesticity, the modern novel owes him
much. But modern journalism owes him more,
since — to use some words of his great adversary — he " refined it first, and showed its
use."

Mr. Aitken's book has been described in the
title to this paper as the "latest" Life of Steele.
It will probably be the " last." No one, at all
events, is likely to approach the subject again
with the same indefatigable energy of research.
To many of us, indeed, Biography, conceived in
this uncompromising fashion, would be a thing
impossible. To shrink from no investigation,
however tedious, to take nothing at second-
hand, to verify everything, to cross-examine
everything, to leave no smallest stone unturned
in the establishment of the most infinitesimal
fact — these are conditions which presuppose a
literary constitution of iron. It is but just to
note that the method has its drawbacks. So narrow an attention to minutiæ tends to impair the
selective power, and the defect of Mr. Aitken's
work is, almost of necessity, its superabundance.
It will be said that his determination to discover

has sometimes carried him too far afield; that
much of these two handsome volumes might
with advantage have been committed to the safe-
keeping of an appendix; that the mass of detail,
in short, is out of proportion to its actual rele-
vance.   To this, in all likelihood, the author
would answer that his book is not designed (in
Landor's phrase) to lie —

> "With summer sweets, with albums gaily drest,
>   Where poodle snifts at flower between the leaves;"

that he does not put it forward as a study or
critical monograph; but that it is a leisurely
and conscientious effort, reproducing much out-
of-the-way information which is the lawful prize
of his individual bow and spear; and that,
rather than lose again what has been so painfully
acquired, he is prepared to risk the charge of
surplusage, content if his labours be recognised
as the fullest and most trustworthy existing contribution towards the life and achievements of
a distinguished man of letters who died nearly
one hundred and seventy years ago.   And this
recognition his labours undoubtedly deserve.

THE AUTHOR OF "MONSIEUR TONSON."

"NEVER have a porch to your paper." Acting upon this excellent maxim of the late Master of Balliol, we may at once explain that "Monsieur Tonson" is the title of a long-popular recitation. It recounts, in rhyme of the Wolcot and Colman order, how, in the heyday of hoaxes and practical joking, a wag, called King in the verses, persecutes an unhappy French refugee in St. Giles's with repeated nightly inquiries for an imaginary "Mr. Thompson," until at length his maddened victim flies the house. And here comes in the effective point of the story. After a protracted absence abroad, the tormentor returns to London, when the whim seizes him to knock once more at the old door with the old question. By an extraordinary coincidence the Frenchman has just resumed residence in his former dwelling.

Without one thought of the relentless foe,
Who, fiend-like, haunted him so long ago,
	Just in his former trim he now appears :
The waistcoat and the nightcap seemed the same,
With rushlight, as before, he creeping came,
	And KING's detested voice astonish'd hears, —

the result being that he takes flight again, " and
ne'er is heard of more." The author of this *jeu
d'esprit* was John Taylor, the oculist and jour-
nalist ; and it originated in a current anecdote,
either actually founded on fact or invented by a
Governor of Jamaica. After a prosperous career
in prose, Taylor versified it for Fawcett, the
comedian, who was giving recitations at the
Freemasons' Tavern. It had an extraordinary
vogue ; was turned by Moncrieff into a farce
(in which Gatti, and afterwards Matthews, took
the leading part of Monsieur Morbleu, the
Frenchman) ; was illustrated by Robert Cruikshank, and still, we are told, makes furtive
appearance in popular " Reciters." By describing himself on the title-page of his memoirs as
" Author of ' Monsieur Tonson,' " its writer
plainly regarded the poem as his passport to
fame ; and whether one agrees with him or not,
it may safely be taken as a pretext for some account of the gossiping and discursive volumes
which contain his recollections.

John Taylor's grandfather, also John, was a person of considerable importance in his day, being indeed none other than the notorious oculist, or "Ophthalmiater," known as the "Chevalier" Taylor. Irreverent persons seem to have hinted that, as a matter of fact, this new-fangled Ophthalmiater meant no more than old Quack "writ large;" and one William Hogarth, generally on the side of the irreverent, hitched the Chevalier into a well-known satirical etching which collectors entitle indifferently "Consultation of Physicians" or "Company of Undertakers." Here the gifted recipient (as *per* advertisement) of so many distinctions "Pontifical, Imperial, and Royal," appears ignobly with Mrs. Sarah Mapp, the Epsom bone-setter, and that famous Dr. Joshua Ward, referred to by Fielding, whose pill (like a much-vaunted nostrum of our own day) had the property of posting at once to the part affected. Yet the Chevalier, despite inordinate vanity, and a fondness for fine clothes which made him fair game for the mocker, was undoubtedly a man of ability. "He has a good person, is a natural orator, and has a facility of learning foreign languages"— says Dr. King, who met him at Tunbridge; and apart from the circumstance that he had been a pupil of Cheselden the anatomist, he was really a very skilful operator for cataract, and wrote a long list of works or pamphlets on the eye. He was a familiar figure in the different Courts of Europe for his cures, real and imaginary, the story of which he relates — without showing any " remarkable diffidence in recording his own talents and attainments," says his grandson — in three volumes of Memoirs,[1] having a longer title-page than that of " Pamela." Judging from his own account (which should probably be taken with the fullest allowance of cautionary salt), his experiences must have been peculiar, and his visiting list unusually varied. He asserts, without much detail, that he knew Lord Bath and Jack Sheppard ; Mary Tofts, the Godalming rabbit-breeder, and Sarah, Duchess of Marlborough.

---

[1] " The History of the Travels and Adventures of the Chevalier John Taylor, Ophthalmiater . . . Author of 45 works in different Languages : the Produce for upwards of Thirty years, of the greatest Practice in the Cure of distempered Eyes, of any in the Age we live [*sic*] — Who has been in every Court, Kingdom, Province, State, City, and Town of the least Consideration in all Europe, without exception. Written by Himself . . . *Qui Visum Vitam Dat.* London : J. Williams, 1761–2." This must not be confounded with the " Life " in two volumes published by Cooper in 1761, a coarse catchpenny invention by Lord Chesterfield's profligate protégé, the bricklayer poet, Henry Jones.

He also professed acquaintance with Marshals Saxe and Keith ; with Pöllnitz of the " Virginians ; " with Theodore, the bankrupt King of Corsica ; with Boerhaave, Albinus, Linnæus, Pope, Voltaire, Metastasio, La Fontaine, etc. (If the fabulist be intended, there is clearly some mistake, since La Fontaine departed this life about eight years before the Chevalier was born.) He was a witness, he says, of the execution of Counsellor Christopher Layer for high treason, and he affirms that he was actually present in the Old Bailey upon that memorable occasion when Blake (*alias* Blue-skin) tried to cut the throat of Jonathan Wild. Having seen many men and cities, and full of honours — chiefly of foreign manufacture — the Chevalier died in a convent at Prague in 1780. At the time of his death, it may be noted, the famous Ophthalmiater was himself blind. He can scarcely be said to have wanted a *vates sacer*, for Churchill mentions him in " The Ghost : " —

> Behold the CHEVALIER —
> As well prepar'd, beyond all doubt,
> To put Eyes in, as put them out.

And Walpole gave him a not very happy epigram : —

> Why Taylor the quack calls himself *Chevalier*,
>   'T is not easy a reason to render;
> Unless blinding eyes, that he thinks to make clear,
>   Demonstrates he 's but a *Pretender*.

His only son, John Taylor the Second, was
also an oculist, but not of equal eminence, although one of his cures — that of a boy born
blind — obtained the honours of a pamphlet by
Oldys the antiquary, and a portrait by Worlidge
the etcher.   At the Chevalier's death John Taylor applied for the post, which his father had
held, of oculist to the King, but the appointment was given to the Baron de Wenzel, one of
the Chevalier's pupils, who had been fortunate
enough to operate successfully on the old Duke
of Bedford, of " Junius " notoriety.   To John
Taylor the Second succeeded John Taylor the
Third, the " Author of ' Monsieur Tonson.' "
Beginning life as an oculist, like his father and
grandfather, he achieved considerable reputation
in that capacity, and by good luck obtained at
Wenzel's death the very appointment which his
father had failed to secure.   But in mid-career
he relinquished his profession for journalism.
For many years he was proprietor and editor of
the *Sun* newspaper, and in 1827 he also published a couple of volumes of prologues, epilogues, sonnets, and occasional verses.   His

chief reputation, however, was that of a *racon-teur*. "In his latter days," says the *Literary Gazette*, in its obituary notice of May 19, 1832, he " was, perhaps, as entertaining in conversation, with anecdote, playfulness, and satire, as any man within the bills of mortality." Many of his good things are preserved in the two volumes of " Records of My Life " which appeared shortly after his death,[1] to the compilation of which he was impelled by the perfidy of a former partner and the invitation of an " eminent publisher," presumably Mr. Edward Bull, of Holles Street, whose imprint the volumes bear. His recollections are set down without any other method than a certain rough grouping ; they have the garrulity and the repetitions of the advanced age at which they were penned ; but they contain, in addition to a good deal that he had heard from others, much that had come within his own experiences. As he professes strict veracity, it is from the latter class that we shall chiefly make selection, beginning as in duty bound, with the anecdotes of literary men.

[1] " Records of my Life ; by the late John Taylor, Esquire, Author of ' Monsieur Tonson.' " 2 vols. London : Bull, 1832. The copy belonging to the present writer contains, besides inserted photographs, " Addenda " by John Stirling Taylor, the author's son.

Concerning Johnson and Goldsmith he has not much to say beyond the fact that, as a boy, he had once delivered a letter for the latter at the Temple, but without seeing him. It is, however, to the " Author of ' Monsieur Tonson ' " that we owe the historic episode of the borrowed guinea slipped under the door, which recurs so prominently in all Goldsmith's biographies; while he tells one anecdote of Johnson which, as far as we can discover, has escaped Dr. Birkbeck Hill. According to Dr. Messenger Monsey, physician of Chelsea Hospital — a rough, Abernethy sort of man, whom his admirers compared with Swift — upon one occasion, when the age of George III. was under discussion, Johnson burst in with a " Pooh! what does it signify when such an animal was born, or whether he had ever been born at all? " — an ultra-Jacobital utterance which the Whig narrator did not neglect to accentuate by reminding his hearers that to this very " usurper " Johnson subsequently owed his pension. But as Monsey did not like the Doctor, and Taylor calls him a " literary hippopotamus," the incident is probably exaggerated. Then there is a story of Dr. Parr, in which is concerned another of the Johnson circle, Edmund Burke. During the Hastings trial Parr was effusive (Taylor says " diffusive ") about the

speeches of Sheridan and Fox, but silent as to
Burke's, a circumstance which led that distinguished orator to suggest interrogatively that he
presumed Parr found it faultless. "Not so,
Edmund," was the reply, in Parr's best Johnsonese ; " your speech was oppressed by epithet,
dislocated by parenthesis, and debilitated by
amplification," — a knock-me-down answer to
which "Edmund" made no recorded re-
joinder. There is a touch of the lexicographic
manner in another anecdote, this time of Hugh
Kelly, the stay-maker turned dramatist and bar-
rister, who was so proud of his silver that he
kept even his spurs upon the sideboard. Ex-
amining a lady at the trial of George Barring-
ton, the pick-pocket, Kelly inquired elaborately,
" Pray, madam, how could you, in the immensity
of the crowd, determine the identity of the man ? "
As he found that his question was wholly unintelligible to the witness, he reduced it to " How
do you know he was the man ? " "Because,"
came the prompt reply, " I caught his hand in my
pocket." Taylor apparently knew both the Bos-
wells, father and son, and, indeed, playfully claims
part-authorship in the famous " Life " upon the
ground that he had suggested the substitution
of " comprehending " for " containing " in the
title-page ; and certainly — if that be proof —

" comprehending " is there, and " containing " is
not.[1] He had also relations with Wilkes, whom
he praises for his wit and learning. For his
learning we have the evidence of his " Catullus,"
but his wit seems, like much wit of his day, to
have been largely based upon bad manners.
Once a certain over-goaded Sir Watkin Lewes
said angrily to him, " I 'll be your butt no
longer." Wilkes at once mercilessly retorted,
" With all my heart. I never like an empty
one."

Wolcot and Caleb Whitefoord of the " Cross
Readings," Richard Owen Cambridge and Richard Cumberland — all figure in the " Records."
Taylor thinks that the famous Whitefoord addition to " Retaliation " was really by Goldsmith
— a supposition which is not shared by modern
Goldsmith critics. Of Wolcot there is a lengthy
account, the most striking part of which refers
to his last hours. Taylor asked him, on his
death-bed, whether anything could be done for
him. " His answer, delivered in a deep and
strong tone, was, ' Bring back my youth,' " after
which futile request he fell into the sleep in
which he died. Cambridge Taylor seems to
have known but slightly, and apart from a long

[1] For exact title, see *post*, " Boswell's Predecessors and
Editors."

story, for the authenticity of which he does not
vouch, has nothing memorable to say of him,
except that he declared he had written his
" Scribleriad " while under the hands of his
hairdresser, — a piece of fine-gentleman affecta-
tion which recalls Molière's poetaster.   But
Taylor tells a story of Cumberland which is at
least well invented.   Once — so it runs — Cumberland stumbled on entering a box at Drury
Lane Theatre, and Sheridan sprang to his assistance.   " Ah, sir! " said the writer of the " West
Indian," " you are the only man to assist a *falling* author."   " Rising, you mean," returned
Sheridan, thus, either by malice or misadventure,
employing almost the exact words which, in the
Critic, he had put into the mouth of " Sir Fret-
ful Plagiary," — a character admittedly modelled
upon Cumberland himself.   Sheridan, too, supplies more than one page of these recollections,
and their writer professes to have been present
when he (Sheridan) spoke as follows concerning
a pamphleteer who had written against him :
" I suppose that Mr. —— thinks I am angry
with him, but he is mistaken, for I never harbour resentment.   If his punishment depended
on me, I would show him that the dignity of
my mind was superior to all vindictive feelings.
Far should I be from wishing to inflict a capital

punishment upon him, grounded on his attack upon me ; but yet on account of his general character and conduct, and as a warning to others, I would merely order him to be publicly whipped three times, to be placed in the pillory four times, to be confined in prison seven years, and then, as he would enjoy freedom the more after so long a confinement, I would have him transported for life."

At the date of the above deliverance, the scene of which was a tavern in Portugal Street, — perhaps the now vanished Grange public house, — Sheridan was lessee of Drury Lane Theatre. In later years Taylor was to become acquainted with another Drury Lane magnate, Lord Byron, with whom he corresponded and exchanged poems. Concerning Lady Byron he reports that Mrs. Siddons, whom he regarded as an unimpeachable authority, assured him that if she had no other reason to admire his Lordship's judgment and taste, she should be fully convinced of both by his choice of a wife, — a sentiment which should certainly be set down to the credit of a lady who is by no means over-praised. Among the Portugal Street roisterers was Richard Wilson, the painter. According to Taylor he must have been vintner as well, since most of the wine came from his cellar in Lin-

coln's Inn Fields (Great Queen Street), the
company having condemned the tavern bever-
ages. Apart from the fact that Wilson's " favourite fluid," like Churchill's, was porter, this
particular is more out of keeping with his traditional lack of pence than another, also related
by Taylor, in which he says that, upon one
occasion, having procured Wilson a commission,
he was obliged to lend him the money to buy
brushes and canvas. With artists, however,
Taylor's acquaintance was not large. He knew
Peters the academician, afterwards the Rev. ;
and he knew Ozias Humphry the miniaturist,
who in his old age became totally blind. With
West and his rival Opie (who, like Wilson, lived
in Queen Street) he was apparently on familiar
terms, and he was often the guest of the former at
the dinners which the Royal Academy of that day
were accustomed to have on the anniversary of
Queen Charlotte's birthday. Of West he speaks
warmly ; does not mention his vanity, and attributes much of his baiting by Peter Pindar to
that satirist's partiality for Opie. Fuseli, another resident in Great Queen Street, and
Northcote, also flit through the record ; and
there is reference to a supper at Reynolds's,
where it was idly debated whether Johnson
would have written the " Reflections on the

French Revolution " better than Burke, and where — on the topic *De mortuis* — Reynolds propounded the practical dictum that " the dead were nothing, and the living everything, " — a sentiment which shows him to have been in agreement with the *On doit des égards aux vivants* of Voltaire. But, on the whole, the annalist's memories of artists are of meagre interest, and the only compact anecdote related of a member of the profession refers to the architect known popularly as " Capability " Brown. Once when Lord Chatham, disabled by the gout, was hobbling painfully down the stairs of St. James's Palace, Brown had the good fortune to assist him to his carriage.   Lord Chatham thanked him, adding pleasantly, " Now, sir, go and adorn your country."   To which Brown the capable retorted neatly, " Go you, my Lord, and save it."

Of anecdotes of actors and actresses the Author of " Monsieur Tonson " has no lack. As already stated, he was much in request for prologues and epilogues ; he was an active and intelligent dramatic critic, and he was, moreover, intimate with most of the leading players of his day.   To make any adequate summary of so large a body of theatrical gossip would be difficult ; but a few stories may be selected con-

cerning some of the older men. Of Garrick,
whom Taylor's father had seen when he first
came out at Goodman's Fields, and regarded as
the Shakespeare of actors, he tells a number of
stories which, unfamiliar when the " Records "
were published, are now fairly well-known.
Taylor was, however, the first, we believe, to
record that effective anecdote of Mrs. Clive,
who, watching Garrick from behind the scenes,
between smiles and tears, burst at last into emphatic and audible expression of her belief that
he could " act a gridiron ; " and Taylor also
says that once, when his father was performing
an operation for cataract, Garrick, who was
present, so enthralled the nervous patient by
his humour, that he forgot both his fears and
his pain. Of Garrick's Lady Macbeth, Mrs.
Pritchard, Taylor, deriving his information from
his father, speaks highly, and considers that
Johnson degraded her memory by describing
her as " an ignorant woman, who talked of her
gownd." (Mrs. Pritchard had acted the heroine in the great man's *Irene*, and it is possible
that he was prejudiced.) To Macklin, another
celebrated Macbeth, — being, indeed, the first
who performed that part in the old Scottish garb,
— Taylor makes frequent reference. He saw
him in Iago, in Sir Paul Pliant of the *Double*

Dealer, and in other characters ; but held that
he was "too theoretical for nature. He had
three pauses in his acting — the first, moderate ;
the second, twice as long ; but his last, or
'grand pause,' as he styled it, was so long that
the prompter on one occasion, thinking his
memory failed, repeated the cue . . . several
times, and at last so loud as to be heard by the
audience." Whereupon Macklin in a passion
rushed from the stage and knocked him down,
exclaiming, "The fellow interrupted me in my
grand pause ! " Quin, Macklin's rival, was also
given to inordinate pauses, and once, while acting Horatio in Rowe's "Fair Penitent" (the
play in which George Primrose of Wakefield
was to have made his début), he delayed so long
to reply to the challenge of Lothario that a man
in the gallery bawled out, "Why don't you give
the gentleman an answer, whether you will or
no ?" Taylor cites a good many instances of
Quin's *gourmandise*, and of his ready, but rather
full-flavoured wit. He is perhaps best when on
his dignity. Once at Allen's of Prior Park
(Fielding's "Allworthy"), the imperious Warburton attempted to degrade the guest into the
actor by insidiously pressing Quin to recite
something. Quin accordingly spoke a speech
from Otway's "Venice Preserved" which contained the lines, —

> *" Honest men*
> Are the soft easy cushions on which knaves
> Repose and fatten, " —

delivering them with so unmistakable an application to Allen and Warburton respectively that
he was never again troubled by the divine for a
specimen of his declamatory powers.   Another
story told by Taylor of Quin may be quoted,
because it introduces Mrs. Clive.   She had invited Quin to stay at Cliveden (Little Strawberry), of which the appointments were on as
minute a scale as those of Petit-Trianon.   When
he had inspected the garden, she asked him if
he had noticed a tiny piece of water which she
called her pond.   " Yes, Kate," he replied, " I
have seen your *basin*, but did not see a wash-
ball."   Taylor seems surprised that Walpole
should have been so much attracted to Mrs.
Clive, whose personal charms were small, and
whose manners, he alleges, were rough and vulgar.   He quotes, with apparent approval, some
unpublished lines by Peter Pindar, criticis-
ing the epitaph in which Walpole declared that
Comedy had died with his friend : —

> " Horace, of Strawberry Hill I mean, not Rome,
> Lo ! all thy geese are swans, I do presume;
>   Truth and thy verses seem not to agree;

Know Comedy is hearty, all alive ;
The Comic Muse no more expired with Clive
Than dame Humility will die with thee."

But one need no more swear to the truth of
an epitaph than of a song.   Catharine Clive had
both humour and good-humour ; her indefatigable needle was continually employed in the
decoration of Walpole's Gothic museum, and it
may be concluded that he knew perfectly what
he was about.   As a near neighbour, a blue
stocking might have been wearisome, a beauty
dangerous, and she was probably of far more
use to him than either.

Except for the " gridiron " anecdote, however, Mrs. Clive does not play any material part
in Taylor's chronicle.   With a later luminary,
Miss Farren, he was not actually acquainted,
although he had met her once with Lord Derby
(whom she ultimately married), and had admired
her genuine sensibility in Miss Lee's " Chapter
of Accidents."   But he seems to have been on
intimate terms with Mrs. Abington, both in her
prime and also in her decline, for he was present when she degraded herself by acting Scrub
in the " Beaux' Stratagem ; "[1] and he had dined
with her at Mrs. Jordan's, when she talked

[1] There is a caricature of Mrs. Abington in this part
by James Sayer.

unceasingly and enthusiastically of Garrick, — a
circumstance which, considering the trouble she
had given him in his lifetime, may perhaps be
regarded in the light of an expiatory exercise.
Taylor also knew Mrs. Siddons, of whom he
speaks warmly, saying that he had been intimate with her for years, and had " many of her
letters, with which even her request would not
induce him to part " He was, as a matter of
fact, connected with the Kemble family by marriage, his first wife, Mrs. Duill, having been a
Miss Satchell, whose sister had married Stephen
Kemble, a huge Trulliber of a man who could
act Falstaff without stuffing, and had gone
through all the experiences of a strolling player,
even to lunching in a Yorkshire turnip-field.[1]
Of John Kemble, and Charles Kemble and his
wife there is much in the " Records," but most
of it has grown familiar by repetition. There
is also much of other actors and actresses, as
might be expected from one who had seen
Dodd as Sir Andrew Aguecheek, Lewis as Mer-
cutio, " Gentleman " Smith as Charles in the
" School for Scandal," and Palmer — Lamb's

[1] Stephen George Kemble died in June, 1822. While
manager of the Newcastle Theatre, he was on intimate
terms with Thomas Bewick, who engraved a portrait of
him as Falstaff for a benefit ticket.

Jack Palmer — as Sneer in the " Critic." Taylor's portrait, in the poem called " The Stage," of the last-named performer may serve as an example of its writer's powers as a rival of Lloyd and Churchill : —

> " Where travell'd fops, too nice for nature grown,
>   Are sway'd by affectation's whims alone ;
>   Where the sly knave, usurping honour's guise,
>   By secret villainy attempts to rise ;
>   Or where the footman, negligently gay,
>   His master's modish airs would fain display ;
>   But chiefly where the rake, in higher life,
>   Cajoles the husband to seduce the wife,
>   And, fraught with art, but plausible to sight,
>   The libertine and hypocrite unite —
>   PALMER from life the faithful portrait draws,
>   And calls unrivall'd for our warm applause."

In the foregoing plunges into the Taylorian bran-pie, we have, as promised at the outset, depended rather upon the writer's personal experiences than upon his miscellaneous anecdotes. But we have by no means exhausted the personal experiences. Not to mention political magnates like Lord Chatham and Lord Chesterfield, whom we have almost entirely neglected, there are many references to characters difficult to classify, but no less diverting to recall. As a boy, Taylor had seen Coan, the Norfolk dwarf of Churchill's *Rosciad*

("Whilst to six feet the vig'rous stripling grown,
Declares that GARRICK is another COAN "),

then lodging at a tavern in the Five Fields (now
Eaton Square) kept by one of the Pinchbecks
who Invented the metal of that name ; and he
remembered the boxer Buckhorse, a debased
specimen of humanity, whose humour consisted
in permitting the Eton and Westminster boys
to punch his battered features at the modest
rate of a shilling the blow.[1] He had also
visited the famous Mrs. Teresa Cornelys, when
that favourite of the Nobility and Gentry had
fallen upon evil days, and was subsisting pre-
cariously as a purveyor of asses' milk at Knights-
bridge ; he had known intimately a certain Mr.
Donaldson, who, like Horace Walpole, had gone
in danger of his life from the "gentleman high-
wayman," James Maclean ; and at Angelo's in
Carlisle Street, Soho, he had frequently met the
Chevalier D'Eon in his woman's dress, but old,
and equally decayed in manners and means. It
is singular that the Author of " Monsieur Tonson," with all his dramatic proclivities, should

[1] Buckhorse can hardly have been familiar with Roman
law. But twenty-five pieces of copper (about the value
of a shilling) was the legal tender, or solatium, for a blow
on the face (*cf.* the story of Veratius in Gibbon's forty-
fourth chapter).

never have attempted a play.   As far as can be
ascertained, however, his sole contribution to
stage literature, prologues and epilogues excepted, was the lines for the rhyming Butler in
Mrs. Inchbald's " Lovers' Vows," that version
of Kotzebue's "Das Kind der Liebe " which
figures so conspicuously in Miss Austen's
" Mansfield Park."   " Lovers' Vows " would
appear to be fertile in suggestion, for it was in
playing this piece that Charles Kean fell in love
with his future wife, Miss Ellen Tree, sister of
the musical Maria (Mrs. Bradshaw), who lives
for ever in Henry Luttrell's happy epigram : —

> " On this Tree when a nightingale settles and sings,
> The Tree will return her as good as she brings."

BOSWELL'S PREDECESSORS AND EDITORS.

WRITING to Pope in July, 1728, concerning the annotation of the *Dunciad*, Swift comments upon the prompt oblivion which overtakes the minor details of contemporary history. "Twenty miles from London nobody understands hints, initial letters, or town facts and passages; and in a few years not even those who live in London." A somewhat similar opinion was expressed by Johnson. "In sixty or seventy years, or less," he said, "all works which describe manners require notes." His own biography is a striking case in point. Almost from the beginning the editorial pen was freely exercised upon it, and long before the lesser term he mentions, it was already — to use an expressive phrase of Beaumarchais — "*rongée d'extraits et couverte de critiques.*" With Mr. Croker's edition of 1831 it might have been thought that the endurable limits of illustration and interpretation had been reached, and for some time, indeed, that opinion seems to have obtained. But within a comparatively brief period three other editions of importance have made their appearance, each of which has its specific merits, while four and twenty years ago was published another (reissued in 1888), which had, at least, the merit of an excellent plan. Boswell's book itself may now, in Parliamentary language, be taken for " read." As Johnson said of Goldsmith's *Traveller*, "its merit is established, and individual praise or censure can neither augment nor diminish it." But the publication, in Colonel Grant's excellent brief memoir, of the first systematic bibliography of Johnson's works, coupled with the almost simultaneous issue by Mr. H. R. Tedder, the able and accomplished librarian to the Athenæum Club, of a bibliography of Boswell's masterpiece, affords a sufficient pretext for some review of Boswell's editors and predecessors.

Johnson died on the evening of Monday, December 13, 1784. According to a letter dated May 5, 1785, from Michael Lort to Bishop Percy, printed in Nichols' " Literary Illustrations," the first Life appeared on the day following the death. But this is a manifest mistake, as reference to contemporary newspapers, or even to the pamphlet itself, should have sufficed to show. At p. 120 is an account

of Johnson's funeral, which did not take place
until Monday, December 20. Moreover, the
portrait by T. Trotter, for which Johnson is
said to have sat " some time since," is dated
the 16th, and in an article in the *Gentleman's
Magazine* for December it is expressly stated
that the book "was announced before the
Doctor had been two days dead," and appeared
on the ninth morning after his death. It may
even be doubtful if this is strictly accurate, as
the first notification of the pamphlet in the *Public Advertiser* appears on Thursday, the 23rd,
and promises its publication that week. Its
title is " The Life of Samuel Johnson, LL.D.,
with Occasional Remarks on his Writings, an
Authentic Copy of his Will, and a Catalogue
of his Works, &c.," 1785. It is an octavo of iv-
144 pages, and its publisher was the G. Kears-
ley, of 46 Fleet Street, who issued so many of
Goldsmith's works. Its author, too, is supposed to have been the William Cook who
subsequently wrote recollections of Goldsmith
in the *European Magazine* for 1793. In Kears-
ley's advertisement great pains are taken to
avert the possible charge of catchpenny haste,
by the statement that the book had been drawn
up for some time, but had been withheld from
motives of delicacy. This anticipatory defence

is, however, somewhat neutralized by a communication in the *Gentleman's Magazine* for December, in which certain of its errors are excused upon the ground of "hurry." It professes, nevertheless, to be "a sketch, warm from the life," and, although speedily superseded by more leisurely efforts, is certainly not without interest as the earliest of its kind, even if it be not quite so early as it has hitherto been affirmed to be.

Cook's Life was followed by articles in the *European* and the *Gentleman's Magazines* for December, which, according to the fashion of those days, appeared at the end and not at the beginning of the month. That in the *European Magazine*, which was more critical than biographical, was continued through several numbers, and contains nothing to distinguish it from the respectable and laborious journey-work of the period. The sketch in the *Gentleman's Magazine* is of a far more meritorious character, and was from the pen of Tom Tyers, the "Tom Restless" of the *Idler*, and the son of Jonathan, "the founder of that excellent place of publick amusement, Vauxhall Gardens." Tyers had really known Johnson with a certain degree of intimacy, and even Boswell is obliged to admit that Tyers lived with his illustrious friend "in as easy a manner as almost any of his very numerous acquaintance." He has certainly not caught Johnson's style, as his memories are couched in abrupt shorthand sentences which are the reverse of Johnsonese. But apart from a certain vanity of classical quotation, with which he seems to have been twitted by his contemporaries, "Tom Restless" writes like a gentleman, and is fully entitled to the praise of having produced the first animated sketch of Johnson, who, from a sentence towards the close, appears to have anticipated that Tyers might be one day "called upon to assist a posthumous account of him." Mr. Napier says that Tyers continued his sketch in the *Gentleman's Magazine* for January, 1785. This is not quite exact, and is indeed practically contradicted by Mrs. Napier, since in the valuable volume of "Johnsoniana" which accompanies her husband's edition, she prints no more than is to be found in the December number. What Tyers really did was to insert a number of minor corrections in the annual supplement to the *Gentleman's Magazine*, and in the following number.

Without a close examination of contemporary advertisement sheets it would be difficult to fix precisely the date of publication of the next biography. It is a small duodecimo of 197 pages, entitled " Memoirs of the Life and Writings of the Late Dr. Samuel Johnson." The title-page is dated 1785. In the Preface mention is made of assistance rendered by Thomas Davies, the actor-bookseller of Russell Street, Covent Garden, who is described as "the late." The book must therefore have appeared after Thursday, May 5, when Davies died. Its author is supposed to have been the Rev. William Shaw, "a modest and a decent man," referred to in Boswell as the compiler of "an Erse Grammar," subsequently issued in 1788 as " An Analysis of the Gaelic Language." Colour is given to this supposition by the fact that another of the persons who supplied information was Mr. Elphinston, by whom Shaw was introduced to Johnson, and by the references made to the Ossianic controversy, in which Shaw did battle on Johnson's side against Macpherson. For the book itself, it is, like most of the pre-Boswellian efforts, Tyers's sketch excepted, mainly critical, and makes no attempt to reproduce Johnson's talk or sayings.

Chit-chat and personal characteristics are, however, somewhat more fully represented in what — neglecting for the moment Boswell's " Journal of a Tour to the Hebrides " — may be regarded as the next effort in the biographical sequence, the famous "Anecdotes of the Late Samuel Johnson, LL.D., during the Last Twenty Years of his Life," by Hesther Lynch Piozzi, which was published in March, 1766. Written in Italy, where she was then living, it was printed in London. Its success, as might perhaps have been anticipated from the author's long connection with Johnson, was exceptional. The first edition, like that of Fielding's "Amelia," was exhausted on the day of publication, and other editions followed rapidly. Boswell, as may be guessed, was not well disposed towards the work of his fortunate rival, and in his own book is at considerable pains to expose her "mistaken notion of Dr. Johnson's character," while his coadjutor, Malone, who tells us that she made £500 by the "Anecdotes," plainly calls her both "inaccurate and artful." We, who are neither editors nor biographers of Boswell, need not assume so censorious an attitude. That Mrs. Piozzi, by habit of mind, and from the circumstances under which her narrative was compiled, was negligent in her facts (she even blunders as to the date when she first met Johnson) may be admitted, and it is not inconceivable that, as Mrs. Napier says in the "Prefatory Notice" to her "Johnsoniana," her account would have been "more tender and true if it had been given by Mrs. Thrale instead of Mrs. Piozzi." But the cumulative effect of her vivacious and disconnected recollections (even Malone admits them to be "lively") is rather corroborative of, than at variance with, that produced by Johnson's more serious biographers. Her opportunities were great, — perhaps greater than those of any of her contemporaries, — her intercourse with Johnson was most unrestrained and unconventional, and notwithstanding all its faults, her little volume remains an essential part of Johnsonian literature.

Boswell, whose *magnum opus* we are now approaching, so fills the foreground with his fame that the partial obliteration of his predecessors is almost a necessary consequence. In this way Sir John Hawkins, whose " Life of Samuel Johnson, LL.D.," 1787, comes next in importance to Mrs. Piozzi's " Anecdotes," has suffered considerably ; and his book, which immediately after Johnson's death was advertised as " forthcoming," is, to use the words of a recent writer, " spoken of with contempt by many who have never taken the trouble to do more than turn over its leaves." That the author seems to have been extremely unpopular can scarcely be denied. Malone, who accumulates a page of his characteristics, says that Percy

called him "most detestable," Reynolds, "ab-
solutely dishonest," and Dyer, "mischievous,
uncharitable, and malignant," to which garland
of dispraise the recorder adds, as his own contribution, that he was "rigid and sanctimonious."
Johnson, too, styled him "an unclubable man."
But against all this censure it must be remembered that he was selected as one of the first
members of "The Club" (to whose promoters
his peculiarities can scarcely have been unknown,
for he had belonged to the earlier association
in Ivy Lane), and that Johnson appointed him
one of his executors. Boswell, whose vanity
Hawkins had wounded by the slight and
supercilious way in which he spoke of him in
the "Life," could scarcely be supposed to feel
kindly to him ; and though he professes to have
modified what he said of this particular rival on
account of his death, we have no means of
knowing how much he suppressed. He gives,
nevertheless, what on the whole is a not unfair
idea of Hawkins's volume. "However inadequate and improper," he says, "as a Life of Dr.
Johnson, and however discredited by unpardon-
able inaccuracies in other respects, [it] contains
a collection of curious anecdotes and observations which few men but its authour could have
brought together." What is commendatory in

this verdict is not exaggerated, and those who
care enough for Johnson to travel beyond Boswell will certainly find Hawkins by no means
so "ponderous" as Boswell would have us to
believe. Many of the particulars he gives are
certainly not to be found elsewhere, and his
knowledge of the seamy side of letters in Georgian London was "extensive and peculiar."

To speak of Hawkins after Mrs. Piozzi is a
course more convenient than chronological, as
it involves the neglect of an intermediate biographer. But the " Essay on the Life, Character,
and Writings of Dr. Samuel Johnson," from the
pen of the Rev. Joseph Towers, which comes
between them in 1786, has no serious import.
It treats more of the writings than the character
and life, and, except as the respectable effort
of an educated man, need not detain us from
Boswell himself, whose first offering at the
shrine of his adoration was made in September,
1785, when he published the "Journal of a
Tour to the Hebrides with Samuel Johnson,
LL.D." The tour, of which Johnson had himself given an account in his "Journey to the
Western Islands of Scotland," had taken place
as far back as 1773, and Boswell's journal had
lain by him ever since. But the manuscript had
been lent to different persons, — to Mrs. Thrale

among the rest. " I am glad you read Boswell's journal," said Johnson to her; "you are now sufficiently informed of the whole transaction, and need not regret that you did not make the tour to the Hebrides." A more emphatic testimony is contained in the "Journal" itself. Johnson, we are told, perused it diligently from day to day, and declared that he took great delight in doing so. " It might be printed," he said, "were the subject fit for printing," and further on he forbade Boswell to contract it. In his dedication to Malone, whose acquaintance he made in Baldwin's printing office while correcting the proofs, Boswell showed that he was conscious of the strong point of his work, "the numerous conversations, which (he said) form the most valuable part." In the third edition, dated August, 1786, the success of the book justified an ampler note of gratification: " I will venture to predict, that this specimen of the colloquial talents and extemporaneous effusions of my illustrious fellow-traveller will become still more valuable, when, by the lapse of time, he shall have become an ANCIENT; when all those who can now bear testimony to the transcendent powers of his mind shall have passed away; and no other memorial of this great and good man shall remain but the follow-

ing Journal, the other anecdotes and letters
preserved by his friends, and those incomparable works, which have for many years been
in the highest estimation, and will be read and
admired as long as the English language shall
be spoken or understood." Whether this variation of *Exegi monumentum* is justifiable or not —
and certainly some of the "incomparable works,"
have but faintly fulfilled their promise of perpe-
tuity — Boswell's accentuation of his distinctive
excellence, his admirably characteristic records
of conversations, is unanswerable evidence of a
settled purpose and a definite aim.

On a fly-leaf of the "Tour to the Hebrides"
(not as Mr. Napier seems to suppose, confined
to the third edition) was announced as "preparing for the press" the greater work by which
the "Tour" was succeeded in 1791. At first
it was to have been comprised in one quarto
volume, but it ultimately made its appearance in
two. The publisher was Charles Dilly, in the
Poultry, and the title-page ran as follows : —

"The Life of Samuel Johnson, LL.D., comprehending an Account of his Studies and numerous Works, in chronological Order ; a Series of
his Epistolary Correspondence and Conversations with many eminent Persons ; and various
original Pieces of his Composition, never be-

fore published. The whole exhibiting a View
of Literature and Literary Men in Great-Brit-
ain, for near half a Century, during which he
flourished."

In the dedication to Sir Joshua Reynolds,
referring to the earlier book, Boswell dwells
upon a difference of treatment which distinguishes
the "Life" from its predecessor. In the
"Tour" he had, it seems, been too open in his
communications, freely exhibiting to the world
the dexterity of Johnson's wit, even when that
wit was exercised upon himself. His frankness
had in some quarters been mistaken for insensi-
bility, and he has therefore in the "Life" been
"more reserved," and though he tells nothing
but the truth, has still kept in his mind that the
whole truth is not always to be exposed. In
the Advertisement which succeeds he enlarges
upon the difficulties of his task, and the labour
involved in the arrangement and collection of
material ; and he expresses his obligations to
Malone, who had heard nearly all the book in
manuscript, and had revised about half of it in
type. Seventeen hundred copies of it were
printed, and although the price in boards was
two guineas, between May (when the book
appeared) and August twelve hundred of these
had been sold. Boswell, who gives this infor-

mation to his friend Temple, in a letter dated the 22nd of the latter month, expected that the entire impression would be disposed of before Christmas.

This hope, however, does not appear to have been realised, since the second edition in three volumes octavo, considerably revised, and including "eight sheets of additional matter," was not published until July, 1793. During the progress of the work through the press many additional letters and anecdotes had come to hand, which were inserted in an introduction and appendix. These numerous improvements were at the same time printed in quarto form for the benefit of the purchasers of the issue of 1791, and sold at half-a-crown, under the title of "The Principal Corrections and Additions to the First Edition of Mr. Boswell's Life of Dr. Johnson." As in the "Tour to the Hebrides," the success of his labours inspired their author with a greater exultation of prefatory language. Referring to the death of Reynolds, which had taken place in the interval between the first and second editions, he says that Sir Joshua had read the book, and given "the strongest testimony to its fidelity." He has *Johnsonised* the land, he says farther on, and he trusts "they will not only talk but think Johnson."

He was still busily amending and retouching for a third edition when he died, on May 19, 1795, at his house, then No. 47, but now (or recently) No. 122, Great Portland Street. His task was taken up by Malone, who had been his adviser from the first, and under Malone's superintendence was issued, "revised and augmented," the third edition of 1799. From the fact that it contains Boswell's latest touches, this edition is held to be the most desirable by Johnson students. Boswell's friends contributed several notes, some of which were the work of the author's second son, James, then a student at Brasenose College, Oxford. Fourth, fifth, and sixth editions followed, all under the editorship of Malone. Then, shortly after the publication in 1811 of the last of these, Malone himself died. Seventh, eighth, and ninth editions, all avowedly or unavowedly reproducing Malone's last issue, subsequently appeared, the ninth having some additions by Alexander Chalmers. Then came what is known as the "Oxford" edition, by F. P. Walesby, of Wadham College, which contained some fresh recollections of Johnson and some stray particulars as to Boswell, whose portrait, for the first time, is added. A tiny issue in one volume, small octavo, beautifully printed in double col-

umns at the Chiswick Press, is the only one
that needs mention previous to the historical
edition by the Right Honourable John Wilson
Croker, published in 1831.

As will be seen, the foregoing paragraphs
deal more with Johnson's earlier biographers
than with the main subject of this paper, Boswell's editors.   But the earlier biographers are,
if not the chief, at least no inconsiderable part
of the material employed by those editors, and
by none more conspicuously, more ably, and at
the same time more unhappily, than by the one
whose labours attracted the censure of Macaulay
and Carlyle.   What is most distinctive in Boswell is Boswell's method and Boswell's manner.
Long before, Johnson had touched upon this
personal quality when writing of the Corsican
tour.   " Your History," he said, " is like other
histories, but your Journal is in a very high
degree curious and delightful. . . . Your History was copied from books ; your Journal rose
out of your own experience and observation.
You express images which operated strongly
upon yourself, and you have impressed them
with great force upon your readers."   From
less friendly critics the verdict was the same.
Walpole, though caustic and flippant, speaks to
like purport ; and Gray, who has been " pleased

and moved strangely," declares it proves what
he has always maintained, "that any fool may
write a most valuable book by chance, if he
will only tell us what he heard and saw with
veracity." This faculty of communicating his
impressions accurately to his reader is Boswell's
most conspicuous gift. Present in his first
book, it was more present in his second, and
when he began his great biography it had
reached its highest point. So individual is his
manner, so unique his method of collecting and
arranging his information, that to disturb the
native character of his narrative by interpolating
foreign material, must of necessity impair its
specific character and imperil its personal note.
Yet, by some strange freak of fate, this was just
the very treatment to which it was subjected.

From the very outset indeed, it would seem,
his text was considerably "edited." Boswell,
like many writers of his temperament, was fond
of stimulating his flagging invention by miscellaneous advice, and it is plain from the comparison
of his finished work with his rough notes, that
in order to make his anecdotes more direct and
effective he freely manipulated his reminiscences.
But it is quite probable — and this is a point
that we do not remember to have seen touched
on — that much of the trimming which his

records received is attributable to Malone. At all events, when Malone took up the editing after Boswell's death, he is known to have made many minor alterations in the process of "settling the text," and it is only reasonable to suppose that he had done the same thing in the author's lifetime, a supposition which would account for some at least of the variations which have been observed between Boswell's anecdotes in their earliest and their latest forms. But the admitted alterations of Malone were but trifles compared with the extraordinary readjustment which the book, as Malone left it, received at the hands of Mr. Croker. Not content with working freely upon the text itself — compressing, omitting, transposing, as seemed good in his eyes — by a process almost inconceivable in a critic and *littérateur* of admitted experience, he liberally interlarded it with long extracts and letters from Hawkins, Piozzi, Cumberland, Murphy, and others of Boswell's predecessors and successors, and so turned into an irregular patchwork what the author had left a continuous and methodical design. Furthermore he incorporated with it, among other things, under its date of occurrence, the separate volume of the "Tour to the Hebrides," having first polled and trimmed that work according to his taste and fancy. Finally, he added — and this is the least questionable of his acts — an inordinate number of footnotes. Many of these, it must be conceded, are of the highest value. Penned at a time when memories of Johnson and his contemporaries were still fresh in men's minds, and collected by a writer whose industry and curiosity were as exceptional as his equipment and opportunities, they must always remain an inestimable magazine of Johnsoniana. Their worst fault is that they are more a warehouse than a treasury, and that they exhibit less of literary resource than literary incontinence.

But if the intrinsic worth of Croker's voluminous annotations has survived the verbal artillery of Macaulay and Carlyle, it has luckily been otherwise with his remodelling of Boswell's text, the principles of which were virtually abandoned in the second edition of 1835. Unfortunately, the execution of this concession to popular opinion was only partial. Although the majority of the passages added to the text were rearranged as foot-notes or distributed into appendices, the Scotch " tour " still upreared itself in the midst as a huge stumbling-block, while the journey to Wales and the letters of Johnson and Mrs. Thrale were retained. In 1847, when Mr. Croker prepared his definite edition, he continued impenitent to this extent, although he speaks in his " Advertisement " of abridgment and alteration. Nay, he even acquiesced in the perpetuation of another enormity which dates from the edition of 1835 (an edition which he only partly superintended), the breaking up of the book into chapters. This was a violation of Boswell's plan which it is impossible to describe except as an act of Vandalism. " Divisions into books and chapters," says Mr. Napier, unanswerably (if somewhat grandiloquently), " are, as it were, articulations in the organic whole of a literary composition ; and this special form cannot be super-induced merely externally." Yet, all these drawbacks to the contrary, Mr. Croker's edition enjoyed a long popularity, and the edition just referred to was reprinted as late as 1876.

It would be beyond our province to trace the post-Crokerian issues of Boswell's book, which, with the exception of an illustrated edition under the superintendence of Dr. Robert Carruthers, author of the life of Pope, were mainly reprints of Malone. But from what has gone before, it will be surmised that the presentation, as far as practicable, of Boswell's unsophisticated text must sooner or later become the ambition of the modern editor. In this praiseworthy enterprise the pioneer appears to have been Mr. Percy Fitzgerald. In May, 1874, acting with the encouragement and countenance of Carlyle, to whom his work was dedicated, he published with Messrs. Bickers an edition of Boswell's " Life " in three volumes, of which the object was to exhibit Boswell's text in its first published form, and at the same time to show the alterations made or contemplated by him in the two subsequent editions with which he was concerned. Thus the reader was enabled to follow the process of revision in the author's mind, and to derive additional satisfaction from the spectacle of the *naïf* and highly ingenuous motives which prompted many of Boswell's rectifications and re-adjustments. As was inevitable in such a plan, the " tour to the Hebrides " was placed by itself at the end, an arrangement which had also been followed by Carruthers ; the " Diary of a Tour in Wales," which Mr. Croker had turned into chap. xlvi. of his compilation, disappeared altogether ; and the interpolated letters knew their place no more. The division into chapters also vanished with the restoration of the original text, which, together with Boswell's spelling, punctuation, paragraphs, and other special characteristics, were religiously preserved. By this arrange-

9

ment, taken in connection with the foot-notes
exhibiting the variations, the reader was placed
in the position of a person having before him
at one view the editions of 1791, 1793, and
1799, as well as the separate " Corrections and
Additions" issued by Boswell in 1793. Mr.
Fitzgerald also appended certain notes of his
own ; but, wherever they occurred on the same
page as Boswell's work, carefully fenced them
off by a line of demarcation from what was
legitimate Boswell. Upon these notes, generally brief and apposite, it is not necessary to
dwell. The noticeable characteristic of Mr.
Fitzgerald's edition is its loyalty to Boswell,
and for that, if for that only, the lovers of Johnson owe him a deep debt of gratitude.[1]

In 1880, six years after the first appearance
of the above edition of Boswell's " Life," Mr.
Fitzgerald published, under the title of " Croker's Boswell and Boswell," a volume which was
apparently the outcome of his earlier labours
in this field. With the first part of this, which
treats mainly of the feud between Macaulay
and Croker, and the peculiarities and defects

[1] Mr. Fitzgerald's edition of Boswell was re-issued in
1888, with a new and interesting preface, to which was
added the valuable Bibliography by Mr. H. R. Tedder,
referred to at the beginning of this paper.

of the latter as an editor, we have no immediate concern. But the second part, which
exhibits Boswell at his work, collects much
valuable information with respect to his method
of note-making, and, with the assistance of the
curious memoranda belonging to the late Lord
Houghton, published in 1874 by the Grampian
Club under the title of " Boswelliana," shows
how much judicious correction and adroit com-
pression went to produce these " literary and
characteristical anecdotes . . . told with authenticity, and in a lively manner," which, as
Boswell explained to his friend Temple, were to
form the staple of his work. Other chapters
of equal interest deal with Boswell's strange
antipathies and second thoughts, both of which
themes, and the former especially, are of no
small importance to the minute student of his
labours. We have mentioned this book of Mr.
Fitzgerald's, because, among the many pro-
ductions of his indefatigable pen, it is the one
which has always interested us most, and it is
obviously, as he declares in his preface, written
con amore.

That the reproduction of Boswell neat — to
use a convenient vulgarism — had attracted
closer attention to the defects of Croker's con-
coction may be fairly assumed, and the volume

just mentioned probably, and certainly among specialists, enforced this impression. Accordingly, in 1884, a new edition of the " Life," upon which the editor, the late Rev. Alexander Napier, vicar of Holkham, had been engaged for many years, was issued by Messrs. George Bell and Sons. It was illustrated by facsimiles, steel engravings and portraits, and was received with considerable, and even, in some quarters, exaggerated, enthusiasm. In this edition the arrangement of Boswell's text was strictly followed, and the tours in Wales and Scotland were printed separately. Many of Croker's notes were withdrawn or abridged, and Mr. Napier, in pursuance of a theory, which is as sound as it is unusual, also omitted all those in which his predecessor had considered it his duty " to act as censor on Boswell " and even on Johnson himself. The editor's duty, said Mr. Napier, " is to subordinate himself to his author, and admit that only which elucidates his author's meaning. . . . It cannot be the duty of an editor to insult the writer whose book he edits. I confess that the notes of Mr. Croker which most offend are those in which, not seldom, he delights — let me be allowed to use a familiar colloquialism — to snub ' Mr. Boswell.'" In this deliverance no reasonable reader can fail

to concur. Besides the editing of Croker, however, Mr. Napier added many useful notes of
his own, as well as some very interesting appendices. One of these reproduces the autobiographical sketch of Johnson prefixed by
Richard Wright of Lichfield, in 1805, to Miss
Hill Boothby's letters ; another deals with that
mysterious " History of Prince Titi" which
figures in Macaulay's review of Croker's first
edition ; a third successfully dissipates the leg-
endary account of a meeting between Ursa
Major and Adam Smith, which represents those
"grave and reverend seignors" as engaged in
competitive Billingsgate. " Carleton's Memoirs," Theophilus Cibber's " Lives of the
Poets," and the daughters of Mauritius Lowe
are also treated of in this, the newest part of
Mr. Napier's labours.

But his edition also includes a valuable supplement in the shape of a volume of " Johnsoniana,"
collected and edited by Mrs. Napier, whose
praiseworthy plan is to avoid merely fragmentary
" sayings " and " anecdotes," and, as far as possible, to give only complete articles. Thus
Mrs. Napier opens with Mrs. Piozzi's book, and
then goes on to reprint Hawkins' collection of
apophthegms, the Hill Boothby correspondence,
Tyers' sketch from the *Gentleman's Magazine*,

the essay published by Arthur Murphy in 1792
for his edition of Johnson's works, and various
recollections and so forth collected from Reynolds, Cumberland, Madame D'Arblay, Hannah
More, Percy, and others. But her freshest
trouvaille is the diary of a certain Dr. Thomas
Campbell, an Irishman who visited England in
1775, and, after the fashion of the time, recorded
his impressions. This diary has a curious history. Carried to Australia by some of its writer's
descendants, it was peaceably travelling towards
dissolution when it was unearthed behind an old
press in one of the offices of the Supreme Court
of New South Wales. In 1854 it was published
at Sydney by Mr. Samuel Raymond, and from
that date until 1884 does not seem to have been
reprinted in England. Dr. Campbell had some
repute as an historian, and it was he who prepared for Percy the memoir of Goldsmith which,
in 1837, was in the possession of Mr. Prior, and
formed the first sketch for the straggling compilation afterwards prefixed to the well-known
edition of Goldsmith's works dated 1801.
Campbell's avowed object in coming to London
was to " see the lions," and his notes are sufficiently amusing. He lodged at the Grecian
Coffee House, and at the Hummums in Covent
Garden, where once appeared the ghost of

Johnson's dissolute relative, Parson Ford, the

" fortem validumque combibonem
Lœtantem super amphora repleta "

of Vincent Bourne's hendecasyllabics; he saw
Woodward in Hoadly's " Suspicious Husband,"
and Garrick as Lusignan and Lear, in which
latter character Dr. Campbell, contradicting all
received tradition, considered " he could not
display himself." He went to the auction-rooms
in the Piazza; he went to the Foundling and
the Temple and Dr. Dodd's Chapel; he went to
Ranelagh and the Pantheon, where he watched
those lapsed lovers, Lady Grosvenor and the
Duke of Cumberland, carefully avoiding each
other. He dined often at Thrale's, meeting
Boswell and Baretti, and Murphy and Johnson.
With the great man he was not impressed, and
his portrait affords an example of Johnson as he
struck an unsympathetic contemporary. According to Dr. Campbell this was his picture: —
" He has the aspect of an Idiot, without the
faintest ray of sense gleaming from any one
feature — with the most awkward garb, and un-
powdered grey wig, on one side only of his
head — he is for ever dancing the devil's jig, and
sometimes he makes the most driveling effort to
whistle some thought in his absent paroxisms.

He came up to me and took me by the hand, then sat down upon a sofa, and mumbled out that ' he had heard two papers had appeared against him in the course of this week — one of which was — that he was to go to Ireland next summer in order to abuse the hospitality of that place also [a reference to the recéntly published " Journey to the Western Islands "].' His awkwardness at table is just what Chesterfield described, and his roughness of manners kept pace with that.   When Mrs. Thrale quoted something from Foster's ' Sermons ' he flew in a passion, and said that Foster was a man of mean ability, and of no original thinking.   All which tho' I took to be most true, yet I held it not meet to have it so set down."   From this it will be perceived that Dr. Campbell was of those who identified the "respectable Hottentot" of Chesterfield's letters with the " great Lexicographer," an identification which Dr. Birkbeck Hill, in " Dr. Johnson : His Friends and His Critics," has successfully shown to be untenable.

Towards the close of 1884 Mr. Napier's edition was reissued in the " Standard Library," making six small volumes, in which some only of the portrait illustrations of the first issue were reproduced.   The chief addition consisted of a series of seven letters from Boswell to his friend

Sir David Dalrymple. Extracts from this very interesting correspondence, bearing upon Boswell's first acquaintance with his Mentor, had appeared in the volume of "Boswelliana" already mentioned, but they had been but extracts. Mr. Napier gave the letters *in extenso.* Two years later Professor Henry Morley published, in five exceedingly handsome volumes, what, from the fact of its decoration by portraits from the brush of Sir Joshua, he christened the " Reynolds " edition. In common with all Professor Morley's work, the editing of this issue was thoroughly straightforward and sensible. A new and noticeable feature was the prefixing to each of the prefaces of the different editors a succinct account of the writer. At the end came an essay entitled the " Spirit of Johnson," to which can scarcely be denied the merit claimed for it by a competent critic of being " one of the best descriptions of Johnson's character that has ever been written." There were also elaborate indices, of which one can only say in their dispraise that they were less elaborate than that prepared by the editor who follows Professor Morley. Like Mr. Napier, Mr. Morley was largely indebted to Croker, and like Mr. Napier he freely pruned his predecessor's luxuriance.

Colonel Francis Grant's excellent little memoir in the "Great Writers" series deserves mention, because, although exceedingly unpretentious, it is the work of one who, to borrow Boswell's epithet for Malone, is certainly "Johnsonianissimus." It is impossible to turn his anecdotical pages without seeing that he is steeped in the literature of the period, and that, for him, the personages of the Boswellian drama have all the reality of living friends. His volume, too, includes a valuable bibliography by Mr. John P. Anderson of Johnson's works, which, in point of time, preceded the special bibliography of Boswell's "Life" in Mr. Fitzgerald's reprint. And this brings us to the last work on our list, the sumptuous edition by Dr. George Birkbeck Hill, issued in 1887 from the Clarendon Press, a work which was received with an almost universal chorus of praise.

That Dr. Birkbeck Hill's book is "*un livre de bonne foi,*" there can indeed be little doubt. He is well known as a devoted worshipper at Johnson's shrine. He has been for years a persistent reviewer of books on this subject (especially Mr. Fitzgerald's), and his essays (collected in 1878 from the *Cornhill* and other periodicals under the title of "Dr. Johnson: His Friends and His Critics"), bear that unmistakable stamp

which denotes the writer who has not crammed
his subject for the purpose of preparing an article, but who has, so to speak, let the article
write itself out of the fulness of his resources.
Besides these he edited, in 1879, Boswell's
" Journal of a Tour to Corsica " and his correspondence with Andrew Erskine.   But he has
crowned his former labours by this sumptuous
edition with its excellent typography, its handsome page, and its exhaustive index, which last,
we can well believe, must have cost him, as he
says, "many months' heavy work."   That he
himself executed this " sublunary task," as a
recent writer has described it, is matter for con-
gratulation ; that he has also verified it page by
page in proof almost entitles him to a Montyon
prize for exceptional literary virtue.   Our only
regret is that his " Preface " is touched a little
too strongly with the sense of his unquestioned
industry and conscientiousness.   However legitimate it may be, the public is always somewhat
impatient of the *superbia quæsita meritis*.   Moreover, it is an extremely difficult thing to display
judiciously, and, after all, as Carlyle said of
Croker's attempt, the editing of Boswell is " a
praiseworthy but no miraculous procedure."

This note of self-gratulation in Dr. Birkbeck
Hill's introductory words is, however, but a

trifling drawback when contrasted with the real merits of a work which, in these days of piping-hot publication, has much of the leisurely grace of eighteenth-century scholarship. The labour — not only the labour of which the result remains on record, but that bloomless and fruitless labour with which everyone who has been engaged in editorial drudgery can sympathise — must have been unprecedented. Nothing could be more ungracious than to smear the petty blot of an occasional inaccuracy across the wide field which has been explored so observantly — certainly it could not be the desire of those who have ever experienced the multiplied chances of error involved by transcription, press-correction, revision, and re-revision. At the same time we frankly own that we think Dr. Birkbeck Hill's edition has not escaped a dangerous defect of its qualities. It unquestionably errs on the side of excess. " I have sought," he says, " to follow him [Johnson] wherever a remark of his required illustration, and have read through many a book that I might trace to its source a reference or an allusion." And he has no doubt been frequently very fortunate, notably in his identification of the quotation which Johnson made when he heard the Highland girl of Nairne singing at her spinning-wheel, in his solution of "loplolly," and in half a dozen similar cases. But, as regards "remarks that require illustration," there are manifestly two methods, the moderate and the immoderate. By the one nothing but such reference or elucidation as explains the text is admissible ; by the other anything that can possibly be connected with it is drawn into its train, and the motley notes tread upon each other's heels much as, in the fairy tale, the three girls, the parson, and the sexton follow the fellow with the golden goose. To the latter of these methods rather than the former Dr. Birkbeck Hill "seriously inclines," and almost any portion of his book would serve to supply a case in point. Take, for instance, the note at page 269, vol. i., to the verse which Boswell quotes from Garrick's well-known "Ode on Mr. Pelham." Neither Malone nor Croker has anything upon this, and as Boswell himself tells us that Pelham died on the day on which Mallet's edition of Lord Bolingbroke's works came out, and as the first line of his paragraph gives the exact date of the event, it is difficult to see what ground, and certainly what pressing need, there could be for further comment. Yet Dr. Birkbeck Hill has no less than four "illustrations." First he tells us, from Walpole's letters, that Pelham died of a surfeit. This

suggests another quotation from Johnson himself about the death of Pope, which introduces
the story of the potted lampreys.   Then comes
a passage from Fielding's " Journal of a Voyage
to Lisbon," to the effect that he (Fielding) was
at his worst when Pelham died.   Lastly comes
a second quotation from Walpole, this time from
his " George II.," in which we are told that the
king said he should now " have no more peace,"
because Pelham was dead.   The recondite erudition of all this is incontestable, but its utility
is more than doubtful.   Dr. Birkbeck Hill's
method is seen more serviceably at work in a
note on Reynolds's visit to Devonshire in 1762.
First we get a record how Northcote, "with
great satisfaction to his mind," touched the skirt
of Sir Joshua's coat, and this quite naturally recalls the well-known anecdote how Reynolds
himself in his youth had grasped the hand of the
great Mr. Pope at Christie's.   The transition to
Pope's own visit as a boy of twelve to Dryden
at Will's Coffee House thus becomes an easy
one.   " Who touched old Northcote's hand ? "
says Dr. Birkbeck Hill.   " Has the apostolic succession been continued ? " and then he goes on
to add : " Since writing these lines I have read
with pleasure the following passage in Mr.
Ruskin's ' Præterita,' chap. i. p. 16 : ' When

at three-and-a-half I was taken to have my portrait painted by Mr. Northcote, I had not been
ten minutes alone with him before I asked him
why there were holes in his carpet.' Dryden,
Pope, Reynolds, Northcote, Ruskin, so runs the
chain of genius, with only one weak link in it."

This is an excellent specimen of the concate-
nated process at the best. We are bound to add
that there are many as good. We are moreover
bound to admit that the examples of its abuse
are by no means obtrusive. Dr. Birkbeck Hill,
in short, has done his work thoroughly. His
appendices — *e. g.* those on Johnson's Debates
in Parliament, and on George Psalmanazar —
are practically exhaustive, and he has left no
stone unturned in his labour of interpretation.
If in the result of that labour there is something
of what Croker called "surplusage," it must
also be conceded that Boswell's famous book
has never before been annotated with equal
enthusiasm, learning, and industry.[1]

[1] Since this paper was first published, Dr. Birkbeck
Hill has largely supplemented his Johnson labours by
two volumes of letters (1892), and two more of "Johnsonian Miscellanies" (1897). There have also been several
other issues of Boswell's "Life," — notably an edition in
one volume by Mr. Fitzgerald, which is a marvel of
cheapness, — but that of Dr. Birkbeck Hill is still unrivalled in its kind.

AN ENGLISH ENGRAVER IN PARIS.

IT is a curious fact — and, if it has not been already recorded, must assuredly have been remarked — that Fate seems always to provide the eminent painter with his special and particular interpreter on steel or copper. Thus, around Reynolds are the great mezzotinters, MacArdell, Fisher, Watson, Valentine Green. Gainsborough has his nephew Gainsborough Dupont; Constable his Lucas. For Wilson there is Woollett; for Stothard there are Heath and Finden. To come to later days, there is Turner with his Willmores and Goodalls, and Landseer with his brother and (no pun intended) his Cousens. Similarly, for Wilkie (after Burnet), the born translator into dot and line seems to have been Abraham Raimbach. It was Raimbach who engraved "The Rent Day," "Blind Man's Buff," "The Village Politicians," and the majority of Sir David's chief works, and it is of Raimbach that we now propose to speak. Concerning his work as a craftsman, these pages

could scarcely be expected to treat; and his
life, the life of a man occupied continuously in
a sedentary pursuit, and residing, like Stothard,
almost entirely in one place, affords but little
incident to invite the chronicler of the picturesque. But he nevertheless left behind him a
privately printed memoir, of which a portion at
least is not without its interest, — the interest
attaching to every truthful record of occurrences
which time has pushed backward into that per-
spective which transforms the trivial. In 1802
he went to Paris for a couple of months. The
visits of foreigners to England have not been
unattractive; and the visit of an Englishman to
France, shortly after the Revolution, may also —
with a few preliminary words as to the tourist —
supply its *memorabilia.*

Raimbach was born on February 16, 1776, in
Cecil Court, St. Martin's Lane, Westminster,
a spot remarkable — as far as we can remember —
for nothing but the fact that Mrs. Hogarth *mère*
had died there some forty years before. His
father was a naturalised Swiss; his mother a
Warwickshire woman, who claimed descent from
Richard Burbage, the actor of Shakespeare's
day. His childhood was uneventful, save for
two incidents. One of these was his falling,
as a baby, out of a second-floor window, when

he was miraculously " ballooned " by his long-
clothes ; the other, his being roused as a little
boy of four by the roar of the Gordon rioters as
they rushed through the streets, calling to the
sleeping inhabitants to light up their windows.
After a modest education, chiefly at the Library
School of St. Martin's — where Charles Mathews
the Elder was his schoolfellow, and Liston afterwards held a post as master — he was formally
apprenticed to Ravenet's pupil, John Hall, historical engraver to George the Third, and popularly regarded as the legitimate successor of
Woollett.   Hall was a man of more than ordinary cultivation, one of whose daughters had
married the composer Stephen Storace, — the
Storace who wrote the music to Colman's
" Iron Chest," and (as Raimbach recollected)
superintended the rehearsals thereof from a
sedan-chair, in which, arrayed in flannels, he
was carried on to the stage.   Hall in his day
had been introduced to Garrick ; and he was
sometimes visited by John Kemble, who impressed the young apprentice with his solemn
and sepulchral enunciation, and his manifest
inability to forget, even in private life, that he
was not before the footlights.   Another remembered visitor was Sheridan, nervously solicitous
lest Hall, who was engraving his portrait, should

needlessly emphasise that facial " efflorescence "
— so familiar in Gillray's caricatures — which
the too-truthful Sir Joshua had neglected to
disguise.

Sheridan, however, could only have appeared
occasionally in the altitudes of Hall's study.
But the three flights which ascended to it were
often climbed by other contemporaries. Benjamin West (whose " Cromwell dissolving the
Long Parliament" Hall engraved), Opie and
Northcote, Flaxman and Westall, all came frequently on business and pleasure, while the
eclectic arts were represented by George Steevens (the Shakespeare critic), John Ireland, (the
Hogarth commentator), and Dibdin's " Quis-
quilius," George Baker, the print-collector and
laceman of St. Paul's Churchyard. These, with
Storace and his theatrical circle, must have made
variety enough in a wearisome craft (for Hall's
larger plates were many months in hand), and
their conversation and opinions no doubt con-
spired to fill the young apprentice with a life-
long interest in art and the stage. When at
length, in August, 1796, his period of servitude
came to an end, the professional outlook was by
no means a cheerful one. The French Revolution was engrossing all men's thoughts, and the
peaceful arts — that *ars longa* of the engraver in

particular — were at their lowest ebb, the only
patrons of prints being the booksellers.   Young
Raimbach's first definite employment was on
Cooke's "Tales of the Genii," a task which,
it may be added, was even more precarious than
usual, inasmuch as it was Cooke's custom, by
prearrangement, not to pay for the work if he
did not approve it when finished.   Fortunately,
in this instance, he did approve, and Raimbach
continued from time to time to reproduce for
him in copper the designs for books of Thurston,
the elder Corbould, and Madame D'Arblay's
clever cousin, Edward Burney.   He had long
been an assiduous Royal Academy student, and
he speedily "doubled" his profession by min-
iature-painting, in which — " having," as he
modestly says, " some facility of execution and
the very common power [?] of making an inveterate likeness " (at three guineas a head) —
he attained considerable success.   Then, at the
end of 1801, he procured a commission to exe-
cute three plates from Smirke's paintings for
Forster's " Arabian Nights."   He had for some
time been lodging with a French modeller in
Charles Street, and by this means had improved
an already respectable acquaintance with the
French language.   With the proceeds of his
three plates in his pocket, about £70, he set

out in July, 1802, for a fortnight's visit to Paris.

The short-lived Peace of Amiens, patched up by the Addington ministry, had been signed in the preceding March, and the route to the Continent, closed for ten or twelve years, was again open. The result was a rush across the Channel of all sorts and conditions of Englishmen, eager to note the changes resulting from the Revolution. Among these, the number of painters was considerable, — West, Turner, Flaxman, Shee, and Opie being all included. Securing a passport from the Secretary of State's office — a preliminary precaution which, in those days, meant an outlay of £2,5s. — Raimbach set out *via* Brighton and Dieppe. Competition, at this time, had reduced the coach fare to the former place to half a guinea inside. On July 9 he embarked for Dieppe in a little vessel, landing in France on the following day during a glorious sunrise, but drenched to the skin. His first impressions of the French were not unlike those of Hogarth fifty years before. The filth and slovenliness of the people, the number and shameless importunity of the beggars, the dragging of loaded carts and the bearing of heavy burdens by the weaker sex — all these, with the brusque revolutionary manners and the

savage *sans-culottism* of the men, were things
for which not even the long ear-pendants and
picturesque Norman caps of the women could
entirely atone. From Dieppe the traveller proceeded to Rouen in a ramshackle cabriolet,
drawn by two ill-matched but wiry horses which
went better than they looked. At Rouen he
arrived in time for a bread riot, promptly suppressed by the soldiery ; and he inspected several
churches, among others St. Maclou, being no
doubt attracted thereto by the famous door-
carvings of Jean Goujon. Then, on the *im-
périale* of a diligence, he made his way through
the delightful landscape of Northern France, by
Pontoise and St. Denis, "cemetery of mon-
archs," to Paris, which he reached on the
evening of the 12th.

At Paris he took up his quarters in that "dirt-
iest and noisiest of streets," the Rue Montorgueil, where, twenty-two years before, Béranger
had been born. Here he was keenly sensible
of those exhalations in which the French capital
competed with the "Auld Reekie" of the eighteenth-century, although, in this instance, they
were blended and complicated with another
odour, that of cookery. But, notwithstanding
an abhorrence of "evil smells" quite equal to
that of Queen Elizabeth, he speedily became

acclimatised, and pleasantly appreciative of the bright, cheerful, many-coloured life of the Parisian boulevards and the social attractions of the *table d'hôte.* In the capital, too, he found that the people were less brutal, short-spoken, and surly than in the provinces, and that the Revolution, which had disfigured their palaces and monuments,[1] had not wholly effaced their traditional politeness. On the second day after his arrival took place the annual *fêtes* of July in memory of the destruction of the Bastille. There were to be reviews and illuminations, fireworks on the Pont Neuf, dancing and *mâts de cocagne* in the Champs-Élysées and Place Vendôme, and free plays and concerts in the Tuileries gardens. But the weather was finer than the show. "The fireworks on the bridge would not go off; the concert in the garden could not be heard, and the illuminations, though in good taste, were not sufficiently general to mark a decided national feeling." It is consoling to our insular self-esteem that neither this celebration, nor that inaugurating Bonaparte as First Consul, which took place shortly afterwards, could be com-

[1] The Tuileries still bore the words, "dix d'Août" painted in white letters wherever the cannon-balls had struck. Arthur Moore was looking on (*Journal,* 1793, i. 26)

pared, in the opinion of this observer, with the Jubilee of George the Third, or the Coronation of George the Fourth, at both of which he subsequently assisted.

He was naturally anxious to get a glimpse of the famous First Consul, but of this he had little hope, as Bonaparte seldom appeared in public except at a review or a theatre, and in the latter case always without previous announcement. After fruitless attempts to see the "modern Attila" at the Opera and Théâtre Français, Raimbach was at length fortunate enough to effect his object at an inspection of the garrison of Paris in the Place du Carrousel, where he paid six francs for a seat at a first-floor window. After five-and-thirty years he still remembered vividly the small, thin, grave figure, — in the blue unornamented uniform, plain cocked hat, white pantaloons and jockey boots, — which, surrounded by a brilliant staff (among whom the Mameluke Roustan was conspicuous by his eastern costume), rode rapidly down the lines at a hand-canter on Marengo, made a brief speech to the soldiers, saluted them with military formality, and then passed back under the archway of the Tuileries. Napoleon at this date was about thirty-two. Raimbach never saw him again, and beyond a casual inspection

of the ladies of the Bonaparte family at Notre
Dame, enjoyed no second opportunity of studying the ruling race. But there were many things
of compensating interest. At the Jardin des
Plantes, for instance, there was an enormous
female elephant, which had been transferred by
right of conquest from the Stadtholder's collection at the Hague, and had brought its English
keeper with it into captivity. Then there were
the noble halls and galleries of the Louvre,
crowded with the fruits of French victories
("les fruits de nos victoires!"), statues and
pictures of all countries, and all exhibited free
of charge to an exultant public. The Apollo
Belvedere from the Vatican was already in-
stalled, and while Raimbach was still at Paris
arrived the famous Venus de' Médici. Probably so splendid a "loan collection" had never
before been brought together.

It was this no doubt which attracted so many
English artists to Paris, where French spolia-
tion enabled them to study comparatively a pictorial collocation which nothing but the Grand
Tour could otherwise have presented to them.
Here, in all their glory, were Rembrandt and
Rubens, with the best of the Dutch and Flemish
schools. Raphael's glorious "Transfiguration;"
the great rival altarpiece of Domenichino, the

"Communion of St. Jerome;" Correggio's "Marriage of St. Catherine," — all these, together with many of the choicest specimens of the Carracci, of Guido, of Albano, of Guercino, were at this time to be seen in the long gallery of the Louvre, which Raimbach not only visited frequently, but drew in almost daily. In the magnificent Hall of Antiques, besides, he made the acquaintance of more than one contemporary French painter. Isabey, the miniaturist; Carle Vernet; his greater son, Horace, at this time a bright boy of thirteen or fourteen, were all then living in apartments adjoining the galleries, and in some cases at Government expense To the illustrious leader of the new Imperio-Classical School, which had succeeded with its wide-striding and brickdust-coloured nudities to the rosy *mignardises* of Fragonard and Boucher, Raimbach was not, however, introduced. M. Jacques Louis David, whose friendship with Robespierre had not only acquainted him with the interior of a prison, but had also brought him perilously close to the guillotine itself, was for the moment living in prudent seclusion, dividing his attentions between his palette and his violoncello. Meanwhile, a good example of his manner, "The Sabines" (which Raimbach calls "Rape of the Sabines"), executed immediately after his release from the Luxembourg, and popularly supposed to allude to the heroic efforts which Madame David had made for her husband's safety, was at this time being exhibited to a public who were divided between enthusiasm for the subject and indignation at the door-money — door-money apparently having never before been charged for showing a picture. Of David's pupils and followers, Gérard, Girodet, Gros, Guérin, Ingres, and the rest, Raimbach also speaks, but, as in the case of the master himself, more from hearsay than personal experience. On the other hand, one of his own compatriots, Benjamin West, the favourite painter of George the Third

> (Of modern works he makes a jest
> Except the works of Mr. West),

was very much *en évidence* in public places. He had succeeded Reynolds as President of the Royal Academy, and the diplomatic French notabilities were doing their best to flatter him into the belief that Bonaparte was not only the greatest of men but of art collectors. Indeed, the First Consul himself favoured this idea by personally commending West's own " Death on the Pale Horse," the finished sketch of which he had brought with him from England to exhibit at the Salon. West, whose weakness was "more than female vanity," was by no means backward in acknowledging these politic, if not perfidious, attentions, which he accepted without suspicion. "Wherever I went," he said simply, "people looked at me, and ministers and men of influence in the State were constantly in my company. I was one day in the Louvre — all eyes were upon me, and I could not help observing to Charles Fox, *who happened to be walking with me*, how strong was the love of Art and admiration of its professors in France." Fox, whose reputation as an orator and a patriot had preceded him, was naturally the observed of all observers, and he was besides the object of special attentions on the part of Bonaparte.

Fox's chief mission to Paris, according to his biographer, Lord Russell, was to search the archives for his " History of the Revolution of 1688." But transcribing the correspondence of Barillon did not so exclusively occupy him as to divert him from the charms of the Théâtre Français, or, as it was at this time called, the "Théâtre de la République." Fox went frequently to see that queen of tragedy Mlle. Duchesnois, of whom it was said, " qu'elle avait des larmes dans la voix." [1]   He saw her

---

[1] Thackeray, who applies this to Gay, quotes it of Rubini.

in "Andromaque" and "Phèdre," and as
Roxane in "Bajazet." Raimbach also, as
might be anticipated from the schoolfellow of
Charles Mathews and the admirer of Kemble,
did not neglect the French theatres, which,
he notes, were at this time more numerous
than in all the other capitals of Europe put together. At the Grand Opéra, then rechristened
"Théâtre de la République et des Arts," he
heard the opera of "Anacréon," in which the
principal male singer was François Lays, or
Lais, and the foremost female that Mlle. Maill-
ard to whom tradition assigned the part of the
Goddess of Reason at the celebration of 1793,
which celebration, indeed, had been arranged
by Lais with the prophet of the cult, Chaumette.
Raimbach, however, thought little, as a singer,
of the lady, who had just succeeded to the
place of her preceptress, the accomplished Mlle.
St. Huberti, who, as Countess d'Entraigues,
was cruelly murdered with her husband at
Barnes Terrace some few years later by an
Italian valet.[1] But he was charmed with the
vocalisation of Lais, and delighted with the
ballet, which included the elder Vestris ("*Diou*"

[1] In 1812. There is an account of this tragedy in the
"Walk from London to Kew" of Sir Richard Phillips,
1817.

de la danse) and Mme. Gardel. In particular
the young engraver remembered an English
hornpipe, executed in a jockey's dress by one
Beaupré, which excelled anything of the kind
he had ever seen in his own country. At the
Théâtre Français, — possibly because his tastes
lay rather in comedy than tragedy, — Raimbach
says nothing of Racine and Mlle. Duchesnois.
But he speaks of Monvel, the sole survivor of
the old school of the Lekains and Prévilles and
Barons, as still charming in spite of age and loss
of teeth ; and he also saw that practical joker
and pet of the Parisians, Dugazon, who must
have been almost as diminutive as Addison's
"little Dickey," Henry Morris.[1] But after
Préville he was the prince of stage valets,
and despite a tendency to exaggeration (which
Raimbach duly chronicles), almost perfect in
his own line. Another stage luminary mentioned by Raimbach is Monvel's daughter,
Mlle. Mars, at this time only three-and-twenty,

---

[1] It was Dugazon who cajoled the original Bartholo
of the *Barbier*, Desessarts (who was enormously fat), into
applying for the post of elephant to the Court. When the
irate Desessarts afterwards challenged him, Dugazon, by
gravely chalking a circle upon his adversary, and propos-
ing that all punctures outside the ring should count for
nothing, turned the whole affair into ridicule.

and not yet displaying those supreme qualities which afterwards made her unrivalled in
Europe. But she was already seductive as an
ingénue ; and her performance of Angélique in
" La Fausse Agnès " of Néricault Destouches
(which Arthur Murphy afterwards borrowed for
his farce of the " Citizen)," is declared by
Raimbach to have been " replete with grace
and good taste." Finally, Raimbach saw the
First Consul's tragedian, Talma, then in the
height of his powers, and continuing successfully those reforms of costume and declamation
which he was supposed to have learned in
England. John Kemble, who was also visiting
Paris, where he was hospitably entertained by
the French actors, was now in his turn taking
hints from Talma, for it was observable that
when he got back to London he adopted
Talma's costume for the Orestes of the " Dis-
tressed Mother."

The Italian Opera, of course, was not open,
and of the remaining actors Raimbach says not
very much. At the Vaudeville he saw Laporte,
the leading harlequin of the day, and at Picart's
Theatre in the Rue Feydeau witnessed what
must have been the " Tom Jones à Londres "
of M. Desforges, in which Picart himself, who
was a better author than actor, took the part of

the so-called "Squire Westiern." This representation, as might be expected, was amusing
for its absurdities rather than its merits. But
it can hardly have been more ridiculous to an
Englishman than Poinsinet's earlier Comédie
Lyrique, where Western and "l'ami Jone"
pursue the flying hart to the accompaniment of
cors de chasse and the orthodox French *hallali.*
Another (unconsciously) theatrical exhibition
which Raimbach occasionally attended, was the
Tribunat, one of the new Legislative bodies
that at this time held its sittings in the Palais
Royal, then, on that account, re-christened
Palais du Tribunat. Here he met with the
notorious Lewis Goldsmith, not, as afterwards,
the inveterate assailant of Napoleon, but for
the moment actively engaged in editing a paper
called "The Argus ; or, London Reviewed in
Paris," which attacked the war and the English Government. At the Tribunat Goldsmith
pointed out several of the minor men of the
Revolution to Raimbach. But it was a colour-
less assembly, wholly in the power of the imperious First Consul, and its meetings had little
instruction for a stranger. Goldsmith, however,
was not the sole compatriot Raimbach met in
the Palais Royal. In the *salons littéraires* he
came frequently in contact with Thomas Hol-

croft, of the " Road to Ruin." Holcroft had
married a French wife, had a family, and was
engaged in preparing those " Travels in France,"
which Sir Richard Phillips afterwards published.
Holcroft was a friend of Opie (then also in
Paris), who painted the portrait of him now at St.
Martin's Place ; but from Raimbach's account
he must have been far more petulant and irri-
table than befitted the austere philosopher of his
writings. Of another person whom Raimbach
mentions he gives a rosier account than is given
generally. At the Café Jacob in the Rue
Jacob, an obscure *cabaret* in an obscure street,
was frequently to be seen the once redoubtable
Thomas Paine, then about sixty-five. Contemporaries represent him at this date as not only
fallen upon evil days, but dirty in his person
and unduly addicted to spirits. That the
general appearance of the author of the " Rights
of Man " was " mean and poverty-stricken,"
and that he was " much withered and care-
worn," Raimbach admits, and he moreover
adds that " he had sunk into complete insignifi-
cance, and was quite unnoticed by the Government." But he also describes him as " fluent
in speech, of mild and gentle demeanour, clear
and distinct in enunciation," and endowed with
an " exceedingly soft and agreeable voice " —

words which, in this connection, somehow remind one of Lord Foppington's philosophic eulogy of Miss Hoyden. Certainly they scarcely suggest the red-nosed and dilapidated personage who drank brandy and declaimed against Religion in his cups with whom modern records have acquainted us.

Raimbach's remaining experiences must be rapidly summarised. He attended the Palais de Justice, and was much impressed by the French forensic oratory. Concerning the oratory of the pulpit he is not equally enthusiastic, observing, indeed, that he should think the cause of religion derived little support from the eloquence of the clergy. But it must be remembered that at this period most of the priests were expatriated, and many of the churches were still used as warehouses and stables. One close by him in the Rue Montorgueil was, as a matter of fact, employed as a saddler's shop. He was much interested in the now dispersed collection brought together in the Musée des Monuments in the Petits-Augustins by M. Alexandre Lenoir, the artist and antiquary. This consisted of such monumental efforts as had escaped the fury of the Terror — escaping, it should be added, only miserably mutilated and defaced. Lenoir, who had received a severe bayonet

wound in attempting to defend the tomb of
Richelieu, had admirably arranged these waifs
and strays, and the collection of eighteenth
century sculpture was especially notable, as were
also the specimens of stained glass. Among
Raimbach's personal experiences came the successful consumption at Véry's in the Palais
Royal of a *fricassée* of frogs. But this was done
in ignorance, and not of set purpose, as in the
case of the epicure, Charles Lamb, who speaks
of them as "the nicest little delicate things."
Raimbach's return to England, somewhat precipitated by the fury of the First Consul at the attacks
upon him in the *Morning Chronicle*, was made
by the Picardy route. At Calais he spent a day
at the historical Lion d'Argent,[1] where Hogarth
and so many of his fellow countrymen had been
before him, and he reached Dover shortly afterwards, giving, with his party, three ringing cheers
at once more treading upon English soil. He
had been absent two months instead of two
weeks. His *impressions de voyage*, which occupy nearly half his "Memoirs," would have
gained in permanent charm if he had described
more and reflected less. All the same, his trip

[1] Mrs. Carter (*Memoirs,* i. 253) says, in June, 1763:
"I am sorry to say it, but it is fact, that the Lion d'Argent
at Calais is a much better inn than any I saw at Dover."

to Paris as a young man in 1802 was the one
event of his career, for though he went abroad
again on two or three occasions, received a gold
medal from the Salon in 1814, for his engraving
of "The Village Politicians," was fêted by
Baron Gérard in 1825, and made a Corresponding Member of the Institute ten years later, the
rest of his recollections are comparatively un-
interesting, except for his intercourse with
Wilkie, of whom he wrote a brief biography.
He died in January, 1843, in his sixty-seventh
year.

THE " VICAR OF WAKEFIELD" AND
ITS ILLUSTRATORS.

NOT many years since, *à propos* of a certain
volume of epistolary parodies, the para-
graphists were busily discussing the different
aspects which the characters of fiction present
to different readers. It was shown that, not
only as regards the fainter and less strongly
drawn figures, — the Frank Osbaldistones, the
Clive Newcomes, the David Copperfields, —
but even as regards what Gautier would have
called " the grotesques," — the Costigans, the
Swivellers, the Gamps, — each admirer, in his
separate " study of imagination," had his own
idea, which was not that of another. What is
true of the intellectual perception is equally true
of the pictorial. Nothing is more notable than
the diversities afforded by the same book when
illustrated by different artists. Contrast for a
moment the Don Quixotes of Smirke, of Tony
Johannot, of Gustave Doré ; contrast the Fal-
staffs of Kenny Meadows, of Sir John Gilbert,

of Mr. Edwin A. Abbey.   Or, to take a better
instance, compare the contemporary illustrations
of Dickens with the modern designs of (say)
Charles Green or Frederick Barnard.   The
variations, it will at once be manifest, are not
the mere variations arising from ampler resource
or from fuller academic skill on the part of the
younger men.   It is not alone that they have
conquered the inner secret of Du Maurier's
artistic   stumbling-blocks — the   irreconcilable
chimney-pot hat, the "terrible trousers," the
unspeakable evening clothes of the Victorian
era : it is that their point of view is different.
Nay, in the case of Barnard, one of the first, if
not the first, of modern humorous designers,
although he is studiously loyal to the Dickens
tradition as revealed by "Phiz" and Cruikshank, he is at the same time as unlike them as
it is well possible to be.   To this individual and
personal attitude of the artist must be added,
among other things, the further fact that each
age has a trick of investing the book it decorates
with something of its own temperament and atmosphere.   It may faithfully endeavour to revive
costume ; it may reproduce accessory with the
utmost care ; but it can never look with the old
eyes, or see exactly in the old way.   Of these
positions, the "Vicar of Wakefield" is as good

an example as any. Between its earlier illustrated editions and those of the last half century
the gulf is wide; while the portraits of Dr.
Primrose as presented by Rowlandson on the
one hand and Stothard on the other are as strik-
ingly in contrast as any of the cases above indicated. We shall add what is practically a fresh
chapter to a hackneyed history if for a page or
two we attempt to give some account of Goldsmith's story considered exclusively in its aspect
as an illustrated book.

To the first edition of 1766 there were no
illustrations. The two *duodecimo* volumes "on
grey paper with blunt type," printed at Salisbury in that year " by B. Collins, for F. New-
bery," were without embellishments of any kind;
and the sixth issue of 1779 had been reached before we come to the earliest native attempt at
any pictorial realisation of the characters. In
the following year appeared the first illustrated
English edition, being two tiny booklets bearing
the imprint of one J. Wenman, of 144 Fleet
Street, and containing a couple of poorly-exe-
cuted frontispieces by the miniaturist, Daniel
Dodd. They represent the Vicar taking leave
of George, and Olivia and the Landlady — a
choice of subjects in which the artist had many
subsequent imitators. The designs have little

distinction but that of priority, and can claim no higher merit than attaches to the cheap adornments of a cheap publication. Dodd is seen to greater advantage in one of the two plates which, about the same date, figured in Harrison's " Novelist's Magazine," and also in the *octavo* edition of the " Vicar," printed for the same publisher in 1781. These plates have the pretty old-fashioned ornamental framework which the elder Heath and his colleagues had borrowed from the French vignettists. Dodd illustrates the episode of the pocket-book, while his companion Walker, at once engraver and designer, selects the second rescue of Sophia at the precise moment when Burchell's " great stick " has shivered the small sword of Mr. Timothy Baxter. Walker's design is the better of the two ; but their main interest is that of costume-pieces, and in both the story is told by gesture rather than by expression.

So natural is it to associate the grace of Stothard with the grace of Goldsmith, that one almost resents the fact that, in the collection for which he did so much, the task of illustrating the " Vicar " fell into other hands. But as his first relations with Harrison's " Magazine " are alleged to have originated in an application made to him to correct a drawing by Dodd for " Joseph

Andrews," [1] it is probable that, before he began to work regularly for the publisher, the plates for the " Vicar " had already been arranged for. Yet it was not long before he was engaged upon the book. In 1792 [2] was published an *octavo* edition, the plates of which were beautifully engraved by Basire's pupil and Blake's partner, James Parker. Stothard's designs, six in number, illustrate the Vicar taking leave of George, the Rescue of Sophia from Drowning, the Honeysuckle Arbour, the Vicar and Olivia, the Prison Sermon, and the Family Party at the end. The best of them, perhaps, is that in which Olivia's father, with an inexpressible tenderness of gesture, lifts the half-sinking, half-kneeling form of his repentant daughter. But though none can be said to be wanting in that grace which is the unfailing characteristic of the artist, upon the whole they are not *chefs-d'œuvre*. Certainly they are not as good as the best of the " Clarissa " series in Harrison ; they are not even better than the illustrations to Sterne, the originals of which are at South Kensington. In-

[1] Pye's " Patronage of British Art," 1845, pp. 247–8.

[2] An imaginary frontispiece portrait of the Vicar, prefixed to a one-volume issue of 1790, has not been here regarded as entitling the book to rank as an " illustrated " edition. There is no artist's name to the print.

deed, there is at South Kensington a circular composition by Stothard from the " Vicar " — a lightly-washed sketch in Indian ink — which surpasses them all. The moment selected is obscure ; but the persons represented are plainly the Wakefield family, Sir William Thornhill and the 'Squire. The 'Squire is speaking, Olivia hides her face in her mother's lap, Dr. Primrose listens with bent head, and the *ci-devant* Mr. Burchell looks sternly at his nephew. The entire group, which is admirable in refinement and composition, has all the serene gravity of a drawing by Flaxman. Besides the above, and a pair of plates to be mentioned presently, Stothard did a set of twenty-four minute headpieces to a Memorandum Book for 1805 (or thereabouts), all of which were derived from Goldsmith's novel, and these probably do not exhaust his efforts in this direction.

After the Stothard of 1792 comes a succession of editions more or less illustrated. In 1793 Cooke published the " Vicar " in his " Select Novels," with a vignette and plate by R. Corbould, and a plate by Anker Smith. The last, which depicts " Olivia rejecting with disdain the offer of a Purse of Money from 'Squire Thornhill," is not only a dainty little picture, but serves to exemplify some of the remarks at the

outset of this paper. Seven-and-twenty years
later, the same design was re-engraved as the
frontispiece of an edition published by Dean and
Munday, and the costumes were modernised to
date. The 'Squire Thornhill of 1793 has a three-
cornered hat and ruffles ; in 1820 he wears
whiskers, a stiff cravat with a little collar, and
a cocked hat set athwartships. Olivia, who disdained him in 1793 in a cap and sash, disdains
him in 1820 in her own hair and a high waist.
Corbould's illustrations to these volumes are
commonplace. But he does better in the five
plates which he supplied to Whittingham's edition of 1800, three of which, the Honeysuckle
Arbour, Moses starting on his Journey, and
Olivia and the Landlady, are pleasant enough.
In 1808 followed an edition with a charming
frontispiece by Stothard, in which the Vicar
with his arm in a sling is endeavouring to recon-
cile Mrs. Primrose to Olivia. There is also a
vignette by the same hand. These, engraved at
first by Heath, were repeated in 1813 by J.
Romney. In the same year the book appeared
in the " Mirror of Amusement " with three
plates by that artistic Jack-of-all-trades, William
Marshall Craig, sometime drawing-master to the
Princess Charlotte of Wales. There are also editions in 1812, 1823, and 1824, with frontispieces

by the Academician, Thomas Uwins. But, as
an interpreter of Goldsmith, the painter of the
once-popular " Chapeau de Brigand " is not
inspiriting.

In following the line of engravers on copper,
soon to be superseded by steel, we have neglected the sister art of engraving upon wood,
of which the revival is practically synchronous
with Harrison's " Magazine." The first edition
of the " Vicar " decorated with what Horace
Walpole contemptuously called " wooden cuts,"
is dated 1798. It has seven designs, three of
which are by an unknown person called Eginton, and the remainder by Thomas Bewick, by
whom all of them are engraved. Eginton may
be at once dismissed ; but Bewick's own work,
notwithstanding his genuine admiration for
Goldsmith, arouses no particular enthusiasm.
He was too original to be the illustrator of other
men's ideas, and his designs, though fair specimens of his *technique* as a xylographer, are poor
as artistic conceptions. The most successful is
the Procession to Church, the stubbornness of
Blackberry, as may be imagined, being effectively rendered. Frontispieces by Bewick also
appear in editions of 1810 and 1812 ; and between 1807 and 1810 the records speak of three
American issues with woodcuts by Bewick's

trans-Atlantic imitator, Alexander Anderson. Whether these were or were not merely copies of Bewick, like much of Anderson's work, cannot be affirmed without inspection. Nor, for the same reason, is it possible to refer with certainty to the edition illustrated by Thurston and engraved by Bewick's pupil, Luke Clennell, of which Linton speaks in his " Masters of Wood Engraving " as containing a "' Mr. Burchell in the hayfield reading to the two Primrose girls,' full of drawing and daylight," which should be worth seeing. But the triumph of woodcut copies at this date is undoubtedly the so-called " Whittingham's edition " of 1815. This is illustrated by thirty-seven woodcuts and tailpieces engraved by the prince of modern wood-engravers, John Thompson. The artist's name has been modestly withheld, and the designs are sometimes attributed to Thurston, but they are not entirely in his manner, and we are inclined to assign them to Samuel Williams. In any case, they are unpretending little pieces, simple in treatment, and sympathetic in character. The Vicar Consoled by his Little Boys, and the Two Girls and the Fortune-teller, may be cited as favourable examples. But the scale is too small for much play of expression. " Whittingham's edition " was very popular, and copies are by no means rare. It was certainly republished in 1822 and 1825, and probably there are other issues. And so we come to that most extraordinary of contributions by a popular designer to the embellishment of a popular author, the " Vicar " of Thomas Rowlandson.

Rowlandson was primarily a caricaturist, and his " Vicar " is a caricature. He was not without artistic power; he could, if he liked, draw a beautiful woman (it is true that his ideal generally deserves those epithets of " *plantureux, luxuri-ant, exubérant* " which the painter in " Gerfaut " gives to the charms of Mlle. Reine Gobillot) ; but he did not care to modify his ordinary style. Consequently he illustrated Goldsmith's master-piece as he illustrated Combe's " Doctor Syn-tax," and the result is a pictorial outrage. The unhappy Primrose family romp through his pages, vulgarised by all sorts of indignities, and the reader reaches the last of the " twenty-four coloured plates " which Ackermann put forth in 1817, and again in 1823, as one escaping from a nightmare. It is only necessary to glance at Stothard's charming little plate of Hunt the Slipper in Rogers's " Pleasures of Memory " of 1802 to see how far from the Goldsmith spirit is Rowlandson's treatment of the same pastime. Where he is most endurable, is where his de-

signs to the " Vicar " have the least relation
to the personages of the book, as, for example,
in " A Connoisseur Mellowing the Tone of a
Picture," which is simply a humorous print
neither better nor worse than any of the other
humorous prints with which he was wont to fill
the windows of the " Repository of Arts " in
Piccadilly.

It is a relief to turn from the rotundities of
Rowlandson to the edition which immediately
followed — that known to collectors as Sharpe's.
It contains five illustrations by Richard Westall,
engraved on copper by Corbould, Warren,
Romney, and others. Westall's designs are of
the school of Stothard — that is to say, they are
graceful and elegant rather than humorous ;
but they are most beautifully rendered by their
engravers. The Honeysuckle Arbour (George
Corbould), where the girls lean across the table
to watch the labouring stag as it pants past,
is one of the most brilliant little pictures we
can remember. In 1829, William Finden re-
engraved the whole of these designs on steel,
slightly reducing them in size, and the merits
of the two methods may be compared. It is
hard to adjudge the palm. Finden's fifth plate
especially, depicting Sophia's return to the Vicar
in Prison, is a miracle of executive delicacy.

Goldsmith's next illustrators of importance are Cruikshank and Mulready. The contributions of the former are limited to two plates for vol. x. (1832) of Roscoe's "Novelist's Library." They are not successes. The kindly Genius of Broadgrin is hardly as coarse as Rowlandson, but his efforts to make his subjects "comic" at all hazards are not the less disastrous, and there is little of the Vicar, or Mrs. Primrose, or even Moses, in the sketch with which he illustrates the tragedy of the gross of green spectacles; while the most salient characteristic of the somewhat more successful Hunt the Slipper is the artist's inveterate tendency to make the waists of his women (in the words of Pope's imitation of Prior), "fine by defect, and delicately weak." Mulready's designs (1843), excellently interpreted by John Thompson, have a far greater reputation, — a reputation heightened not a little by the familiar group of pictures which he elaborated from three of the sketches. Choosing the Wedding Gown, the Whistonian Controversy, and Sophia and Burchell Haymaking, with their unrivalled rendering of texture and material, are among the painter's most successful works in oil; and it is the fashion to speak of his illustrated "Vicar" as if all of its designs were at the same artistic level. This is by no means the case. Some of them, *e.g.*, Olivia measuring herself with the 'Squire, have playfulness and charm, but the majority, besides being crowded in composition, are heavy and unattractive. Mulready's paintings, however, and the generally diffused feeling that the domestic note in his work should make him a born illustrator of Goldsmith, have given him a prestige which cannot now be gainsaid.

After Mulready follows a crowd of minor illustrators. One of the most successful of these was the clever artist George Thomas; one of the most disappointing, because his gifts were of so high an order, was G. J. Pinwell. Of Absolon, Anelay, Gilbert, and the rest, it is impossible to speak here, and we must close this rapid summary with brief reference to some of the foreign editions.

At the beginning of this paper, in enumerating certain of the causes for the diversities, pleasing or otherwise, which prevail in illustrated copies of the classics, we purposely reserved one which it is more convenient to treat in connection with those books when "embellished" by foreign artists. If, even in the country of birth, each age (as has been well said of translations) "*a eu de ce côté son belvé-*

dère différent," it follows that every other country will have its point of view, which will be at
variance with that of a native. To say that no
book dealing with human nature in the abstract
is capable of being adequately illustrated except
in the country of its origin, would be to state
a proposition in imminent danger of prompt
contradiction. But it may be safely asserted,
that, except by an artist who, from long residence or familiarity, has enjoyed unusual facili-
ties for assimilating the national atmosphere, no
novel of manners (to which class the " Vicar "
must undoubtedly be held to belong) can be
illustrated with complete success by a foreigner.
For this reason, it will not be necessary here to
do more than refer briefly to the principal French
and German editions. In either country the
" Vicar " has had the advantage of being artisti-
cally interpreted by draughtsmen of marked
ability ; but in both cases the solecisms are
thicker than the beauties.

It must be admitted, notwithstanding, for
Germany, that it was earlier in the field than
England. Wenman's edition is dated 1780 ; but
it was in 1776 that August Mylius of Berlin
issued the first frontispiece of the " Vicar." It
is an etching by the " Berlin Hogarth," Daniel
Chodowiecki, prefixed to an English reprint of

the second edition, and it represents the popular
episode of Mr. Burchell and the pocket-book.
The poor Vicar is transformed into a loose-
lipped, heavy-jowled German pastor in a dress-
ing-gown and slippers, while Mr. Burchell
becomes a slim personage in top-boots, and
such a huntsman's cap as stage tradition assigns
to Tony Lumpkin. In the " Almanac Généalogique " for 1777, Chodowiecki returned to this
subject, and produced a series of twelve charming plates — little marvels of delicate execution
— upon the same theme. Some of these, *e. g.*,
the " Conversation brillante des Dames de la
ville " and " George sur le Téatre (*sic*) recon-
noit son Père " — are delightfully quaint. But
they are not illustrations of the text — and there
is no more to say. The same radical objection
applies to the illustrations, full of fancy, ingenuity, and playfulness as they are, of another
German, Ludwig Richter. His edition has
often been reprinted. But it is sufficient to
glance at his barefooted Sophia, making hay,
with her straw hat at her back, in order to decide against it. One crosses out " Sophia "
and writes in " Frederika." She may have
lived at Sesenheim, but never at Wakefield. In
like manner, the insular mind recoils from the
spectacle of the patriarchal Jenkinson studying

the Cosmogony in company with a tankard of a pattern unmistakably Teutonic.

In France, to judge by certain entries in Cohen's invaluable " Guide de l'Amateur de Livres à Vignettes," the book seems to have been illustrated as early as the end of the last century. Huot and Texier are mentioned as artists, but their works have escaped us. The chief French edition, however, is that which belongs to the famous series of books with " *images incrustées en plein texte* " (as Jules Janin says), inaugurated in 1835 by the " Gil Blas " of Jean Gigoux. The " Vicaire de Wakefield " (Bourgueleret, 1838), admirably paraphrased by Charles Nodier, was accompanied by ten engravings on steel by William Finden after Tony Johannot, and a number of small woodcuts, *entêtes* and *culs-de-lampe* by Janet Lange, Charles Jacque, and C. Marville.[1] As compositions, Johannot's contributions are effective, but highly theatrical, while his types are frankly French. Of the woodcuts it may be sufficient to note that when the Vicar and Mrs. Primrose discuss the prospects of the family in the privacy of their own chamber, they do so (in the picture) from two separate four-posters with twisted uprights,

[1] To the edition of 1843, which does not contain these woodcuts, is added one by Meissonier.

and a crucifix between them. The same eccentricities, though scarcely so naïvely ignorant,
are not entirely absent from the work of two
much more modern artists, M. V. A. Poirson
and M. Adolphe Lalauze. M. Poirson (Quan-
tin, 1885) who, in his own domain, has extraordinary skill as a decorative artist, depicts 'Squire
Thornhill as a gay young French *chasseur* with
many-buttoned gaiters and a *fusil en bandoulière*,
while the hero of the " Elegy on a Mad Dog "
appears in those " wooden shoes " (with straw
in them) which for so long a period were to
English cobblers the chief terror of a French
invasion. M. Lalauze again (Jouaust, 1888),
for whose distinguished gifts (in their place) we
have the keenest admiration, promotes the whole
Wakefield family into the *haute noblesse.* An
elegant Dr. Primrose blesses an elegant George
with the air of a Rochefoucauld, while Mrs.
Primrose, in the background, with the Bible and
cane, is a *grande dame.* Under the same treatment, the scene in the hayfield becomes a *fête
galante* after the fashion of Lancret or Watteau.

Upon the whole, dismissing foreign artists for
the reason given above, one is forced to the conclusion that Goldsmith has not hitherto found
his fitting pictorial interpreter. Stothard and
Mulready have accentuated his graver side;

Cruikshank and Rowlandson have exaggerated his humour. But no single artist in the past, as far as we are aware, has, in any just proportion, combined them both. By the delicate quality of his art, by the alliance in his work of a simplicity and playfulness which has a kind of parallel in Goldsmith's literary style, the late Randolph Caldecott seemed always to suggest that he could, if he would, supply this want. But, apart from the captivating play-book of the " Mad Dog," and a frontispiece in the " Parchment Library," Caldecott contributed nothing to the illustration of Goldsmith's novel.[1]

---

[1] The foregoing paper, which appeared in the " English Illustrated Magazine," for October, 1890, was afterwards reprinted as the Preface to Mr. Hugh Thomson's admirable illustrated edition of the " Vicar " (Macmillan, same year).

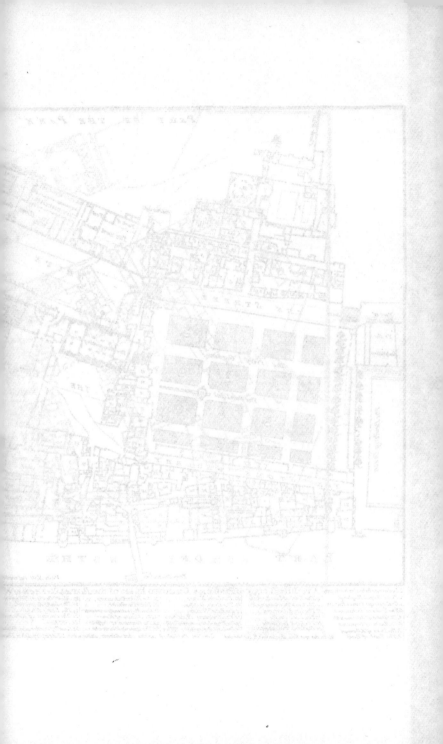

OLD WHITEHALL.

NOW, when the widening of Parliament Street promises to afford an adequate approach to St. Stephen's, and another imposing range of buildings has arisen at Spring Gardens to match the Foreign and India Offices, it may be worth while to linger for a moment upon some former features of this much-changing locality. In such a retrospect, the Old Banqueting-House of Inigo Jones naturally becomes a prominent object. Its massive Northamptonshire stone and classic columns invest it with a dignity of which the towering pile of Whitehall Court can scarcely deprive it ; and it seems to overlook Kent's stumpy Horse Guards opposite much as a nobleman with a pedigree might be expected to survey a neighbour of a newer creation. And yet, impressive though it is, it represents but an insignificant portion of the architect's original design, the imaginative extent of which may be studied in Campbell's " Vitruvius Britannicus " and elsewhere. As a matter of fact, the present Banqueting-House was only one out of

four similar pavilions in a vast structure of
which the ground plan would have extended
from the river bank to a point far beyond the
Horse Guards, and would have occupied all the
space on either side of the road from Horse
Guards Avenue to the Mews of Richmond
Terrace. It included no fewer than seven
splendid internal courts, and the façades towards
the park and the Thames — the latter especially
— were of great beauty. But the scheme was
beyond the pocket of the first James, for whom,
in 1619, it was designed ; and a cheaper modifi-
cation, reaching only to the roadway, and prepared twenty years later, fared no better with
Charles I. The Banqueting-House, which was
built in 1619–22, and is common to both schemes,
is consequently all that was ever executed of
what, in its completed form, would have been
a palace among palaces, surpassing the Louvre
and the Escurial.

Apart from its existing employment as a military museum,[1] the Banqueting-House to-day
serves chiefly as a landmark or key by help of
which its ancient environments may be mentally
re-constructed. With Gibbons' fine bronze statue
of James II., now erected in the enclosure at

---

[1] *I. e.*, that of the Royal United Service Institution.

the side of Gwydyr House,[1] it practically con-
stitutes the sole surviving portion of Old Whitehall as it appears in John Fisher's famous
" Survey and Ground-Plot " of 1680 ;[2] and
about it was dispersed irregularly that pell-mell
of buildings dating from Henry VIII. and
Elizabeth, which, in Jacobean and Caroline days,
was known as " our Palace of Westminster."
Roughly speaking, this aggregation might be
defined geographically as bounded on the north[3]
by St. James's Park ; on the south by the
Thames ; to the east by Scotland Yard and
Spring Gardens, and to the west by Richmond
Terrace Mews. It was traversed throughout
its entire extent by the old roadway leading
to Westminster Abbey, and this divided it into
two portions, the larger and more important of
which lay on the side of the Thames. From
Scotland Yard to the Banqueting-House the
road was fairly wide and open ; but at the western end of the Banqueting-House it suddenly
narrowed, passing through the gate popularly

[1] This originally stood at the back of the Banqueting-
House in Whitehall Gardens ; but was moved to its
present site in 1897.

[2] There are anachronisms which seem to indicate an
earlier date.

[3] By "north," "south," etc., the north and south of
Fisher's plan are here intended.

known as Holbein's, and afterwards entering
King Street through a second or King Street
Gate. " K[ing] Cha[rles]," the Marquis of Nor-
manby told Evelyn, " had a designe to buy
all King Street, and build it nobly, it being
the streete leading to Westm^r." Once, too,
when Evelyn had presented him with a copy
of his " book of Architecture," he sketched a
rough plan for the future building of Whitehall
itself, " together with the roomes of state, and
other particulars." But His Majesty's promises
were better than his performances ; and he had
more pressing and less worshipful ways of
spending his money.

It will be convenient to speak first of that
part of the palace buildings which lay to the
north of King Street and the road to Charing
Cross. Here was the old Cockpit, which, in
the time of Fisher's Plan, was included in the
apartments of Monk, Duke of Albemarle, and
from which the Earl of Pembroke and Montgomery saw the first Charles walk from St.
James's Palace to the scaffold. Later it became
the Privy-Council Office, where, in Anne's reign,
Harley was stabbed by Guiscard. Here also
was the Tennis Court ; and (fronting the Banqueting-House) the Tilt-Yard, where with such
" laudable Courtesy and pardonable Insolence,"

Sir Roger de Coverley's ancestor defeated his opponent.[1] On the site of the present Treasury, and looking upon the street, were the apartments of the Dukes of Monmouth and Ormond ; to the left of these, the quarters of Captain Henry Cooke, " Master of the Children [choir boys] of the Chapel Royal." The remainder of the buildings on this side seem to have been chiefly occupied by Albemarle, though the Duchess of Cleveland had kitchens near the Tennis Court, while between the Horse Guard Yard and the Spring Garden were the rooms of one of the maids of honour, Mrs. Kirk, under whose auspices took place some of those lively and scandalous *petits soupers*, of which record is to be found in the veracious pages of Anthony Hamilton. At the back of all these buildings stretched St. James's Park, where Charles II. made many improvements, and built his famous decoy for waterfowl. In Evelyn's days this must have almost attained the proportions of a menagerie. " Here," says he, " was a curious sort of poultry not much exceeding the size of a tame pidgeon, with legs so short as their crops seem'd to touch ye earth ; a milk-white raven ; a stork which was a rarity at this season, seeing he was loose and could

[1] *Spectator*, No. 109.

flie loftily ; two Balearian [Balearic ?] cranes, one
of which having one of his leggs broken and cut
off above the knee, had a wooden or boxen leg
and thigh, with a joynt so accurately made that
ye creature could walke and use it as well as
if it had ben natural ; it was made by a souldier.
The parke was at this time stored with numerous
flocks of severall sorts of ordinary and extraordinary wild fowle, breeding about the Decoy,
which for being neere so greate a citty, and
among such a concourse of souldiers and people,
is a singular and diverting thing. There were
also deere of severall countries, white ; spotted
like leopards ; antelopes, an elk, red deere,
roebucks, staggs, Guinea goates, Arabian
sheepe, &c. There were withy-potts or nests
for the wild fowle to lay their eggs in, a little
above ye surface of ye water." [1]

Thus we come to that larger and more important portion of Old Whitehall which lay to
the south of the road between Westminster and
Charing Cross. To the west of the Banqueting-House, and corresponding in width to the
distance between the two great gates, was the
Privy Garden, where in May, 1662, Mr. Pepys,
to his great solace and content, saw my Lady
Castlemaine's laced smocks and linen petticoats

[1] " Memoirs of John Evelyn," etc., 1827, ii. 234.

floating gaily to the breeze. According to Hatton, the Privy Garden occupied about three and a quarter acres, and (as the plan shows) was laid out in sixteen grass-plots with statues in the centre of each. To the north a wall separated it from the roadway, to the west was a line of trees, and to the east a straggling range of buildings nearly at right angles to the Banqueting-House. Here lived Evelyn's friend, Sir Robert Murray; and here were the apartments of the Lord Chamberlain, where, in November, 1679, Evelyn witnessed the re-marriage of his Lordship's daughter, a child of twelve years old, to the Duke of Grafton, the king's natural son by Barbara Palmer. Here, again, were the Council Office, the Lord Keeper's Office, and the Treasury. Opposite the Treasury, in the central walk of the garden, was a famous dial, which had been set up in James's reign, but had fallen into ruin in that of his grandson. By King James's order it was fully described in a quarto published in 1624, by one Edmund Gunter, and it was of it that Andrew Marvell wrote the bitter lines : —

" This place for a dial was too insecure,
   Since a guard and a garden could not it defend;
 For so near to the Court they will never endure
   Any witness to show how their time they mispend."

To the south of the Privy Garden, and communicating with the Bowling Green, which lay to the west of it (presumably on the site now occupied by Richmond Terrace), was the famous Stone Gallery. On its northern side were domiciled the Earl of Lauderdale, Lord Peterborough, Prince Rupert, and Mr. Hyde ; and somewhere in its vicinity, although not indicated upon Fisher's plan, doubtless because granted subsequently to the date of its execution, must have been the " luxuriously-furnished " lodgings of that " baby-faced " (but not guileless) Breton beauty, Louise Renée de Kéroualle. This, indeed, is clear from Evelyn's diary. " 4th Oct. [1683] . . . Following his Majesty this morning *thro' the gallerie*, I went, with the few who attended him, into the Dutchesse of Portsmouth's [1] dressing-roome within her bed-chamber, where she was in her morning loose garment, her maids combing her, newly out of her bed, his Maty and the gallants standing about her ; but that which engag'd my curiosity was the rich and splendid furniture of this woman's apartment, now twice or thrice pull'd down and rebuilt to satisfie her prodigal and expensive pleasures, whilst her Matys does not exceede some

[1] From an autograph in the French National Archives, she signed herself " L duchesse de Portsmout."

gentlemen's ladies in furniture and accommodation.   Here I saw the new fabriq of French tapissry, for designe, tenderness of worke, and incomparable imitation of the best paintings, beyond anything I had ever beheld.   Some pieces had Versailles, St. Germain's and other palaces of the French King, with huntings, figures and landskips, exotiq fowls, and all to the life rarely don.   Then for Japan cabinets, screenes, pendule clocks, greate vases of wrought plate, tables, stands, chimney furniture, sconces, branches, braseras, &c. all of massie silver, and out of number, besides some of her Ma^{tys} best paintings."   " 10 April [1691].   This night a sudden and terrible fire burnt down all the buildings *over the stone gallery* at White-hall to the water-side, beginning at the apartment of the late Dutchesse of Portsmouth [1] (wch had ben pull'd down and rebuilt no lesse than three times to please her)."

Between the Stone Gallery and the old river-line, now obliterated by the Embankment, and covering a site which extended as far as White-hall Palace Stairs, were the apartments of the King, the Queen, the Duke of York, and the

---

[1] What Evelyn intends by " late " is not clear, as the Duchess did not die until 1734.   Probably he only means that she had withdrawn to France.

great officers of the Court. The King's rooms, in suggestive proximity to those of the Maids of Honour, and with the notorious Chiffinch conveniently at hand, were to the left of the Privy Stairs ; those of Catherine of Braganza, which, on the plan, look small and unimportant, lay to the right. Neither Pepys nor Evelyn gives us much information with regard to this part of the Palace. Mention is indeed made by them and others of the Shield Gallery, the Matted Gallery, the Boarded Gallery, the Vane Room, the Robe Chamber, the Green Chamber, the Theatre, the Adam and Eve Gallery (which took its name from a picture by Mabuse), and so forth ; but the indications are too vague to enable us to fix their locality with certainty. By favour, however, of " an ancient woman who made these lodgings cleane, and had all yᵉ keys," Evelyn seems to have minutely examined the King's private library, with which, though he spent three or four days over it, he was not greatly impressed. " I went," he says, " with expectation of finding some curiosities, but though there were about 1000 volumes, there were few of importance which I had not perus'd before." He found, nevertheless, a folio MS. containing the school exercises of Edward VI., together with his Journal, which Burnet after-

wards made use of in his " History of the Reformation." [1]   Towards Whitehall Stairs, between
the Banqueting House and the river, were the
Great Hall, and the Chapel where King of Chi-
chester, and the witty South, and the eloquent
Stillingfleet preached to a unedified congregation,
and where inquisitive Mr. Pepys " observed,"
on a certain Sunday in October, 1660, " how
the Duke of York and Mrs. Palmer did talk to
one another very wantonly through the hangings
that parts the King's closet and the closet where
the ladies sit."   An old view of Whitehall, from
the Thames, gives a fair idea of its aspect at this
time.   To the right are the Chapel and Hall, with
the loftier Banqueting-House appearing above
them, and Holbein's gate just distinguishable at
its side.   To the left is the covered Privy Stairs,
whence the Royal Barge with its flags and
trumpeters is just putting off.   Here it must
have been, that, little more than two months before Charles II.'s unexpected death, Evelyn
witnessed the water celebration which took
place in front of the Queen's apartments : —
" [Nov.] 15, [1684] Being the Queene's birthday, there were fire-works on the Thames before White-hall, with pageants of castles, forts,
and other devices of gyrandolas, serpents, the

[1] " Memoirs of John Evelyn," etc., 1827, iii. 33–35.

13

King and Queene's armes and mottos, all represented in fire, such as had not ben seen here.
But the most remarkable was the several fires
and skirmishes in the very water, which actually
mov'd a long way, burning under the water,
now and then appearing above it, giving reports
like muskets and cannon, with granados and in-
numerable other devices.   It is said it cost
£1,500.   It was concluded with a ball, where
all the young ladys and gallants daunced in the
greate hall.   The court had not ben seene so
brave and rich in apparell since his Ma^tys re-
stauration." [1]   To this may succeed that memorable and oft-cited entry, which occurs only a
few pages farther on, when Charles was lying
dead : " I can never forget the inexpressible
luxury and prophanenesse, gaming and all disso-
luteness, and as it were total forgetfullnesse of
God (it being Sunday evening) which this day
se'nnight [25 January, 1685] I was witnesse of,
the King sitting and toying with his concubines,
Portsmouth, Cleaveland and Mazarine, &c., a
French boy [François Duperrier] singing love
songs, in that glorious gallery, whilst about 20
of the greate courtiers and other dissolute persons were at basset round a large table, a bank
of at least 2,000 in gold before them, upon which

[1] " Memoirs of John Evelyn," etc., 1827, iii. 121–2.

two gentlemen who were with me made reflexions with astonishment. Six days after was all in the dust!" The next three lines with their note of official anti climax are not so generally reprinted: — "It was enjoyn'd that those who put on mourning should wear it as for a father, in yᵉ most solemn manner."

From Whitehall Palace Stairs a roadway went, past the Chapel and Great Hall, through a wide open court to the Palace Gate, close to what was the site of the old Wardrobe (afterwards Lord Carrington's). To the right of this road, and extending as far as Scotland Yard, were groups of inferior buildings and offices, — kitchens, butteries, pastries, spiceries, bakehouses, slaughter-houses, charcoal-houses, and the like, — traces of which may still be identified. The present Board of Trade, and the adjacent buildings in Horse Guards Avenue, occupy portions of the sites of the Wine-Cellar, Hall, and Chapel; the Confectionary is said to have been a white house between the former Museum of the United Service Institution and Lord Carrington's stables, and the old Beer Buttery long existed near the gates of Fife House, the place of which is now covered by part of Whitehall Court.

Standing in the entrance to Horse Guards

Avenue (once Whitehall Yard), one may still, with the aid of an old view or two, and Fisher's indispensable plan, obtain a fair idea of the place in the time of the Stuarts. Opposite — where the Scottish Office and Horse Guards are at present — was the boundary wall of the old Tilt and Horse Guard Yards. To the left, immediately in front of the Banqueting-House, extended a row of posts, a little in advance of which — "in the open street before Whitehall" — was the spot where, after much controversy, Charles I. is now allowed to have been beheaded. At right angles to the façade a line of buildings ran out to Whitehall Gate. These, which also looked into the Privy Garden, were, as already explained, the apartments of Lord Arlington, the Lord Chamberlain. Of Whitehall Gate itself, — for, according to Mr. Wornum, we are scarcely justified in styling it Holbein's, — Pennant, who seems to have seen it, gives the following account : — " To *Holbein* was owing the most beautiful gate at *Whitehall*, built with bricks of two colours, glazed, and disposed in a tesselated fashion. The top, as well as that of an elegant tower on each side, were [*sic*] embattled. On each front were four busts in baked clay, which resisted to the last every attack of the weather: possibly the arti-

ficial stone revived in this century. These, I
have been lately informed, are preserved in a
private hand. This charming structure fell a
sacrifice to conveniency within my memory:
as did another in 1723, built at the same time,
but of far inferior beauty. The last blocked
up the road to *King's-Street*, and was called
King's-Gate. *Henry* built it as a passage to
the park, the tennis court, bowling-green, the
cock-pit, and tilting-yard; for he was extremely
fond of athletic exercises ; they suited his
strength and his temper." [1]

Both these gates were engraved by Vertue in
the " Vetusta Monumenta " published by the
Society of Antiquaries. The so-called Holbein's Gate, which long survived the buildings
that connected it with the Banqueting-House,
was pulled down in August, 1759, to make room
for Parliament Street. The Duke of Cumberland had it removed to Windsor, with the intention of re-erecting it at the top of the Long
Walk, and his Deputy Ranger, Thomas Sandby
(the architect), was to have made some additions at the sides, the designs for which are still
to be seen in J. T. Smith's " Westminster."
But, as seems generally the case after removals
of this kind, nothing was ever done in the mat-

[1] " Some Account of London," 3d ed., 1793, pp. 99, 100.

ter.   Meanwhile the medallions of which Pennant speaks were dispersed.   Three of them,
according to Smith, were, when he published
his book, at Hatfield Peverell in Essex ; two
more got worked into keepers' lodges at Windsor.   These, said Cunningham in 1849, " are
now, by Mr. Jesse's [*i. e.* the late J. Heneage
Jesse's] exertions, at Hampton Court, where
they are made to do duty as two of the Roman
Emperors, described by Hentzner, in his Travels,
as then at Hampton Court."   They are of Italian
workmanship, and may probably be attributed to
John de Maiano.

Those who, having sufficiently examined the
Palladian exterior of the Banqueting-House,
and duly noted the famous weather-cock on the
eastern end, which James II. is said to have set
up to warn him of the approach of the Dutch
fleet, desire farther to inspect the interior, can
easily do so, since (as already stated) the building is now a museum.   Its chief feature of
interest is the ceiling, which represents the
apotheosis of James I.   It is painted black,
partly gilded, and divided into panels by bands,
ornamented with a guilloche.   Of the three
central compartments, that at one end represents the British Solomon on his throne, "point-
ing to Prince Charles, who is being perfected

by Wisdom." The middle compartment shows
him " trampling on the globe and flying on the
wings of Justice (an eagle) to heaven." In the
third he is " embracing Minerva, and routing
Rebellion and Envy." These panels, and others
at the sides, were painted by Rubens in 1635,
with the assistance of Jordaens. They were
restored by Cipriani. In 1837, the whole building, which had been closed since 1829, was
refitted and repaired under the direction of Sir
Robert Smirke.

It would occupy too large a space to trace
the history of the Banqueting-House from its
first erection to its Georgian transformation into
an unconsecrated chapel, seductive as it might
be to speak of it as the theatre of Ben Jonson's
masques and the buffooneries of Cromwell. In
Charles II.'s time, to which, in the foregoing
remarks, we have mainly confined ourselves, it
was the scene of many impressive ceremonies
and state receptions. It was in the Banqueting-
House that Charles begged his Honourable
House of Commons to amend the ways about
Whitehall, so that Catherine of Braganza might
not upon her arrival find it " surrounded by
water ; " it was in the Banqueting-House that
he gravely went through that half solemn half
ludicrous business of touching for the evil ; it

was in the Banqueting-House that, coming from
the Tower of London with a splendid cavalcade,
he created at one time six Earls and six Barons.
Under its storied roof he magnificently entertained the French Ambassador, Charles Colbert,
Marquis de Croissy, on which occasion he presented Mr. Evelyn, from his own royal plate, with
a piece of that newly-imported Barbadian luxury,
the King-pine; [1] it was here also that he received the Russian Ambassador with his pres-
ents of " tapissry " and sables, and the swarthy
envoys from Morocco, with their scymetars and
white *alhagas*, and their lions and " estridges "
[ostriches].   But perhaps the brightest and most
vivid page in connection with this famous old
building is that in which Samuel Pepys relates
what he saw from its roof on the 23rd of
August 1662 : —

" . . Mr. Creed . . and I . . walked down
to the Styllyard [Steel Yard] and so all along
Thames-street, but could not get a boat: I
offered eight shillings for a boat to attend me this

[1] In the Breakfast Room at Strawberry Hill, Horace
Walpole had a picture representing Rose, the Royal
gardener, in the act of presenting to Charles II. the first
pineapple raised in England. It (the painting) was attributed to Danckers; and had belonged to a descendant
of one of the firm of London and Wise, Nursery-men,
mentioned in the fifth number of the *Spectator*.

afternoon, and they would not, it being the day
of the Queen's coming to town from Hampton
Court. So we fairly walked it to White Hall,
and through my Lord's [Lord Sandwich's] lodgings we got into White Hall garden, and so to
the Bowling-green, and up to the top of the new
Banqueting-House[1] there, over the Thames,
which was a most pleasant place as any I could
have got ; and all the show consisted chiefly in
the number of boats and barges ; and two pageants, one of a King, and another of a Queen,
with her Maydes of Honour sitting at her feet
very prettily; and they tell me the Queen is Sir
Richard Ford's daughter. Anon come the King
and Queen in a barge under a canopy with
10,000 barges and boats, I think, for we could
see no water for them, nor discern the King nor
Queen. And so they landed at White Hall
Bridge [Privy Stairs] and the great guns on the
other side went off. But that which pleased me
best was, that my Lady Castlemaine stood over
against us upon a piece of White Hall, where I
glutted myself with looking on her. But methought it was strange to see her Lord and her
upon the same place walking up and down with-

[1] No doubt still so called by habit, as it succeeded to an
earlier Banqueting-House which was burnt in January,
1619.

out taking notice one of another, only at first
entry he put off his hat, and she made him a very
civil salute, but afterwards took no notice one of
another ; but both of them now and then would
take their child, which the nurse held in her
armes, and dandle it.   One thing more ; there
happened a scaffold below to fall, and we feared
some hurt, but there was none, but she of all the
great ladies only run down among the common
rabble to see what hurt was done, and did take
care of a child that received some little hurt,
which methought was so noble.   Anon there
came one there booted and spurred that she
talked long with.   And by and by, she being in
her hair, she put on his hat, which was but an
ordinary one, to keep the wind off.   But me-
thinks it became her mightily, as every thing
else do." [1]

Evelyn's last entry respecting the old palace
is as follows : " 2 [4 ?] Jan. [1698]. . . .
White-hall burnt, nothing but walls and ruins
left."   Thus it comes about that the Banqueting-House (which, notwithstanding the above,
escaped), besides being the sole relic of a never-
existent Whitehall, is also the sole relic of the
Whitehall that was.

[1] Pepys' "Diary," by Wheatley, ii (1893), 316, 317.

LUTTRELL'S "LETTERS TO JULIA."

NOTHING (‥ melancholy truism) fades
with suc . rapidity as the reputation of the
mere favourite of society. If he be a dandy
his name, perh ps, may linger here and there in
the circular of a fashionable tailor ; if a wit,
his sayings, although — like those of Praed's
Belle — " extremely quoted " during his lifetime, scarcely survive his contemporaries and
boon-companions. It may be that he secures
to himself some notice from posterity by posthumous " Memoirs " put together by a friend —
perhaps a valet ; or he may leave behind him
some literary legacy which now and then is
disinterred from the shelves of the British
Museum Library (if, indeed, it has found an
asylum there) by an enquirer curious in forgotten follies, or anxious to elucidate the caricatures of Gillray and " HB." But, as a rule, if
he does not die early, he passes " into the line
of outworn faces," and his place knows him no
more. Only from a magazine obituary, or a
stray paragraph in a provincial paper, does one

learn, half-a-century afterwards, that an old vale-
tudinarian has died at Bath, or Cheltenham, or
Boulogne, who, in his earlier days, was a favourite
with the Prince Regent, a well-known *habitué*
of Brooks's and White's, a member of the Neapolitan Club, and a frequent figure at Crockford's. These remarks, applicable, it should
be observed, more exactly to the Georgian than
the Victorian era, are mainly prompted by the
difficulty experienced in obtaining particulars
respecting the career of the once-famous wit
and writer of *vers de société*, whose chief work
forms the subject of this paper. Yet, if we
may trust a manuscript note in our copy of the
" Letters to Julia," the author of that book and
" Crockford House " attained the ripe age of
eighty-six ; and seventy years ago no one was
better known in the higher classes of society
as — to use a phrase which would have been
employed in the days when " Pelham " was
penned — a man of the world *du meilleur crû.*
The friend of Jekyll and Lord Alvanley, of
Mackintosh and Sydney Smith, of Lord Holland and Jeffery, of Greville, of Moore, of
Rogers ; a wit with the wits, a scholar with the
scholars ; fairly earning a hearing, even in those
days of " Whistlecraft " burlesques and " Two-
penny Postboys," as a writer of sparkling verse ;

an admirable talker and a polished gentleman —
HENRY LUTTRELL must have been one of the
most delightful of social companions.   Yet,
secluded in those inner circles to which admis-
sion was as difficult as getting on the list of
" Almack's," he lies entirely beyond the range
of the ordinary life-taker ; and the few references to his character and works are only to be
found sparsely scattered through the pages of
contemporary, and, alas ! often unindexed " memoirs."   In Lady Holland's life of Sydney
Smith, for example, there are some brief references to his lightness of hand, his willingness
to be pleased, his amusing Irish stories.   " Luttrell," says Smith, warning Lady Davy against
overlooking the difficulties and embarrassments
of life, " before I taught him better, imagined
muffins grew.   He was wholly ignorant of all
the intermediate processes of sowing, reaping,
grinding, kneading, and baking."   This is not
much of a contribution to a portrait, no doubt ;
but it affords a hint of that sublime and generally affected indifference to the homelier phe-
nomena of life which forms an indispensable
part of the equipment of the man of the world, —
du meilleur crû.   Yet, although we find Rogers
regretting his attachment to, and monopoly by,
" persons of mere fashion," Luttrell, it is only

fair to infer, must have been considerably more than this. Everywhere, by happy allusion, and fine turns of expression, his work shows an intimate knowledge of classic authors ; and, as might be anticipated, of Horace in particular.

"Tickler," in the "Noctes Ambrosianæ," calls him "one of the most accomplished men in all England — a wit and a scholar." "Of course you know Luttrell," said Byron to Lady Blessington ; "he is the best sayer of good things, and the most epigrammatic conversationist I ever met. There is a terseness and wit, mingled with fancy, in his observations that no one else possesses, and no one so peculiarly understands the *apropos*. Then, unlike all, or most other wits, Luttrell is never obtrusive ; even the choicest *bons mots* are only brought forth when perfectly applicable, and they are given in a tone of good breeding which enhances their value." "None of the *talkers* whom I meet in London society," says Rogers, "can slide in a brilliant thing with such readiness as he does." The impression here given is rather of a wit than a humourist ; there is more in it of Chamfort or Rivarol than Thackeray or Sydney Smith ; but, in default of more definite information, it enables us to form an idea of the easy, fluent *causeur*, touching all topics lightly,

quick to catch the fleeting fancy and crystallise
it into an epigram, to turn a dull corner with an
adroit quotation from the classics (such things
were possible formerly), to light up a mediocre
story with a happy setting ; — able and ready,
in short, to give that sparkling ripple to the flow
of conversation which made the gifted possessor
of these rare qualities the envy of diners-out,
and the delight of hostesses. The more conventional type of such a character Luttrell has
himself sketched in easy octosyllabics : —

> How much at home was Charles in all
> The talk aforesaid — nicknamed *small !*
> Never embarrassed, seldom slow,
> His maxim always " touch and go."
> Chanced he to falter ?   A grimace
> Was ready in the proper place ;
> Or a chased snuff-box, with its gems
> And gold, to mask his has and hems,
> Was offered round, and duly rapped,
> Till a fresh topic could be tapped.
> What if his envious rivals swore
> 'T was jargon all, and he a bore ?
> The surly sentence was outvoted,
> His jokes retailed, his jargon quoted ;
> And while he sneered or quizzed or flirted,
> The world, half-angry, was diverted.

It would be of no service to reproduce here
any of the half-dozen good things of Luttrell that

linger in Moore's " Diary." Many of these
are of that class whose prosperity lies emphatically in the ear of the listener ; and we are too
far removed from the speaker to be able to
revive those niceties of manner and delivery
which were essential to a just appreciation of
them. With his verse the case is different.
That, at least, was intended to be read ; and
although some of the allusions are necessarily
obscure, we can, by a slight effort, place ourselves in the position of the audience to whom
it was originally addressed. We must frankly
confess, however, that, doubtless from the absence of those individual advantages of address
and opportunity which gave him grace as a con-
versationalist, Luttrell's work, easy and polished
though it be, scarcely impresses one as com-
mensurate with the praise he received from his
contemporaries. But of this the reader must
judge from the specimens here reproduced.

The " Letters to Julia," [1] Luttrell's longest
and most ambitious effort, is an amplification of

---

[1] In the first edition of the poem, issued in 1820, it
bore the title of "Advice to Julia," and the lady addressed corresponded more exactly with the Lydia of
Horace. But we are dealing with the later edition
of 1822, published under the title we quote above, and
in this we are told that " the first Julia must be forgiven
and forgotten."

that pleasant little ode in the first book of Horace, in which Lydia is enjoined by the poet not to ruin Sybaris by a too exclusive attach- ment to her apron-strings. The reader who recalls the sixteen lines of the original, may perhaps wonder how it was possible to expand so brief a lyric into a poem of two hundred pages. And, indeed, under the digressions of the author, the primary motive almost entirely disappears. But as he himself gives us the above explanation of the origin of his work, we are bound to regard it. His first conception, he says, was " by filling up such an outline on a wider canvas, to exhibit a picture, if imperfect not unfaithful, of modern habits and manners, and of the amusements and lighter occupations of the higher classes of society in England."

Viewed in this aspect, it matters little how the idea was first suggested. In the four epis- tles of which the book consists, the parts of Lydia and Sybaris are taken by Charles, a man of fashion and pleasure, embarrassed, as a mat- ter of course, but " at the head of the *suprême bon ton;*" and Julia, a young widow of two-and- twenty, rather lower in the social scale, but rich and spoiled by flattery, who quite intends to marry her desirable admirer whenever it suits her to do so, but in the meantime subjects him to all the petty tyrannies of coquetry and caprice. The writer of the letters is a cousin of the lady, who undertakes to remonstrate with her upon her harsh treatment of her lover. In this task, thanks to numberless digressions, he manages to ramble from " Almack's " to Newmarket, from Brighton to Paris — where you will — sketching lightly picture after picture of the fashionable life of the first quarter of the century. Now he amplifies *cur vitat olivum* into a score of lines, descriptive of his recreant hero's avoidance of Moulsey and the Fives Court; of —

> — rubbing, racing and raw meat;

now mourns that no longer —

> with pliant arm he stems
> The tide or current of the Thames;

now laments his abdication of his proud supremacy as a dresser, and master of the awful mysteries of the Cravat of our grandfathers. Readers will recall the anecdote of Brummell's tray-full of failures in the following:

> Yet weak, he felt, were the attacks
> Of his voluminous Cossacks; [1]

---

[1] Those trowsers named from the barbarians
Nursed in the Steppes — the Crim-Tartarians,
Who, when they scour a country, under
Those ample folds conceal their plunder.

In vain to suffocation braced
And bandaged was his wasp-like waist;
In vain his buckram-wadded shoulders
And chest astonished all beholders,
Wear any coat he might, 't was fruitless;
Those shoes, those very boots were bootless
Whose tops ('t was he enjoined the mixture)
Are moveable, and spurs a fixture;
All was unprofitable, flat,
And stale without a smart CRAVAT,
Muslined enough to hold its starch;
That last key-stone of Fashion's arch !

" Have you, my friend," I 've heard him say,
" Been lucky in your turns to-day ? —
Think not that what I ask alludes
To Fortune's stale vicissitudes.
Or that I 'm driven from *you* to learn
How cards, and dice, and women turn,
And what prodigious contributions
They levy, in their revolutions :
I ask not if, in times so critical,
You 've managed well your turns political,
Knowing your aptitude to rat.
My question points to — your Cravat.
These are the only turns I mean.
Tell me if these have lucky been ?

How strange their destiny has been !
Promoted, since the year fifteen,
In honour of these fierce allies,
To grace our British legs and thighs.
But fashion's tide no barrier stems ;
So the *Don* mingles with the *Thames !*

If round your neck, in every fold
Exact, the muslin has been rolled,
And, dexterously in front confined,
Preserved the proper set behind ;
In short, by dint of hand and eye,
Have you achieved a perfect tie ?

" Should yours (kind heaven, avert the omen !)
Like the cravats of vulgar, low men,
Asunder start — and, yawning wide,
Disclose a chasm on either side ;
Or should it stubbornly persist,
To take some awkward tasteless twist,
Some crease indelible, and look
Just like a dunce's dog's-eared book,
How would you parry the disgrace ?
In what assembly show your face ?
How brook your rival's scornful glance,
Or partner's titter in the dance ?
How in the morning dare to meet
The quizzers of the park or street ?
Your occupation 's gone, — in vain
Hope to dine out, or flirt again.
The LADIES from their lists will put you !
And even *I*, my friend, must cut you ! "

This is a good sample of Luttrell's lighter manner. Here is another — a wail from " Almack's "
over the substitution of tea for supper : —

" How niggardly," they cry, " to stoop
To paltry black and green from soup !
Once, every novice could obtain
A hearing over iced Champagne,

And claret, ev'n of second growth,
Gave credit to an amorous oath.
But now, such lifeless love is made
On cakes, orgeat, and lemonade,
That hungry women grow unkind,
And men too faint to speak their mind.
Tea mars all mirth, makes evenings drag,
And talk grow flat, and courtship flag ;
Tea, mawkish beverage, is the reason
Why fifty flirtings in a season
Swell with ten marriages, at most,
The columns of the Morning-Post."

We might easily multiply extracts of this kind. And jaunty and fluent as are the above passages, there are others which suggest that the author had a first-rate talent for natural description and quiet landscape, points which here and there seem to rise above his pictures of men and women — or rather, *belles* and *exquisites.* Here is a picture of a storm in the Park, which is close and effective, and quite as truthful in its realism as Swift's " City Shower " : —

How suddenly the day 's obscured !
Bless me, how dark ! — Thou threatening cloud,
Pity the *un-umbrella'd* crowd.
The cloud rolls onward with the breeze.
First, pattering on the distant trees
The rain-drops fall — then quicker, denser,
On many a parasol and spencer ;
Soon drenching, with no mercy on it,
The straw and silk of many a bonnet.

Think of their hapless owners fretting,
While feathers, crape, and gauze are wetting !
Think of the pang to well-dressed girls,
When, pinched in vain, their hair uncurls,
And ringlets from each lovely pate
Hang mathematically straight !
As off, on every side, they scour,
Still beats the persecuting shower,
Till, on the thirsty gravel smoking,
It fairly earns the name of soaking.
Breathless they scud; some helter-skelter
To carriages, and some for shelter ;
Lisping to coachmen drunk or dumb
In *numbers* — while no numbers come.

And what dweller in London will not recognise the accuracy of this : —

Have you not seen (you must remember)
A fog in London — time, November ?
That non-descript elsewhere, and grown
In our congenial soil alone ?
First, at the dawn of lingering day
It rises, of an ashen grey,
Then, deepening with a sordid stain
Of yellow, like a lion's mane,
Vapour importunate and dense,
It wars at once with every sense,
Invades the eyes, is tasted, smelt,
And, like Egyptian darkness, felt.
The ears escape not.   All around
Returns a dull unwonted sound.
Loth to stand still, afraid to stir,
The chilled and puzzled passenger,

> Oft-blundering from the pavement, fails
> To feel his way along the rails,
> Or, at the crossings, in the roll
> Of every carriage dreads its pole.

Here again — in a picture of the Serpentine in winter — are some lines which to us appear to be thoroughly successful in their choice and economy of epithet : —

> What time the slanting wintry sun
> Just skirts th' horizon, and is gone ;
> When from his disk a short-livèd glare
> Is wasted on the clear cold air ;
> When the snow sparkles, on the sight
> Flashing intolerable white ;
> And, swept by hurried feet, the ground
> Returns a crisp and crushing sound.

The main defect of the " Letters to Julia " is its length. One of the poet's contemporaries (Kenney, the creator of Jeremy Diddler) complained indeed, that, besides being too long, it was " not broad enough ; " but with the absence of the latter dimension, we need not quarrel. In point of even execution, and that air of reticent good breeding which Byron declared to be characteristic of the author's style in speaking, little is wanting. The *purpureus pannus* is, in truth, carefully kept out of sight ; and yet, notwithstanding the strict observance of the Horatian precept, there is a certain lack of colour and variety, which begets an impatient desire for discordance of some sort. One is reminded, in turning over the pages of faultlessly rhymed couplets, of that " Cymodocée " of Chateaubriand, in which there was not a single elision, and concerning which the irreverent said, — " *Tant pis pour Cymodocée !* " That the poem treats solely of trivial pursuits and amusements cannot justly be counted as a defect, since the author's intention was to depict the habits of the merely fashionable world. This his graver contemporaries fully recognised when they nicknamed the book, " Letters from a Dandy to a Dolly." A less excusable fault is, that Luttrell nowhere opposes to his picture of frivolity any hint of higher or worthier employment ; nor is there, as in these days there assuredly would be if the theme were treated by a modern, any subtle indication of a graver side to the story, or any skilful suggestion as to the unreality of so-called pleasure as an object in life. But these differences are in some respects due to changed conditions of society, and altered points of view. We are sadder than our forefathers, and if we have no longer their hearty appetites, we are not so willingly grave that we do not occasionally envy them their high spirits.

Little room remains to speak of Luttrell's
lesser effort of " Crockford House," even if it
came within our scheme. The defect of tedi-
ousness is more conspicuous in it than in the
former work, although the motive — denun-
ciation of the prevailing vice of Play — is a
better one.   But the author seems to have
had a doubt about making it public, since,
according to Moore, he consulted Lord Sef-
ton, Mr. Greville, and others, as to the expe-
diency of a man of the town publishing such
an attack upon the high priest of the gaming table, — " a deference to society," says
Moore (rather unexpectedly, considering his
antecedents), " for which society will hardly
thank him."   With " Crockford House " are
printed some lines on Rome and the dirtiness of
that Imperial City.   A rhyming *tour de force*
on " Burnham Beeches," and a few more of
Luttrell's fugitive verses are included in the
late Mr. Locker Lampson's " Lyra Elegantia-
rum," where is also to be found the admirable
little epigram upon Miss Ellen Tree, which
has already been reproduced in these pages.[1]
Here, from the same collection, is a graver
specimen : —

[1] See *ante,* " The Author of Monsieur Tonson."

> " O Death, thy certainty is such,
>   The thought of thee so fearful,
> That, musing, I have wondered much
>   How men are ever cheerful."

There is a compactness about this which makes us wish for some other brief examples of Luttrell's serious style. It is his plans that are long, not his art. If, instead of amplifying "Lydia, dic per omnes," he had simply translated it, or "Vixi puellis," or "Vitas hinnuleo," or any of the lighter of Horace's odes, we should have had nearly perfect versions, for no man could have done them better.

We add one more of his lesser pieces, because the first lines alone are generally quoted. They are the quatrains to Moore about his " Lallah Rookh." Luttrell wrote them in the name of Rogers, whose " Human Life " Lord Lauderdale was said to have by heart : —

> " I 'm told, dear Moore, your lays are sung
>   (Can it be true, you lucky man ?)
> By moonlight in the Persian tongue,
>   Along the streets of Ispahan.

> " 'T is hard, but one reflexion cures,
>   At once, a jealous poet's smart :
> The Persians have translated yours,
>   But Lauderdale has mine by heart."

Not the least piquant thing connected with this little *jeu d'esprit*, so carefully transferred to

his Preface and Diary by the author of the
" Irish Melodies," is, that Luttrell's informant
was none other than Thomas Moore himself.[1]

[1] Henry Luttrell was a natural son of Colonel Luttrell,
afterwards second Earl of Carhampton. He died as late
as December, 1851. Those who desire further particulars
concerning this " Old Society Wit " will do well to consult a most interesting paper with that title in *Temple
Bar* for January, 1895, by a charming writer of reminiscences, the late Mrs. Andrew Crosse.

CHANGES AT CHARING CROSS.

LOOKING from that "coign of vantage," the portico of the National Gallery, upon what Peel called "the finest site in Europe," it is impossible not to think of its vicissitudes. With the exception of St. Martin's Church, which is comparatively modern, the only antiquity now left to link the present with the past is the statue of Charles I., riding unhasting, unresting, to his former Palace of Westminster, and dating from a day when Trafalgar Square was but an irregular range of houses surrounding a royal mews. Only a quarter of a century ago stood in its vicinity an older relic still. If the stones that formed the fine Jacobean frontage of Northumberland House could have spoken, they would have pleaded that they knew of a remoter time when, in place of the royal martyr proclaiming from his pedestal, in Waller's turncoat line, that

"Rebellion, though successful, is but vain,"

had risen the time-honoured cross which marked the last halting place of Queen Eleanor's body

in its progress to the Abbey. The old Cross
again had more ancient memories than Northumberland House. It could recall a falconry —
not unhaunted of a certain rhyming Clerk of
Works called Geoffrey Chaucer — which was
long anterior to the royal mews ; and it remembered how —

> " Ere yet, in scorn of Peter's pence,
>   And number'd bead, and shrift,
> Bluff Harry broke into the spence
>   And turn'd the cowls adrift," —

the hospital of St. Mary Rounceval had preceded
the great palace of the Percies.

In any retrospect of Charing Cross, Queen
Eleanor's monument forms a convenient starting point, and from Ralph Agas's well-known
survey of 1592 we get a fair idea of its environ-
ment in the reign of Elizabeth. At this date
there were, comparatively speaking, few buildings in its neighbourhood. On the river side,
indeed, houses straggled from the Strand towards
Whitehall ; but St. Martin's was actually " in
the fields," Spring Gardens was as open as " S^t
Jemes Parke," and where to-day stand Covent
Garden and Her Majesty's Theatre, laundresses
laid their clothes to dry. Along Hedge Lane,
which began at the present Union Club and fol-

lowed the line of Dorset Place and Whitcomb
Street, you might, if so minded, carry your
Corinna through green pastures to eat tarts at
Hampstead or Highgate, passing, it may be, on
the road, Master Ben Jonson from Hartshorne
Lane (now Northumberland Street), unconscious
for the moment of any other " humour " in life
than the unlimited consumption of blackberries.
By the windmill at St. Giles's you might find
him flying his kite, or (and why not, since the
child is father to the man ?) displaying prema-
turely his " Roman infirmity " of boasting to his
ragged playmates of the parish school.

But to the sober antiquary the pleasures of
imagination are forbidden ; and the Cross itself
has yet to be described. Unfortunately, there
are no really trustworthy representations of it,
and even its designer's name is uncertain.   It
was long ascribed to Pietro Cavallini, to whom
tradition also attributes the monument of Henry
III. in Westminster Abbey. What is undoubted,
however, is that it was one of several similar
crosses erected by the executors of Eleanor of
Castile ; that it was begun by one Richard de
Crundale, *cementarius*, and after his death continued by another of the family ; and that its
material came from Caen in Normandy, and
Corfe in Dorsetshire.   From Agas's map it

seems to have been octagonal in shape with tiers of niches; and it was decorated with paintings and gilt metal figures modelled by Alexander Le Imaginator It stood from 1296 until, by vote of May the 3rd, 1643, the Long Parliament, in the same iconoclastic spirit which prompted the removal of the "Golden Cross" sign as "superstitious and idolatrous," decreed its demolition. "The parliament," says a contemporary Royalist ballad, still to be found in Percy's ' Reliques,'

> " ' The parliament to vote it down
>   Conceived it very fitting,
> For fear it should fall, and kill them all,
>   In the house as they were sitting.
> They were told, God-wot, it had a plot,[1]
>   Which made them so hard-hearted,
> To give command, it should not stand,
>   But be taken down and carted.' "

Other verses bewail its disappearance as a familiar landmark : —

> " Undone, undone, the lawyers are,
>   They wander about the towne,
> Nor can find the way to Westminster,
>   Now Charing-Cros is downe."

[1] This was Waller's plot of June, 1643, to disarm the London militia, etc., for which Tompkins and Chaloner were executed.

As a matter of fact, it was not actually "taken down and carted" till the summer of 1647. Part of its stones, says Charles's biographer, William Lilly, went to pave Whitehall, and others were fashioned into knife-hafts, "which, being well polished, looked like marble." *Sic transit gloria mundi!*

Its site remained unoccupied for seven and twenty years. But here, in the interval, the regicides met their fate. Harrison, Cromwell's chaplain Peters, John Jones, Carew, and others, all suffered "at the railed space where Charing Cross stood." Pepys, between an account of the wantonness of Mrs. Palmer and the episode of "a very pretty lady" who cried out at the playhouse "to see Desdemona smothered," has the following entry of Harrison's death, which he witnessed: — "13th [October, 1660]. I went out to Charing Cross to see Major-general Harrison hanged, drawn, and quartered; which was done there, he looking as cheerful as any man could do in that condition. He was presently cut down, and his head and heart shown to the people, at which there was great shouts of joy. It is said, that he said that he was sure to come shortly at the right hand of Christ to judge them that now had judged him; and that his wife do expect his coming again. Thus it was

my chance to see the King beheaded at White
Hall, and to see the first blood shed in revenge
for the King at Charing Cross."

Grave John Evelyn has also his record:
"17 [October, 1660]. Scot, Scroope, Cook,
and Jones suffered for reward of their iniquities
at Charing Crosse, in sight of the place where
they put to death their natural Prince, and in
the presence of the King his sonn, whom they
also sought to kill. I saw not their execution;
but met their quarters mangl'd and cutt and
reeking as they were brought from the gallows
in baskets on the hurdle. Oh, the miraculous
providence of God!"

For further particulars of these dismal butch-
eries the reader is referred to the State Trials.
In the years to come, less gruesome sights succeeded. From the overseers' books of St.
Martin's, Mr. Peter Cunningham discovered
entries of sums paid in 1666 and 1667 by " Pun-
chinello, ye Italian popet-player for his Booth
at Charing Cross," and in 1668 there are similar records for the " playhouse " of a " Mounsr.
Devone." Then, in 1674, the present "noble
equestrian statue" as Walpole styles it, was
erected, not too promptly, by Charles II.

Its story is singular, — almost as singular as
that of the statue of the Merry Monarch himself,

15

which loyal Sir Robert Viner, "Alderman, Knight
and Baronet," put up in the old Stocks Market.
It appears to have been executed about 1633 by
Hubert Le Sœur, a pupil of John of Bologna,
for the Lord High Treasurer Weston, who intended it to embellish his garden at Roehampton.
By the terms of the commission it was to be of
brass, a foot larger than life, and the sculptor
"was to take advice of his Maj. (Charles I.)
riders of greate horses, as well for the shape of
the horse and action as for the graceful shape
and action of his Maj. figure on the same."
Before the beginning of the Civil War, according
to Walpole, the statue, cast but not erected, was
sold by the Parliament to John Rivett, brazier,
dwelling at the Dial near Holborn Conduit,
who was strictly enjoined to break it up. Rivett,
whose "faith was large in time," carefully
buried it instead, and ingenuously exhibited
some broken brass in earnest of its destruction.
Report further says that, making capital out of
both parties, he turned these mythic fragments
into knife and fork handles, which the Royalists
bought eagerly as relics, and the Puritans as
tokens of the downfall of a despot. In any case
there is evidence to show that the statue was
still in Rivett's possession in 1660, and it is
assumed that it passed from him or his family to

the second Charles. Strype says that he presented it to the King, which is not unlikely.
The pedestal, finely carved with cupids, palms,
armour, and so forth, is attributed to Grinling
Gibbons. Somewhere near it was the Pillory
where, every 10th of August, for several successive years, stood the infamous Titus Oates.
Edmund Curll, too (upon that principle which
makes Jack Sheppard one of the "eminent"
persons buried in St. Martin's), was once its
"distinguished" occupant, for one of his scandalous publications; and later Parsons of the
Cock Lane Ghost suffered here those amenities
so neatly described by Robert Lloyd in his
"Epistle to Churchill" : —

> "Thus, should a wooden collar deck
> Some woefull 'squire's embarrass'd neck,
> When high above the crowd he stands
> With equidistant sprawling hands,
> And without hat, politely bare,
> Pops out his head to take the air;
> The mob his kind acceptance begs,
> Of dirt, and stones, and addle-eggs."

To the right of King Charles's statue, upon a
site now traversed diagonally by Northumberland
Avenue, stood, until 1874, the last of the great
riverside mansions, Northumberland House.
Its façade extended from the statue towards

Northumberland Street, and its gardens went back to Scotland Yard, into which it had a gate. Northampton House, as it was first called, was built about 1605 for Henry Howard, Earl of Northampton, by Bernard Jansen and Gerard Christmas — Christmas, it is supposed, being responsible for the florid gateway or "frontispiece." From the Earl of Northampton it passed to the Suffolks, and changed its name to Suffolk House, a name which it retained until 1670, when becoming the property of the Percies it was again re-christened. Londoners, except upon such special occasions as Exhibition years and the like, saw little of the place beyond the façade. Its original plan was a quadrangle, uncompleted at first on the garden-side. Algernon Percy, tenth Earl of Northumberland, added a new river-front, and a stone flight of stairs, which Mr. Evelyn regarded as clumsy and "without any neat invention." In the interior its chief glory was a double state-staircase with marble steps. There was also a state-gallery of magnificent proportions, a drawing-room decorated by Angelica Kauffman, and a tapestry-chamber by Zuccarelli. The pictures which, with the wonderful stiff-tailed leaden lion so long familiar to passers by, are now transferred to Sion House at Isleworth, including Titian's famous Cornaro family (Evelyn's " Venetian Senators"), and a number of minor masterpieces. One of the show-curiosities was a Sèvres vase nine feet high, presented to the second Duke of Northumberland by Charles X. of France.

It would be easy to accumulate anecdote around this ancient dwelling-place. From this " house with stairs " by Charing Cross set out that merry marriage procession of Boyle and Howard, which Suckling has immortalised in the " Ballad on a Wedding ; " and hence, too, Mr. Horace Walpole, with a hackney-coach full of persons of condition fresh from the opera, started to interview the Cock Lane Ghost. Here again, in the fire of 1780, great part of the library of the Duke's chaplain and relative, Dr. Percy, was destroyed in his apartments, where, doubtless, he often received Reynolds and Johnson. Goldsmith, also, among others, made one very characteristic visit to the same spot, though not on this occasion as the guest of the Bishop of Dromore. Let him tell the story in his own words, *apud* Washington Irving : —

" I dressed myself in the best manner I could, and, after studying some compliments I thought necessary on such an occasion, proceeded to Northumberland House, and acquainted the servants that I had particular business with the duke. They showed me into an ante-chamber, where, after waiting some time, a gentleman, very elegantly dressed, made his appearance ; taking him for the duke, I delivered all the fine things I had composed in order to compliment him on the honour he had done me ; when, to my great astonishment, he told me I had mistaken him for his master, who would see me immediately. At that instant the duke came into the apartment, and I was so confounded on the occasion, that I wanted words barely sufficient to express the sense I entertained of the duke's politeness, and went away exceedingly chagrined at the blunder I had committed." [1]

Fronting Northumberland House, a little to the left, and at some distance from the site of the present hotel of the same name, stood, until the advent of railroads brought about its downfall as a posting-house, that older Golden Cross,[2] whose idolatrous sign scandalised the Puritan House of Commons. But the sign must have been soon restored, for it is distinguishable in Canaletto's view of 1753, though the carriage at the

[1] "Oliver Goldsmith : a Biography," 1849, p. 166.

[2] In that half-authentic, half-romantic book, the " Wine and Walnuts " of Ephraim Hardcastle (Pyne the Artist), he makes Hogarth catch a cold while sketching from the inn window the pageant of the proclamation of George III. at Charing Cross.

door probably hides the long water-trough which, sixty years since, old Londoners still remembered as giving the place something of the air of a country inn. From the Golden Cross, houses extended northward to St. Martin's Church — Duncannon Street being as yet to come. Trafalgar Square and the space now occupied by the National and National Portrait Galleries was covered, as far back as Hemings' Row, by buildings surrounding the King's or royal mews. In the days before Agas's map this had been a falconry, dating from Richard II. or earlier ; but in 1534, when Henry VIII.'s stables at Lomsbery (Bloomsbury) were fired and burned, the royal stables were transferred to the buildings at Charing Cross, which, nevertheless, retained their old name of mews (*i. e.*, a *mewing* place) which they first had " of the King's falcons there kept." Here, in the Caroline days, the famous stallion " Rowley " " champed golden grain " like the horses in the " Iliad," and gave his nickname to a king. Here, too, M. St. Antoine taught the noble art of horsemanship. In 1732, William Kent rebuilt the façade. At this date, as shown in a plan in the British Museum, dated 1690, it still consisted of the " Great Mews," the " Green Mews," and the " Back Mews." It continued to be used for stabling until 1824, when the royal stud, gilt coach, and other paraphernalia were transferred to Pimlico. In 1830, after serving as a temporary shelter to Mr. Cross's menagerie, then ousted from Exeter Change, and to the homeless Public Records of Great Britain, it was pulled down. Not many traditions haunt its past which need a mention here. Its northeastern side, if we may trust Gay's "Trivia," was a chosen resort of thieves and gamblers. "Careful Observers" (he says), "studious of the Town,"

"Pass by the *Meuse*, nor try the Thimble's Cheats;"

and it may be observed that the ill-famed rookery, known in Ben Jonson's day as the "Bermudas" and later, by convenient euphemism, as the "C'ribbee Islands," was close to St. Martin's Church, where it survived until 1829. At the Upper Mews-Gate stood a convivial house of call, celebrated in song by "bright broken Maginn;"[1] and hard by, from 1750 to 1790,

[1] "I miss already, with a tear,
    The Mews-Gate public house,
  Where many a gallant grenadier
    Did lustily carouse ;
  Alas! Macadam's droughty dust
    That honoured spot doth fill,
  Where they were wont the ale robust
    In the King's name to swill."

" Honest Tom Payne " kept the little old book-shop, " in the shape of an L," once so well known to book-lovers in the last century.[1]

Towards 1829–30 the neighbourhood of Charing Cross began to assume something of its present aspect. Already, four years earlier, the College of Physicians, leaving its home in Warwick Lane, had taken up its abode in a handsome building at the bottom of Dorset Place, close by the newly-erected Union Club. Then, about 1830, the ground was cleared for Trafalgar Square, and the C'ribbee Islands and the rookeries were " blotted from the things that be." In 1832, the present National Gallery was begun. Nelson's Column followed, in 1840-9, and then, many years after, was finally completed by the addition of Landseer's lions. Since the National Gallery first became the laughing-stock of cockneys, it has been more than once enlarged ; and even at the present moment further extensions at the back, of considerable importance to the picture-seer, are said to be in contemplation. But it is needless to dwell at any length upon the present aspect of the place. It is too modern for the uses of the antiquary ; and it may be doubted if time can

[1] See " The Two Paynes " in " Eighteenth Century Vignettes," Second Series, pp. 199–202.

ever make it venerable. In justice to its unfortunate architect, Wilkins, it must, nevertheless, be added that his work was done under most unfavourable restrictions. He was vexatiously hampered as to space, and Carlton House having been demolished, it was an express condition that he should avail himself of its fine Corinthian portico.

The only other building near Charing Cross which deserves notice is St. Martin's Church. This, however, will better be reserved for treatment on some future occasion in conjunction with St. Martin's Lane. But Spring Garden, or Gardens, part of which has already disappeared under the new Admiralty buildings, requires and deserves a final paragraph. It lies to the southwest of the Cross, and according to old definitions had a frontage extending from the end of the Haymarket to Wallingford House (the present Admiralty). In the days of James I. and Charles I. it was a pleasure-ground attached to Whitehall Palace, taking its name from one of those *jets d'eau*, the delight of seventeenth century topiarians, which suddenly sprinkled the visitor who unwittingly pressed it with his foot. It contained butts, a bathing-pond, and apparently part of the St. James's Park menagerie, since the State papers contain an order under

date of the 31st January, 1626, for payment to
Philip, Earl of Montgomery, of £72, 5s, 10d,
for "keeping the Spring-Gardens and the beasts
and fowls there." One of the favourite amusements of the place was bowling, and it was
while Charles was watching the players with
his favourite Steenie, who lived at this date in
Wallingford House, that an oft related incident
took place : — "The Duke put on his hat ; one
Wilson, a Scotchman, first kissing the Duke's
hand, snatched it off, saying, ' Off with your
hat before the King ! ' Buckingham, not apt to
restrain his feelings, kicked the Scotchman ;
but the King, interfering, said, ' Let him alone,
George ; he is either mad or a fool.' ' No,
sir,' replied the Scotchman, ' I am a sober man ;
and if your majesty would give me leave I will
tell you that of this man which many know, and
none dare speak.' "

Whether his majesty permitted the proffered
revelation, so significant of the popular estimate
of Buckingham, history has not recorded. But
the garden at this time (1628) must have been
private, for it was not until two years later that
Charles threw it open by proclamation, appoint-
ing one Simon Osbaldeston "keeper of the
King's Garden called the Spring Garden and of
His Majesty's Bowling-green there." Four

years after, it had grown so "scandalous and insufferable" a resort that he closed it again. It must, however, have been reopened, for in June, 1649, Mr. Evelyn tells us that he "treated divers Ladies of my relations, in Spring Garden;" and though Cromwell shut it up once more, it could not have been for long, as ten years after Evelyn's date it was still offering its sheltering thickets to love-makers, and its neats' tongues and bad Rhenish to wandering epicures.

With the Restoration ends its history as a pleasure-ground. To the disgust of the dwellers at Charing Cross, houses began to arise upon it; and its frequenters migrated to the newer "Spring Garden" at Vauxhall. By 1772, when Lord Berkeley was permitted to build over the so-called "Wilderness," its last traces had disappeared. But "the whirligig of time brings in his revenges," and Lord Berkeley's house in its turn has now made way for the office of the Metropolitan Board of Works, and that again for the London County Council.

As a locality Spring Gardens — the Spring Gardens of brick and mortar — has been unusually favoured with distinguished inhabitants. Here Cromwell is said to have had a house; and it was "at one Thomson's," next door to

the Bull Head Tavern, in the thoroughfare leading to the park, that his Latin secretary, John
Milton, wrote his "Joannis Philippi Angli
Responsio," etc. Colley Clbber's home, for
several years, was hard by; so also was the
lodging occupied by the author of the "Sea-
sons," when he first came to London to nego-
tiate his poem of "Winter." In Buckingham
Court lived and died sprightly Mrs. Centlivre,
whose husband (her third) was yeoman of the
mouth to Anne and George I. Locket's ordinary — the "Lackets" of my Lord Foppington
and the "stap-my-vitals" fine gentlemen of
Vanbrugh's day — stood on the site of Drummond's Bank. Two doors from it, towards
Buckingham Court, was the famous "Rummer"
Tavern kept by Matthew Prior's uncle, Samuel
Pryor, also or formerly landlord of that Rhenish
Wine House in Cannon Row where Dorset
first discovered the clever young student of
Horace whom he helped to turn into a statesman and ambassador.[1] The "Rummer" appears in Hogarth's "Night" ("Four Times
of the Day," 1738), which gives a view of
the statue with the houses behind. Hogarth's
"Rummer," however, is on the left, whereas

[1] See Matthew Prior, in "Eighteenth Century Vignettes," Third Series, p. 229.

the tavern (according to Cunningham) was, after
1710, removed to the right or Northumberland House side. Probably in the plate, as
in the one of Covent Garden in the same
series, the view was reversed in the process of
engraving.

Hogarth's name recalls another memory. It
was in an auctioneer's room in Spring Gardens
(now part of the offices of the London County
Council) that the Society of Artists of Great
Britain held their famous second exhibition of
1761, for the catalogue of which Wale and
Hogarth made designs. Hogarth was also a
prominent exhibitor, sending, among other oil
paintings, " The Lady's Last Stake " (Mr.
Huth's), the " Election Entertainment " (Soane
Museum), and the ill-fated " Sigismunda," the
last of which is now gaining, in the National
Gallery, some of the reputation which was denied to it in the painter's lifetime.

JOHN GAY.

NO very material addition, in the way of
supplementary information, can now be
made to the frequently reprinted "Life of Gay"
in Johnson's "Poets," or to the genial and
kindly sketch in Thackeray's "English Hu-
mourists."[1] Gay was born at Barnstaple in
1685, and baptised at the Old Church of that
town on the 16th September. He came of
an ancient but impoverished family, being the
younger son of William Gay, who lived at the
"Red Cross," a house in Joy Street, which,
judging from the church-rate paid by its occupants, must have been one of the best of the

---

[1] This is still practically true. But in an excellent edition of Gay's "Poetical Works," prepared for the "Muses'
Library," in 1893, the late John Underhill, a Barnstaple
man and a Gay enthusiast, besides making certain biographical rectifications, contrived to discover a few new
facts. "Some details that have not been known to former
writers" were also supplied by Mr. George A. Aitken in
an interesting paper prompted by Mr. Underhill's volumes,
and contributed to the *Westminster Review* for January,
1894.

Barnstaple dwellings. He lost his father in
1695, his mother — whose maiden name was
Hanmer — having died in the previous year.
He thus became an orphan at the early age of
ten, and in all probability, fell into the care of
a Barnstaple uncle, Thomas Gay. He was educated at the free grammar school of his native
place, where his master was one Rayner, afterwards succeeded by the "Robert Luck, A. M.,"
whose "Miscellany of New Poems" was published in 1736 (four years after Gay's death) by
Edward Cave. One of the pieces was a Latin
version of Prior's "Female Phaeton," and its
author, in an English introduction to his work,
inscribed to Gay's patron, Charles Douglas,
Duke of Queensberry and Dover, sought
to associate himself with his pupil's metrical
proficiency.

> " O *Queensberry!* cou'd happy *Gay*
>   This Off'ring to thee bring,
> 'T is his, my Lord (he 'd smiling say)
>   Who taught your *Gay* to sing."

It is, moreover, asserted that Gay's dramatic
turn was stimulated by the plays which the
pupils at Barnstaple were in the habit of performing under this rhyming pedagogue. Of his
schooldays, however, nothing is known with

precision ; but it is clear from his subsequent career that he somewhere obtained more than a bowing acquaintance with the classics. There is still preserved, in the " Forster Library" at South Kensington, a large paper copy of Maittaire's " Horace " (Tonson and Watts, 1715), which contains his autograph, and is copiously annotated in his beautiful handwriting. This of itself should be sufficient to refute the aspersions sometimes cast upon his scholarship ; for it affords unanswerable evidence that, even at thirty, and perhaps at a much later period, he remained a diligent student of the charming lyrist and satirist, who, above all others, commends himself to the attention of idle men. In his boyhood, however, it must be assumed that Gay's indolence was more strongly developed than his application, for his friends could find no better opening for him than that of apprentice to a London silk mercer. With this employment he was speedily dissatisfied. Dr. Hill Burton, in his " History of the Reign of Queen Anne," implies that he ran away ; but there is nothing to show that he took any step of so energetic a character. His nephew, the Rev. Joseph Baller, in the little publication entitled " Gay's Chair," explains that, " not being able to bear the confinement of a shop," his uncle became depressed

in spirits and health, and therefore returned to
his native town, taking up his residence, not, as
before, with Thomas Gay, but with his mother's
brother, the Rev. John Hanmer, the Barnstaple
Nonconformist minister.

That Gay should have found the littering of
polished counters with taffeties and watered
tabbies an uncongenial occupation is not surprising, especially if be added thereto that thank-
less service of those feminine " silk-worms "
who (as Swift says in the "City Shower ") " Pre-
tend to cheapen Goods, but nothing buy."   Yet
it is to be feared that the lack of energy which
was his leading characteristic would have equally
disposed him against any continuous or laborious
calling.   When his health was restored, he went
back to town, living for some time (according
to Mr. Baller [1]) " as a private gentleman " — a
statement which is scarcely reconcilable with the
modest opening in life his family had selected
for him.   Already he is supposed to have made
some definite essays in literature, and the swarm-
ing taverns and coffee-houses of the metropolis
afforded easy opportunities of access to notabilities of all sorts.   He had besides some friends
already established in London.   Fortescue,
Pope's correspondent, and later Master of the

[1] " Gay's Chair," 1820, p. 17.

Rolls, had been his schoolmate at Luck's ; while another of Luck's *alumni* was Aaron Hill, the playwright. According to a time-honoured tradition, Gay acted for some time as Hill's secretary. But Hill himself was only embarking in letters when, in May, 1708, Gay published, as an eight-leaf *folio*, his first poem of " Wine," the purport of which may be gathered from the Horatian —

> " Nulla placere diu, nec vivere carmina possunt,
> Quæ scribuntur aquæ potoribus," —

of its motto, a moot theory which seems to have " exercised " the author throughout his life-time, since he is still discussing it in his last letters. " I continue to drink nothing but water," he tells Swift two years before his death, " so that you can't require any poetry from me." The publisher of " Wine " was William Keble, at the Black-Spread-Eagle in Westminster Hall, and it was also pirated by Henry Hills of the " brown sheets and scurvy letter," referred to in Gay's subsequent " Epistle to Bernard Lintott." " Wine " professes to " draw Miltonic air," but the atmosphere inhaled is more suggestive of the " Splendid Shilling " of John Philips. Gay did not reprint the poem in his subscription edition of 1720, perhaps because of its blank

verse ; but the concluding lines, which describe
the breaking up of a " midnight Modern Conversation " at the Devil Tavern by Temple Bar,
already disclose the minute touch of "Trivia": —

> " now all abroad
> Is hush'd and silent, nor the rumbling noise
> Of coach or cart, or smoky link-boys' call
> Is heard — but universal Silence reigns :
> When we in merry plight, airy and gay,
> Surpris'd to find the hours so swiftly fly
> With hasty knock, or twang of pendent cord,
> Alarm the drowsy youth from slumb'ring nod ;
> Startled he flies, and stumbles o'er the stairs
> Erroneous, and with busy knuckles plies
> His yet clung eyelids, and with stagg'ring reel
> Enters confused, and mutt'ring asks our wills ;
> When we with liberal hand the score discharge,
> And homeward each his course with steady step
> Unerring steers, of cares and coin bereft."

As it is expressly stated that the Bordeaux —
the particular vintage specified — was paid for,
it is clear that, at this time, Gay must have succeeded in finding either a purse or a paymaster.
It is equally clear from his next ascertained production that he had acquired more than a slight
familiarity with the world of letters. A year
after the publication of " Wine " Steele established
the *Tatler ;* and in May, 1711, when the *Spectator* was two months old, Gay favoured the

world with his impressions of "the·Histories
and Characters of all our *Periodical Papers,*
whether Monthly, Weekly or Diurnal," in a
threepenny pamphlet, entitled "The Present
State of Wit, in a Letter to a Friend in the
Country." This, which Mr. Arber has reprinted
in volume vi. of his "English Garner," is of
more than fugitive interest. It disclaims politics upon the ground that it does not care "one
farthing either for *Whig* or *Tory*," but it refers
to the *Examiner* as "a Paper which all Men,
who speak without Prejudice, allow to be well
Writ." At this time Swift evidently knew
nothing of his critic, for he tells Stella that
"the author seems to be a Whig" . . . . "Above
all things, he praises the *Tatlers* and *Spectators;*
and I believe Steele and Addison were privy to
the printing of it. Thus is one treated by these
impudent dogs" [with whom his relations were
strained]. Apart from his disclaimer of politics,
nevertheless, Gay, if he was anything, was a Tory,
and Swift was wrong. But Gay was clearly well
informed about the secret history of Steele's ven-
tures, and he gives an excellent account of the
"Esquire's [*i. e.* Bickerstaff's] Lucubrations."
"He has indeed rescued it [Learning] out of
the hands of Pedants, and Fools, and discover'd
the true method of making it amiable and lovely

to all mankind.[1] In the dress he gives it, 't is a
most welcome guest at Tea-tables and Assemblies,
and it is relish'd and caressed by the Merchants on
the Change ; accordingly, there is not a Lady at
Court, nor a Banker in *Lumbard-Street,* who is
not verily perswaded, that *Captain Steele* is the
greatest Scholar, and best Casuist, of any Man
in England." From other passages it is also
plain that the writer (like Swift) knew who was
Steele's unnamed colleague, for he speaks of
Addison's assistance as "no longer a Secret,"
and compares the conjunction of the two
friends to that of Somers and Halifax "in a late
Reign." It may consequently be concluded that
he had at least made Steele's acquaintance, and
that the set of the *Tatlers* in four volumes on
royal paper, which Tonson at this time trans-
mitted to Gay "by Mr. Steel's Orders," is at
once a confirmation of the fact and a tacit recognition of the welcome compliments contained
in "J. G.'s" "Present State of Wit."

But "Mr. Isaac Bickerstaff" was not the
only notability to whom Gay had become known.
In July, 1711, we find Pope sending Henry
Cromwell his "service to all my few friends,

[1] These words seem like an echo of the passage from
Blackmore's Preface to "Prince Arthur," which Steele
quotes admiringly in *Spectator* No. 6.

and to Mr. Gay in particular," and in the same
year Gay wrote the already mentioned "Epistle to Lintott," which contained among other
things, reference to the harmonious "Muse" of
the young author of the "Pastorals" and the
recently-issued "Essay on Criticism."

> "His various numbers charm our ravish'd ears,
> His steady judgment far out-shoots his years,
> And early in the youth the god appears,"

sang this panegyrist in one of those triplets that
Swift abominated. But Pope, who saw the lines
in manuscript, accepted the flattering unction
without reserve, and the epistle accordingly, in
the following May (1712), made its appearance
in Lintott's famous "Rape of the Lock" Miscellany, to which Gay also contributed the Story of
Arachne from Ovid. He was still, it seems, unknown to the general public, for the contemporary announcement of the book, while giving
"bold advertisement" to such lesser lights as
Fenton, Broome, and Henry Cromwell, refrains
from including his name among the eminent hands
who contributed to the collection. Nor is it
probable that his reputation had been greatly
served by the "tragi-comical farce" he had
issued a week or two before under the title
of "The Mohocks,"—*i. e.*, the midnight revel-
lers whose real (or imaginary) misdeeds were

at that time engaging public attention. It was
inscribed to Dennis the critic, who was informed (in his own vocabulary) that its subject
was "*Horrid* and *Tremendous*," that it was
conceived "according to the exactest Rules of
Dramatick Poetry," and that it was based upon
his own "Appius and Virginia." Notwithstanding an intentionally ambiguous title-page,[1]
it was never acted, and its interest, like others
of Gay's efforts, is purely "temporary."

Before 1712 had ended, Pope was able to
congratulate his new ally upon what promised
to be a material stroke of good fortune. He
was appointed "Secretary or Domestic Stew-
ard" to the Duchess of Monmouth, — that
"virtuous and excellent lady," as Evelyn calls
her, whose husband had been beheaded in the
year of Gay's birth. The exact amount of de-
pendence implied by this office is obscure, and
it is differently estimated by different narrators.
It is more material to note that Gay must
already have been engaged upon his next poeti-

[1] The following is the advertisement in the *Spectator*
for 10th April, 1712: —

"This Day is Published, *The Mohocks. A Tragi-
Comical Farce. As it was Acted near the Watch-house in
Covent-Garden. By her Majesty's Servants.* Printed for
Bernard Lintott; at the Cross-Keys between the two
Temple-Gates in Fleet-Street."

cal effort, perhaps his first serious one, the Georgic called "Rural Sports," which he inscribed to Pope. It was published by Tonson on the 13th January, 1713. To the reader of the post-Wordsworthian age, its merit is not remarkable, and Johnson anticipated the *toujours bien, jamais mieux* of Madame Guizot, when he described it as "never contemptible, nor ever excellent." Mr. Underhill, indeed, goes so far as to deny to it any experimental knowledge of country life ; and, as a matter of fact, Gay himself admits that he had long been a town-dweller. Still his childhood must have been passed among rural scenes, and it is by no means certain that if he had written his verses at Barnstaple he would — writing as he did under Anna Augusta — have written them in a different way. We suspect that the germ of the objection, as often, is to be traced, not so much to the poem itself, as to certain preconceived shortcomings in its author. Johnson's disbelief in Goldsmith's ability to distinguish between a cow and a horse no doubt coloured his appreciation of the "Animated Nature;" and Swift (whom Mr. Underhill quotes) doubted if Gay could tell an oak from a crab tree. "You are sensible," Swift went on, "that I know the full extent of your country skill is in fishing for roaches, or gudgeons at the highest." With such a testimony before us, criticism of "Rural Sports" easily becomes a foregone conclusion. Nevertheless, it deserves more consideration than it has received.

Apart from the production at Drury Lane, in May, 1713, of a deplorable play, "The Wife of Bath," and the contribution to Steele's *Guardian* of two brightly written papers on "Flattery" and "Dress" (Nos. 11 and 149), Gay's next ascertained work was "The Fan." It is one of the contradictions of criticism that this poor and ineffectual poem should have been received with greater favour than the (relatively) far superior "Rural Sports." Gay's mythology is never very happy (Mr. Elwin roundly styles it "stupid"), and he always writes best with his eye on the object. Pope, however, interested himself in "The Fan," and even touched on that "little modish machine" in parts, — circumstances which give it a slender interest. A week or two later appeared Steele's "Poetical Miscellany," in which Gay is represented by "A Contemplation upon Death," and by a pair of elegies ("Panthea" and "Araminta"). But his first individual performance, "The Shepherd's Week," belongs to the early part of 1714. This again is closely connected with his friend-

ship with Pope. Pope, smarting under the
praise which Tickell had given in the *Guardian*
to the Pastorals of Ambrose Philips, and not
content with perfidiously reviewing Philips himself in the same periodical, now contrived to
induce the author of " Rural Sports " to aid the
cause by burlesquing his rival in a sequence of
sham eclogues, in which he was to exhibit the
Golden Age with the gilt off, " after the true
ancient guise of Theocritus." " Thou wilt not
find my Shepherdesses " — says the Author's
" Proeme " — " idly piping on oaten Reeds, but
milking the Kine, tying up the Sheaves, or if
the Hogs are astray driving them to their Styes.
My Shepherd gathereth none other Nosegays
but what are the growth of our own Fields ; he
sleepeth not under Myrtle shades, but under a
Hedge, nor doth he vigilantly defend his Flocks
from Wolves " [this was a palpable hit at Philips!]
" because there are none." Like Fielding's
" Joseph Andrews," the execution of " The
Shepherd's Week " was far superior to its avowed
object of mere ridicule. In spite of their bar-
barous " Bumkinets " and " Grubbinols," Gay's
little idylls abound with interesting folk-lore and
(wherever acquired) with closely studied rural
pictures. We see the country girl burning hazel
nuts to find her sweetheart, or presenting the

faithless Colin with a knife with a "posy" on it, or playing at "Hot Cockles," or listening to "Gillian of Croydon," and "Patient Grissel." Nor are there wanting sly strokes of kindly satire, as when the shepherds are represented fencing the grave of Blouzelinda against the prospective inroads of the parson's horse and cow, which have the right of grazing in the churchyard; or when that dignitary, in consideration of the liberal sermon-fee, "Spoke the Hour-glass in her praise — quite out."

From a biographical point of view, however, the most interesting part of "The Shepherd's Week" is its dedicatory prologue to Boling-broke, a circumstance which, according to Swift, constituted that "original sin" against the Court which afterwards interfered so much with Gay's prospects of preferment. But its allusions also show that the former mercer's apprentice had already made the acquaintance of Arbuthnot, and probably of some gentler critics, whose favour was of greater importance. "No more," says the poet,

> "No more I'll sing *Buxoma* brown,
>   Like Goldfinch in her *Sunday* Gown;
>   Nor *Clumsilis*, nor *Marian* bright,
>   Nor Damsel that *Hobnelia* hight.
>   But *Lansdown* fresh as Flow'r of *May*,

And *Berkly* Lady blithe and gay,
And *Anglesey* whose Speech exceeds
The voice of Pipe, or oaten Reeds ;
And blooming *Hide*, with Eyes so rare,
And *Montague* beyond compare."

" Blooming Hide, with eyes so rare," was
Lady Jane Hyde, daughter of the Earl of Clarendon, and elder sister of the Catherine who was
subsequently to be Gay's firmest friend.

The Scriblerus Club, to which his friend
Pope had introduced him, and for which he is
said to have acted as Secretary, had also done
him the greater service of securing him an even
firmer ally in Swift, and it was doubtless to his
connection with this famous association, of which
Lord Oxford was an occasional member, that
he was indebted for his next stroke of good fortune. By June, 1714, he had resigned, or been
dismissed from, his position in the household of
the Duchess of Monmouth. But in that month,
with the aid of his new friends, he was appointed
Secretary to Lord Clarendon, then Envoy Extraordinary to the Court of Hanover, and there
exists a brief rhymed appeal or " Epigrammati-
cal Petition " from the impecunious poet to Lord
Oxford (in his capacity as Lord Treasurer)
for funds to enable him to enter upon his
duties.

> I 'm no more to converse with the swains,
>   But go where fine people resort ;
> One can live without money on plains,
>   But never without it at court.
>
> If, when with the swains I did gambol,
>   I array'd me in silver and blue ;
> When abroad, and in courts, I shall ramble,
>   Pray, my lord, how much money will do ? [1]

He got, not without difficulty, and probably through the instrumentality of Arbuthnot (who handed in his memorial) a grant of £100 for his outfit ; and he also got, from Swift in Ireland, a letter of fatherly advice exhorting him to learn to be a manager, to mind his Latin, to look up Aristotle upon Politics, and Grotius " De Jure Belli et Pacis."   For a brief space we must imagine him strutting in his new clothes through the clipped avenues of Herrenhausen, yawning over the routine life of the petty German Court, and perfecting himself in the diplomatic arts of " bowing profoundly, speaking deliberately, and wearing both sides of his long periwig before." Then the death of Queen Anne put an end to all these halcyon days.   What was worse, the " Shepherd's Week," as already stated, had been dedicated to Bolingbroke, and Bolingbroke — ill-luck would have it — was not in favour with

[1] Letter from Gay to Swift, June 8, 1714.

Her Most Gracious Majesty's successor. In
this juncture, as a course which " could do no
harm, " Pope, who seems always to have treated
Gay with unfailing affection, counselled his de-
jected friend " to write something on the King,
or Prince, or Princess," and Arbuthnot said ditto
to Pope. Gay, cheering up, accordingly, set
about an " Epistle to a Lady [probably Mrs.
Howard, afterwards Lady Suffolk] : Occasion'd
by the arrival of Her Royal Highness [*i. e.* the
Princess of Wales, whom he had seen at Han-
over]." In this he takes opportunity to touch
plaintively upon the forlorn hopes of needy
suitors : —

> " Pensive each night, from room to room I walk'd,
> To one I bow'd, and with another talk'd ;
> Enquir'd what news, or such a Lady's name,
> And did the next day, and the next, the same.
> Places, I found, were daily giv'n away
> And yet no friendly Gazette mentioned *Gay*."

The only appreciable result of this ingenuous
appeal was that Their Royal Highnesses came to
Drury Lane in February, 1715, to witness Gay's
next dramatic effort, the tragic-comi-pastoral farce
of the "What d' ye Call it," a piece after the fashion of Buckingham's "Rehearsal," inasmuch as
it parodies the popular tragedies of the day, and
even roused the ire of Steele by taking liberties

with Addison's "Cato." Without the "Key" which was speedily prepared by Theobald and Griffin the actor, its allusions must at first have fallen rather flat upon an uninstructed audience, especially as its action was grave and its images comic. Gay's matter-of-fact friend, Cromwell, who saw the gestures but, being deaf, could not hear the words, consequently found it hopelessly unintelligible. But it brought its author a hundred pounds, and it contains one of his most musical songs "'T was when the seas were roaring." A few months after its publication in book form, Lord Burlington sent the poet into Devonshire, an expedition which he commemorated in a pleasant tributary epistle published in 1715 with the title of "A Journey to Exeter." He had two travelling companions, no needless precaution when Bagshot Heath swarmed with "broken gamesters" who had taken to the road, and he describes delightfully his *impressions de voyage*, — the fat and garrulous landlord at Hartley-Row, the red trout and "rich metheglin" at Steele's borough of Stockbridge, the "cloak'd shepherd" on Salisbury Plain, the lobsters and "unadulterate wine" at Morecombe-lake,[1] and last of all, the female barber at Axminster : —

[1] A writer in the *Athenæum* for Dec. 1, 1894, points out that this is a mistake. Gay must have stripped

The weighty golden chain adorns her neck,
And three gold rings her skilful hand bedeck:
Smooth o'er our chin her easy fingers move,
Soft as when *Venus* stroak'd the beard of *Jove*."

Incidentally, we learn that Gay could draw, for he sketches the " eyeless " faces of his fellow travellers asleep in two chairs at Dorchester. Also that, at thirty, he was already stout : —

You knew *fat* Bards might tire,
And, mounted, sent me forth your trusty Squire.

It must have been about this time that Gay composed another poem, somewhat akin to the Exeter epistle, inasmuch as both were probably influenced by the verses on " Morning " and " A City Shower," which Swift had contributed to Steele's *Tatler*. Indeed, in the Preface to "Trivia ; or, the Art of Walking the Streets of London," which appeared at the end of January, 1716, Gay specially refers to hints given to him by Dr. Swift. The theme is an unexpected one for an author whose tastes were certainly not pedestrian (" any lady with a coach and six horses would carry him to Japan," said the Dean later) ; but it has still its attraction to

"the lobster of his scarlet mail " a little farther on, at Charmouth. But these references to food at least confirm Congreve's *dictum* of Gay, — *"Edit, ergo est."*

17

the antiquary and the student of the early eighteenth century. Every one who desires to real-
ise the London of the first George, with its
signs and its street cries (that *ramage de la ville*,
which Will. Honeycomb preferred to larks and
nightingales), its link boys and its chairmen, its
sweeps, small-coal men, milk-maids, Mohocks,
and the rest, must give his days and nights to
the study of "Trivia." He will obtain valuable
expert advice as to the ceremony of taking or
giving the wall; learn to distinguish and divide
between a Witney Roquelaure and a Kersey
Wrap-Rascal; and, it may be, discover to his
surprise that there were umbrellas before Jonas
Hanway:—

> Good housewives all the winter's rage despise,
> Defended by the riding-hood's disguise:
> Or underneath th' umbrella's oily shed,
> Safe thro' the wet on clinking pattens tread.

It is consoling to think that Gay made some
£40 by this eighteen-penny poem, and £100
more by the subscriptions which Pope and others, always jealously watching over his interests,
obtained to a large paper edition. But it is
impossible to commend his next production, of
which, indeed, it is suspected that he did no
more than bear the blame. Although he signed

the advertisement of the comedy entitled "Three Hours before Marriage," it is pretty sure that he had Pope and Arbuthnot for active coadjutors. But whether Pope libelled Dennis as "Sir Tremendous," or Arbuthnot Woodward, or Gay himself the Duchess of Monmouth as the very incidental "Countess of Hippokekoana" (Ipecacuanha?) — are questions scarcely worthy of discussion now. It is sufficient that the piece was both gross and silly. It failed ignominiously on the boards in January, 1717, and is not likely to be consulted in type except by fanatics of the fugitive like George Steevens, who reprinted it in the "Additions to Pope" of 1776.

During all this period Gay seems to have been vaguely expecting Court favour, and to have suffered most of the discouragements of hope deferred. Yet, if the Court neglected his pretensions — and it nowhere appears that they were very well grounded — he always found friends whose kindness took a practical form. Lord Burlington had sent him to Exeter; in 1717 Pulteney carried him to Aix as his Secretary, a trip which furnished the occasion of a second Epistle. Then, in 1718, he went with Lord Harcourt to Oxfordshire, where befell that pretty tragedy of the two haymakers struck

dead by lightning, which sentimental **Mr. Pope**
made the subject of a fine and famous letter to
Lady Mary Wortley Montagu, who, unluckily
for sentiment, received it in anything but a sentimental spirit. Both the journeys to Aix and
Exeter were reprinted in the grand quarto edition of Gay's poems which Tonson and Lintott
published in 1720, with a frontispiece by the
eminent William Kent, and with a list of sub-
scribers rivalling in number and exceeding in
interest that prefixed to the Prior of 1718.
Those munificent patrons of literature, the Earl
of Burlington and the Duke of Chandos, took
fifty copies each! In the second volume were
included a number of epistles and miscellaneous
pieces, many of which were published for the
first time, as well as a new pastoral tragedy
called "Dione." One of the ballads, "Sweet
William's Farewell to Black Ey'd Susan," was
long popular, and is still justly ranked among
the best efforts of the writer's muse. Of the
thousand pounds which Gay cleared over this
venture his friends hoped he would make provi-
dent use, suggesting purchase of an annuity,
investment in the funds, and so forth. But
Craggs had given him some South Sea Stock,
and to this he added his new windfall, becoming in short space master of £20,000. Again

his well-wishers clustered about him with prudent counsels. At least, said Fenton, secure as much as will make you certain " of a clean shirt, and a shoulder of mutton every day." But the " most refractory, honest, good-natur'd man," as Swift calls him, was not to be so advised. He was seized with the South Sea madness, and promptly lost both principal and profits.

Among the other names on the subscription list of the volumes of 1720 are two which have a special attraction in Gay's life, for they are those of his kindest friends, the Duke and Duchess of Queensberry. The lady was the charming and wayward Catharine Hyde, — the " Kitty " whose first appearance at Drury Lane playhouse as a triumphant beauty of eighteen Prior had celebrated in some of his brightest and airiest verses, and whose picture, as a milkmaid of quality, painted by Charles Jervas at a later date, is to be seen at the National Portrait Gallery. As already stated, Gay had written of her sister Jane (by this time Countess of Essex) as far back as 1714; and it may be that her own acquaintance with him dated from the same period. In any case, after her marriage to the Duke of Queensberry in 1720, she appears to have taken Gay under her protection. " He [Gay] is always with the Duchess of

Queensberry " — writes Mrs. Bradshaw to Mrs.
Howard in 1721 ; and five years afterwards the
poet himself tells Swift that he has been with
his patrons in Oxfordshire and at Petersham
and " wheresoever they would carry me." In
the interval he is helping Congreve to nurse his
gout " at the *Bath,*" or living almost altogether
with Lord Burlington at Chiswick or Piccadilly
or Tunbridge Wells, or acting as secretary to
Pope at Twickenham (" which you know is no
idle charge "), or borrowing sheets from Jervas
to entertain Swift in those lodgings which had
been granted to him by the Earl of Lincoln,
and were taken from him by Sir Robert Walpole. It says much for the charm of his character that he knew how to acquire and how to
retain friends so constant and so diverse. But
though his life sounds pleasant in the summary,
it must have involved humiliations which would
have been intolerable to a more independent
man. According to Arbuthnot, the Burling-
tons sometimes left their *protégé* in want of the
necessaries of life, and neither they nor his
other great friends were very active to procure
him preferment. "They wonder," says Gay
piteously to Swift in 1722, " at each other for
not providing for me ; and I wonder at them
all." From a letter which he wrote to Pope

two years later, it is nevertheless plain that
somebody had given him a lottery commissionership worth £150 per annum, so that, for a man
whose claims were not urgent, he can hardly
be said to have been culpably neglected.

Previously to his appointment as a lottery
commissioner he had been seriously ill. The
loss of his South Sea Stock preyed upon his
spirits; and his despondency "being attended
with the cholic " — in the unvarnished language
of the " Biographia Britannica " — " brought
his life in danger." Upon his recovery, and
pending the postponed advancement he was
always " lacking " ("the Court keeps him at
hard meat," wrote Swift in 1725), he produced
another play, " The Captives," which ran for
a week in January, 1724, the third or author's
night being expressly commanded by his old
patrons, the Prince and Princess of Wales.
Then at the request of the Princess, he set to
work upon the " Fables " by which his reputation as a writer mainly survives. " Gay is
writing Tales for Prince William," Pope tells
Swift. After many delays, partly in production
by the press, partly owing to Gay's own dilatory
habits, the first series appeared in 1727,[1] and

---

[1] A second series of sixteen fables was published in
1738, after his death, from the manuscripts in the hands of
the Duke of Queensberry.

was well received, although, if Swift is to be
believed, their " nipping turns " upon courtiers
were not best welcomed where the poet most
needed encouragement. To this it is perhaps
to be attributed that when George II. came at
last to the throne nothing better was found for
Gay than the post of gentleman-usher to the
little Princess Louisa — a child under three.
By this time he was more than forty, and he
had self-respect enough to think himself too
old. He therefore politely declined the nomina-
tion. With this, however, his long deferred
expectations finally vanished. " I have no
prospect," he wrote with tardy sagacity to
Swift, " but in depending wholly upon myself,
and my own conduct. As I am used to dis-
appointments, I can bear them ; but as I can
have no more hopes, I can no more be disap-
pointed, so that I am in a blessed condition."

Strangely enough, when he penned this in
October, 1727, he had already completed what
was to be his greatest dramatic success, the
famous " Beggar's Opera," which, produced at
Lincoln's Inn Fields on the 29th of January,
1728, for a season overthrew Italian song, —
" that Dagon of the Nobility and Gentry, who
had so long seduced them to idolatry," as the

" Companion to the Playhouse " puts it, — and
made its Author's name a household word.
How it first occurred to Swift what " an
odd pretty sort of thing a Newgate Pastoral
might make ; " how friends hesitated, and Cibber
rejected, and the public rapturously applauded ;
how it was sung at street corners, and painted
on screens ; how it procured its " Polly "
(Lavinia Fenton) a coronet, and made Rich
(the manager) gay, and Gay (the author) rich —
all these things are the commonplaces of literature. At Mr. John Murray's in Albemarle
Street may still be seen one of the three pictures which William Hogarth painted of that all
conquering company, and which, years afterwards, was engraved by another William —
William Blake. The Coryphæus of the high-
way (Walker) appears in the centre, while
" Lucy " (Mrs. Egleton) pleads for him to the
left, and " Polly " (Miss Fenton) to the right.
Scandal, in the person of John, Lord Hervey,
adds that the opera owed a part of its popularity
to something in the dilemma of Macheath " between his twa Deborahs " which irresistibly
suggested the equally equivocal position of
Walpole between his wife and his mistress.
This is probably exaggerated, as is also the aid
which Gay is reported to have received from

Pope and others,[1] but it accounts in a measure
for the fate which befell Gay's next enterprise.

That some attempt to perpetuate so signal
a success as the " Beggar's Opera " should not
be made was scarcely in the nature of things ;
and Gay set speedily about the preparation of
a sequel, to which he gave the name of the
popular heroine of the earlier piece.   But
" Polly " was saved from the common fate of
continuations by the drastic action of the Lord
Chamberlain, taken, it is surmised, upon the
instruction of Walpole.   When it was almost
ready for rehearsal, the representation was pro-
hibited.   The result of this not very far-sighted
step on the part of the authorities was of course
to invest its publication as a book with an unprecedented   and   wholly   fictitious   interest.
Friends on all sides, and especially those opposed to the Court, strained every nerve to
promote the sale.   The Duchess of Marlborough
(Congreve's Henrietta) gave £100 for a copy ;
and the Duchess of Queensberry, who had the
temerity to solicit subscriptions within the very
precincts of St. James's, was forbidden to return

---

[1] Pope — " *semper ardentes acuens sagittas* " — was supposed to have pointed some of the songs.   But he told
Spence that neither he nor Swift gave any material aid in
the work (" Anecdotes," 1858, pp. 110, 120).

to them. Thereupon the Duke, nothing loth,
threw up his appointments, as Vice Admiral of
Scotland and Lord of the Bedchamber, and
followed his lady, who delivered a Parthian
shaft in the shape of a very indiscreet and
saucy letter to His Majesty King George. In
all this, it is plain that Gay's misfortune was
simply made the instrument of political antag-
onisms : but, for the moment, his name was
on every lip. "The inoffensive *John Gay*" —
writes Arbuthnot to Swift under date of March
19, 1729 — "is now become one of the obstruc-
tions to the peace of *Europe*, the terror of the
ministers, the chief author of the *Craftsman*,
and all the seditious pamphlets, which have
been published against the Government. He
has got several turned out of their places ; the
greatest ornament of the court banished from
it for his sake ;[1] another great lady [Mrs.
Howard] in danger of being *Chassé* [*sic*] like-
wise ; about seven or eight duchesses pressing
forward, like the antient *circumcelliones* in the
church, who shall suffer martyrdom on his account first. He is the darling of the city . . .
I can assure you, this is the very identical

[1] " The gay Amanda let us now behold,
In thy Defence, a lovely *banish'd* Scold."
"The Female Faction," 1729.

John Gay, whom you formerly knew, and lodged with in *Whitehall* two years ago." The gross result was that Gay gained about £1200 by the publication of " Polly " as a six shilling quarto, of which Bowyer, the printer, in one year struck off 10,500 copies ; by the representation of the " Beggar's Opera " he had made, according to his own account, " between £700 and £800 " to Rich's £4000.

During a great part of 1728 Gay resided at Bath with the Duchess of Marlborough. After the prohibition of " Polly," he appears, as usual, to have fallen ill, and to have been tenderly nursed by Arbuthnot. " I may say, without vanity, his life, under God, is due to the unwearied endeavors and care of your humble servant," writes this devoted friend to Swift. Then the Queensberrys took formal charge of John Gay and henceforth he lived either at their town house in Burlington Gardens (where now stands the Western Branch of the Bank of England), or at their pleasant country seat of Amesbury in Wiltshire. The Duke kept the poet's money ; the Duchess watched over the poet and his wardrobe.[1] " I was a long time,"

[1] In these characteristics Gay seems to have imitated La Fontaine, who, after living twenty years with Mme. de la Sablière, passed at her death to the care of M.

he says in 1730, " before I could prevail with her
to let me allow myself a pair of shoes with two
heels ; for I had lost one, and the shoes were
so decayed, that they wore not worth mending."
Elsewhere it is — " I am ordered by the duchess
to grow rich in the manner of Sir *John Cutler*.[1]
I have nothing, at this present writing, but my
frock that was made at *Salisbury*, and a bob-
perriwig." In an earlier paper in these volumes[2]
we have given some account of the joint letters
which at this period Gay and his kind protect-
ress wrote to Swift in Ireland, and they present
a most engaging picture of the alliance between
the author of " The Hare and Many Friends "
and the *grande dame de par le monde* of the
last century. Most of them were written from
Amesbury (where nothing but a summer house
now remains of the buildings as they were in
Gay's time), and their main theme is the invita-

and Mme. de Hervart. " D'autres prenaient soin de lui "
— says M. Taine. " Il se donnait à ses amis, sentant
bien qu'il ne pouvait pourvoir à lui-même. Mme.
d'Hervart, jeune et charmante, veilla à tout, jusqu'à ses
vêtements," etc. . . . " Ses autres amis faisaient de
même," Are all fabulists congenitally feckless?

[1] Cf. Pope's Epistle "Of the Use of Riches," ll.
315–34.

[2] See " Prior's Kitty," in " Eighteenth Century Vignettes," First Series.

tion of Swift to England. The final epistle of
the series is dated November 16, 1732; and in
this Gay reports that he has " come to London
before the family to follow his own inventions,"
which included the production of his recently
written Opera of " Achilles." A few days later,
he was attacked by a constitutional malady to
which he had long been subject, and died on
the 4th of December. After lying in state in
Exeter Change, he was (says Arbuthnot, who
had again nursed and attended him) " interred
at *Westminster*-Abbey, as if he had been
a peer of the realm;" and the Queensberrys
erected a handsome monument to his memory.
By other friends he was mourned as sincerely,
if not as sumptuously. Pope, who had always
loved him, felt a genuine sorrow, and five days
elapsed before Swift at Dublin could summon
courage to open the boding letter which announced his death. His fortune, of which his
patrons had made themselves the voluntary
stewards, amounted to about £6000. It was
divided between his sisters, Mrs. Baller and
Mrs. Fortescue.

His last letter to Swift had ended: — " Believe me, as I am, unchangeable in the regard,
love and esteem I have for you." The words
reveal the chief source of his personal charm.

He was thoroughly kindly and affectionate,
with just that touch of clinging in his character,
and of helplessness in his nature, which, when
it does not inspire contempt (and Gay's parts
saved him from that), makes a man the spoiled
child of men and the playfellow of women.
He had his faults, it is true : he was as indolent as
Thomson, as fond of fine clothes as Goldsmith ;
as great a *gourmand* as La Fontaine. That he
was easily depressed, was probably due in a
measure to his inactive life and his uncertain
health. But at his best, he must have been
a delightfully soothing and unobtrusive companion — invaluable for fêtes and gala days, and
equally well adapted for the half lights and
unrestrained intercourse of familiar life. "You
will never " — writes Swift to the Duchess of
Queensberry, " be able to procure another so
useful, so sincere, so virtuous, so disinterested,
so entertaining, so easy, and so humble a friend,
as that person whose death all good men lament."
The praise is high, but there is little doubt that
it was genuine. Pope's antithetical epitaph,
despite the terrible mangling it has received at
the hands of Johnson, may also be quoted : —

> " Of manners gentle, of affections mild ;
> In wit a man ; simplicity a child ;
> With native humour temp'ring virtuous rage,
> Formed to delight at once and lash the age :

> Above temptation, in a low estate,
> And uncorrupted, e'en among the great :
> A safe companion, and an easy friend,
> Unblamed through life, lamented in thy end,
> These are thy honours! not that here thy bust
> Is mixed with heroes, or with kings thy dust,
> But that the worthy and the good shall say,
> Striking their pensive bosoms —*Here* lies Gay."

The monument in Westminster Abbey, for which the above was composed, bears, in addition, a flippant couplet of Gay's own which can only have been — as indeed it is stated to have been — the expression of a passing mood.

To attempt any detailed examination of Gay's works is unnecessary. Those which are most likely to attract the nineteenth century reader have been mentioned in the course of the foregoing pages. Stripped of the adventitious circumstances which threw the halo of notoriety around them, his two best known plays remain of interest chiefly for their songs,[1] which have all

---

[1] One of the couplets of the " Beggar's Opera " bids fair to live as long as Buridan's two bundles of hay. " How happy could I be with either, Were t' other dear Charmer away ! " — was, not long since, employed by Sir William Harcourt in the House to illustrate a political dilemma. Whereupon Mr. Goschen neatly turned the laugh upon the Leader of the Opposition by continuing the quotation —" But while you thus tease me together, To neither a word will I say ! "

the qualities songs possess when the writer,
besides being a poet, is a musician as well.
This lyric faculty is also present in all Gay's
looser pieces, and is as manifest in the ballad on
Molly Mog of the " Rose " Inn at Wokingham,
as in " Black-Ey'd Susan " or " 'T was when
the Seas were roaring." In his longer poems
he is always happiest when he is most un-
constrained and natural, or treads the *terra
firma* of the world he knows. The " Fan," the
miscellaneous " Eclogues," the " Epistles," are
all more or less forced and conventional. But
exceptions occur even in these. There is a
foretaste of Fielding in " The Birth of the
Squire ; " and the " Welcome from Greece," in
which he exhibits Pope's friends assembling to
greet him after his successful translation of the
" Iliad," has a brightness and vivacity of move-
ment, which seems to be the result of an
unusually fresh inspiration. It is written, moreover, in an *ottava rima* stanza far earlier than
Tennant's or Frere's or Byron's. The " Tales "
are mediocre, and generally indelicate ; the
" Translations " have no special merit. In the
" Fables " Gay finds a more congenial vocation.
The easy octosyllabic measure, not packed and
idiomatic like Swift's, not light and ironical like
Prior's, but ambling, colloquial, and even a

little down-at-heel, after the fashion of the bard
himself, suited his habits and his Muse. An
uncompromising criticism might perhaps be inclined to hint that these little pieces are by no
means faultless ; that they are occasionally
deficient in narrative art, that they lack real
variety of theme, and that they are often
wearisome, almost unmanly, in their querulous
insistence on the vices of servility and the
hollowness of Courts. On the other hand, it
must be admitted that they are full of good
nature and good sense ; and if not characterised
by the highest philosophical wisdom, show
much humorous criticism of life and practical
observation of mankind. They have, too, some
other recommendations, which can scarcely be
ignored. They have given pleasure to several
generations of readers, old and young ; and they
have enriched the language with more than one
indispensable quotation. " While there is life,
there 's Hope," " When a Lady 's in the Case,"
and " Two of a Trade can ne'er agree," — are
still part of the current coin of conversation.

AT LEICESTER FIELDS.

IT is with places as with persons ; they often
attract us more in their youth than in their
maturer years. Apart from the fact that these
papers are mainly confined to the Eighteenth
Century, this threadbare truth affords a sufficient
excuse for speaking of Leicester Square by its
earlier, rather than by its existing name. And,
indeed, the abiding interest of the locality lies
less in the present than in the past. Not even
the addition to the inclosure of busts and a
Shakespeare fountain has been able to regener-
ate entirely the Leicester Square that most of
us remember, with its gloomy back streets, —
its fringe of dingy *cafés* and *restaurants*, — its
ambiguous print- and curiosity-shops, — its in-
corrigibly-unacclimatised Alhambra, whose gar-
ish Saracenic splendours scale and peel perpetually in London's *imber edax*. If we call
anything forcibly to mind in connection with
the spot, it is a certain central statue, long the
mock of the irreverent, — a statue of the first
George, which had come of old, gilded and

magnificent, from "Timon's Villa" at Canons, to fall at last upon evil days and evil tongues, to be rudely spotted with sacrilegious paint, to be crowned with a fool's cap, and, finally, to present itself to the spectator in the generally dishonoured and dilapidated condition in which, some twenty years ago, it was exhibited by the late John O'Connor on the walls of the Royal Academy. But when, travelling rapidly backwards, past the Empire and the Alhambra, past Wylde's Globe and the Panopticon, past Burford's Panorama and Miss Linwood's Needlework, we enter the last century, we are in the Leicester Fields of Reynolds and Hogarth, of Newton and John Hunter, — the Leicester Fields of Sir George Savile and Frederick, Prince of Wales, of Colbert and Prince Eugene. This is the Leicester Fields of which we propose to speak. Leicester Square and its notorieties may be left to the topographers of the future.[1]

[1] The name "Leicester Squaie" — it is but right to say — is also of fairly early date. In "A Journey through England," 4th ed., 1724, i. 178, the writer, speaking of the space before Leicester House, says: "This was till these Fourteen Years always called *Leicester Fields*, but now *Leicester Square.*" There is, however, abundant evidence that the older name continued to be freely used throughout the century. For example, in 1783, Mrs. Hogarth's

It is in Ralph Agas his survey of 1592 (or rather in Mr. W. H. Overall's excellent facsimile) that we make our first acquaintance with the Fields, then really entitled to their name. According to Agas, the ground to the north-west of Charing Cross, and immediately to the east of the present Whitcomb Street (at that time Hedge Lane), was formerly open pasture land, occupied — in the plan — by a pair of pedestrians larger than life, a woman laying out clothes, and two nondescript quadrupeds, of which one is broken-backed beyond the licence of deformity. The only erections to be discovered are the King's Mews, clustering together for company at the back of the Cross. Sixty years later, judging from the map known generally as Faithorne's, the ground had become more populated. To the right of St. Martin's Lane, it is thickly planted with buildings ; to the left also a line of houses is springing up and creeping northward, while in the open space above referred to stand a couple of lordly mansions. One, on a site which must have lain to the north of the present Little Newport Street, is Newport House, the town residence of

house is advertised as " *The Golden Head* in *Leicester Fields*," and it is " at his house in *Leicester Fields*," in 1792, that Malone makes Reynolds die.

Mountjoy Blount, Earl of Newport ; the other, which occupies ground now traversed by Leicester Place, is Leicester House. Its garden at the back extended across the eastern end of Lisle Street, and its boundary wall to the north was also the southern boundary wall of the old Military Garden where King James's son, Prince Henry of Wales — whose gallant and martial presentment you shall see figured in the fore front of Michael Drayton's " Poly-Olbion," — had been wont to exercise his troops, and make the now-discredited welkin ring with the shooting-off of chambers, with alarums, and points of war.

Leicester House the first was built about 1632–6 by Robert Sydney, second Earl of Leicester, the father of Algernon Sydney, and of that beautiful Dorothy, afterwards Countess of Sunderland, whom Van Dyck painted, and Waller " Petrarchised " as Sacharissa. The site (Swan Close) [1] was what is known as Lammas-land, and from the Overseers' Books of the Parish of St. Martin's in the Fields, the Earl seems not only to have paid " Lammas " for " the

[1] Cunningham failed to identify Swan Close. But from a letter in the State Paper Office, quoted in " Temple Bar " for June, 1874, it would seem that this was the actual site of the building.

ground that adjoins to the Military Wall," but also "for the field that is before his house " — *i. e.* Leicester Fields. This latter probably extended to the present Orange Street, so that the grounds of the old mansion may be roughly said to be bounded by the Mews on the south, and by the Military Garden on the north. Few memories cling about the place which belong to Lord Leicester's lifetime. When not engaged in embassies and the like, he was absent at his other and more famous seat of Penshurst in Kent, and Leicester House was " To Let." One of the earliest of its illustrious tenants was that quondam "Queen of Hearts " (as Howell calls her), the unfortunate Elizabeth of Bohemia, who, already smitten with her last illness, died there in February, 1662, after a few days' residence, " in the arms " (says Evelyn) "of her nephew the King" [Charles II.]. Another tenant, some years later, was Charles Colbert, Marquis de Croissy, the French Ambassador, a brother of Louis the Fourteenth's famous minister and financier ; and Pepys records, under date of 21st October, 1668, that he was to have taken part in a deputation from the Royal Society to Lord Leicester's distinguished lessee. But having unhappily been " mighty merry " at a house-warming of his friend Batelier, he arrived too late to accompany the rest, and was fain to console himself (and perhaps to do penance) by carrying his wife to Cow Lane, Smithfield, in order to inspect a proposed new coach, with the splendours of which " she is out of herself for joy almost," although, from the sequel, it was not the one ultimately purchased.

Pepys, as will be seen, did not actually enter Leicester House, at all events upon this occasion. His brother diarist was more fortunate. Going in October, 1672, to take leave of the second Lady Sunderland (Sacharissa's daughter-in-law), whose husband had already set out as ambassador to Paris, grave John Evelyn was entertained by Her Ladyship with the performances of Richardson the fire-eater, who, in those days, enjoyed a vogue sufficient to justify the record of his prowess in the " Journal des Sça-vans " for 1680. " He devour'd brimston on glowing coales before us," says Evelyn, " chewing and swallowing them ; he mealted a beere-glasse and eate it quite up ; then taking a live coale on his tongue, he put on it a raw oyster, the coal was blown on with bellows till it flam'd and sparkl'd in his mouth, and so remain'd till the oyster gaped and was quite boil'd ; then he mealted pitch and wax with sulphur, which he drank downe as it flam'd ; I saw it flaming in his

mouth a good while; he also tooke up a thick
piece of yron, such as laundresses use to put in
their smoothing-boxes, when it was fiery hot,
held it betwoono his tceth, then in his hand, and
threw it about like a stone, but this I observ'd
he car'd not to hold very long; then he stood
on a small pot, and bending his body, tooke a
glowing yron with his mouth from betweene
his feete, without touching the pot or ground
with his hands; with divers other prodigious
feates." [1]

Lord Leicester closed a long life in 1677, and
many other tenants afterwards occupied the
mansion in the Fields. Under Anne it was the
home of the German Ambassador, or " Imperial
Resident," who lived in it far into the reign of
the first George. At this time, judging from a
water-colour bird's-eye view in the Crace Collection at the British Museum, it was a long two-
storied building, with attics above, a court-
yard in front, and a row of small shops or stalls
extending on either side, of its entrance gate.
Behind came the garden, stretching northward,
and decorated in the Dutch fashion with formal
trees and statues. Hither, on a Saturday in
January, 1712, conveyed unostentatiously in a

[1] "Memoirs of John Evelyn," etc., 1827, ii. pp. 375-6.

hackney coach from Whitehall Stairs, came
Eugene of Savoy, who, by desire of the Emperor
Charles VI., had just crossed from the Hague
in Her Majesty's " Yacht ' Fubs ' " (Captain
Desborough), with the intention of preventing,
if possible, what Prior calls that " vile Utrecht
Treaty." His mission was to be fruitless from
the outset, for at the Nore he was greeted with
the news of Marlborough's disgrace, and his
presence in England had little or no effect upon
the pending proposals for peace. But for two
months he was to be fêted and lionised by the
nobility in a way which — modest warrior and
discreet diplomatist as he was — must have taxed
his resources as much as a campaign in Flanders.
His admirers mobbed him on all occasions. " I
could not see Prince Eugene at court to-day," —
writes Swift to Mrs. Johnson at Dublin, — " the
crowd was so great. The Whigs contrive to
have a crowd always about him, and employ the
rabble to give the word when he sets out from
any place." Elsewhere Swift had said — " I hope
and believe he comes too late to do the Whigs
any good." At first His Highness's appearance
prepossessed him. He is not ill-looking, " but
well enough, and a good shape." Later on, he
has revised his opinion. " I saw Prince Eugene
at court to-day very plain. He is plaguy yellow,

and literally ugly besides." A great Tory lady, Lady Strafford (wife of that haughty Envoy to the Hague who declined to serve with Prior in the Utrecht negotiations) goes farther still. She calls him — her Ladyship spells far worse than Stella — a "frittfull creature," and adds, " the Ladys here dont admire Prince Eugene, for he seemes to take very little notis of them," — a sentiment in which we may perhaps detect a spice of the "*spretæ injuria formæ.*"

Much, indeed, depends upon the point of view, political and otherwise. To Steele, with his military instincts and quick enthusiasm, the great Captain, who surprised Cremona and forced the trenches of Turin, comes surrounded with an aura of hyperbole. " He who beholds him," he writes in " Spectator," No. 340, " will easily expect from him anything that is to be imagined or executed by the Wit or Force of Man. The Prince is of that Stature which makes a Man most easily become all Parts of Exercise ; has Height to be graceful on Occasions of State and Ceremony, and no less adapted for Agility and Dispatch ; His Aspect is erect and compos'd ; his Eye lively and thoughtful, yet rather vigilant than sparkling : His Action and Address the most easy imaginable, and his Behaviour in an Assembly peculiarly graceful in a certain Art of mixing insensibly with the rest, and becoming one of the Company, instead of receiving the Courtship of it. The Shape of his Person, and Composure of his Limbs, are remarkably exact and beautiful." Burnet, as staunch a Whig as Steele, writes more moderately to the same effect. " I had the honour to be admitted at several times, to much discourse with him ; his Character is so universally known, that I will say nothing of him, but from what appeared to myself. He has a most unaffected Modesty, and does scarcely bear the Acknowledgments, that all the World pay him : He descends to an easy Equality with those, with whom he converses ; and seems to assume nothing to himself, while he reasons with others : He was treated with great respect by both Parties ; but he put a distinguished Respect on the Duke of *Marlborough*, with whom he passed most of his Time.[1] The Queen used him civilly, but not with the Distinction, that was due to his high Merit : Nor did he gain much ground with the Ministers." [2]

[1] It was for Marlborough, no doubt, that the Prince sat to Kneller. The portrait, in which he wears the Order of the Golden Fleece over a rich coat of armour, and holds a marshal's baton, was mezzotinted by John Simon in 1712.

[2] " History of His Own Time," ii. (1734), pp. 589–90.

Eugene's stay at Leicester House was brief;
but it must have been fully occupied. "Je
caressais beaucoup les gens en place," he writes
in his "Mémoires," and it is clear that, however
attentive he may have been to his fallen comrade-
in-arms of Blenheim and Oudenarde, he did not
omit to pay assiduous court to those in power.
"He has been every day entertain'd at some great
man's," says gossiping Peter Wentworth. Lord
Portland gives him "dinner, musick and a dancing" all at once; the Duke of Shrewsbury has
Nicolini to sing for him; the Duke of Buckingham turns out the militia in his honour. And so
forth. He, in his turn, was not backward in re-
sponding. "Prince Eugene," says Lady Strafford,
"has given an order to six ladys and six men.
The ladys are the four Marlborough daughters
and the Duchess of Bolton and Lady Berkely.
'T is a medall — Cupid on won side with a sword
in won hand and a fann in the othere, and the
othere side is Cupid with a bottle in his hand
with a sword run through it. And the motto's
are in French which I dare not write to you but
the English is 'won don't hinder the othere'
[" L'un n'empêche pas l'autre "]." He had arrived in London on January 5, and he returned to
Holland on March 17, carrying with him nothing
but the diamond hilted sword ("very rich and

genteele, and the diamonds very white," says Lord
Berkeley of Stratton), which, at a cost of £5000,
had been presented to him by Queen Anne.[1]
After this Leicester House continued to be the
home of the German Resident, apparently one
Hoffmann, whom Swift calls a "puppy." But he
had also called Hoffmann's predecessor, Count
Gallas, a "fool," and too much importance may
easily be attached to these mere flowers of speech.
About 1718, the house, being again to let, was
bought for £6000 by George Augustus, Prince of
Wales, who had quarrelled with his father; and
a residence of the Princes of Wales it continued
for forty years to come.

This was perhaps the gayest time in its history.

---

[1] If he received royal gifts, he was also princely in his
acknowledgments. According to Hearne (Doble, 1889,
iii. 329), he paid twenty guineas for Joshua Barnes's quarto
"Homer" of 1711, and fifteen guineas for Whiston's
"Heretical Book." He also paid thirty guineas for Samuel
Clarke's edition of "Cæsar's Commentaries (Tonson,
1712)," then just published with a magnificent portrait of
Marlborough, to whom it was dedicated. A large paper
copy of this, sumptuously bound, fetched sixteen guineas
at Dr. Mead's sale of 1754–5; but though it is praised by
Addison in "Spectator," No. 367, as doing "Honour to the
English Press," Eugene certainly gave too much. Prob-
ably he meant to do so. "Je fis des présens," he says
("Mémoires," 1811, p. 107); "car," he adds significantly,
"on achète beaucoup en Angleterre."

From the precision and decorum of St. James's,
people flocked eagerly to the drawing-rooms and
receptions of Leicester House, where the fiddles
were always going. " Balls, assemblies and masquerades have taken the place of dull formal
visiting," writes my Lord Chesterfield, " and the
women are more agreeable triflers than they were
designed. Puns are extremely in vogue, and the
license very great. The variation of three or
four letters in a word breaks no squares, inasmuch, that an indifferent punster may make a
very good figure in the best companies." He
himself was one of the most brilliant luminaries
of that brilliant gathering, delighting the Prince
and Princess by his mimicry and his caustic
raillery. Another was that eccentric Duchess of
Buckingham, who passed for the daughter of
James II. by Catharine Sedley, Countess of Dorchester, and who always sat in a darkened chamber, in the deepest mourning, on the anniversary
of King Charles's execution. Thus she was discovered by Lord Hervey, surrounded by servants in sables, in a room hung with black, and
lighted only by wax candles. But the most attractive figures of the Prince's Court are the
youthful maids of honour, — charming, good-
humoured Mary Bellenden, Mary Lepel (to
whom an earlier paper in these volumes has

been devoted),[1] and reckless and volatile Sophia Howe. Pope and Gay wrote them verses, — these laughing damsels, — and they are often under contemporary pens. Miss Bellenden married Colonel John Campbell, and became a happy wife ; the " beautiful Molly Lepel " paired off with John, Lord Hervey, whose pen-portrait by Pope exhausts the arts of " conscientious malevolence," while poor Sophia Howe fell in love, but did not marry at all, and died in 1726 of a broken heart.

When, in June, 1727, George II. passed from Leicester House to the throne of England, another Prince of Wales succeeded him, — though not immediately, — and maintained the traditions of an opposition Court. This was Frederick, Prince of Wales. Bubb Dodington, afterwards Lord Melcombe, was the Chesterfield of this new *régime*, and Miss Chudleigh and Lady Middlesex, its Bellenden and Lepel. Political intrigue alternated with gambling and theatricals. One of the *habitués* was the dancing master Desnoyers, whom Hogarth ridiculed ; and French comedians made holiday. " The town," says an historian of the Square, " was at this time full of gaiety — masquerades, ridottos, Ranelagh in full

---

[1] See " Marv Lepel, Lady Hervey," in " Eighteenth Century Vignettes," Third Series, pp. 292–322.

swing, and the Prince a prominent figure at all,
for he loved all sorts of diversion, from the
gipsies at Norwood, the conjurors and fortune-
tellers in the bye-streets about Leicester Fields,
and the bull-baits at Hockley-in-the-Hole, to
Amorevoli at the Opera, and the Faussans in the
ballet. When the news came of the Duke of
Cumberland having lost the battle of Fontenoy
in May, 1745, the Prince was deep in preparation for a performance at Leicester House of
Congreve's masque of "The Judgment of Paris,"
in which he played Paris. He himself wrote a
French song for the part, addressed to the three
rival goddesses, acted by Lady Catherine Hanmer, Lady Fauconberg, and Lady Middlesex,
the *dame régnante* of the time. It is in the high
Regency vein : —

> "'Venez, mes chères Déesses,
> Venez, calmez mon chagrin ;
> Aidez, mes belles Princesses,
> À le noyer dans le vin.
> Poussons cette douce ivresse
> Jusqu'au milieu de la nuit,
> Et n'écoutons que la tendresse
> D'un charmant vis-à-vis.'"

"What signifies if Europe Has a tyrant more
or less, So we but pray Calliope Our verse and
song to bless" — proceeds this Anacreontic per-

formance ; and Walpole copies out its entire five stanzas to send to Mann at Florence.   They miscarry, he says, "in nothing but the language, the thoughts and the poetry," — a judgment which is needlessly severe.

In March, 1751, an end came to these light-hearted junketings, when His Royal Highness quitted the scene almost precipitately from the breaking of an abscess in his side, caused by the blow of a cricket-ball at Cliveden.   The Princess and her children continued to live in Leicester Fields until 1766.   Meanwhile, to the accompaniment of trumpets and kettledrums, the old house witnessed the proclamation of George III., and the marriage, in its great drawing-room, of the Princess Augusta to Ferdinand, Hereditary Prince of Brunswick, one of the most popular heroes ever huzzaed to by an English mob. After this last occurrence, the only important event connected with royalty in the Fields is the death at Savile House on 29th December, 1765, of one of the princes.   "The King's youngest brother, Prince Frederick," writes Walpole (with one of those Gallic affectations of phrase which roused the anger of Macaulay) "is dead of a dropsy and consumption : he was a pretty and promising boy."

The Savile House above referred to stood

next to Leicester House on the west. Savile
House, too, was not without its memories. It
was here that Peter the Great had boozed with
his pot companion, the Marquis of Caermarthen,
who occupied it when the Czar made his famous
visit to this country in 1698. More than one
English home bore dirty testimony to the passage of the imperial savage and his suite, the
decorous dwelling of John Evelyn, in particular,
at Sayes Court, Deptford, being made "right
nasty." There is, however, no special record
of any wrong to Savile House beyond the spill-
ing, down the autocratic throat, of an "intolerable deal of sack" and peppered brandy. In
January, 1718, the house was taken by the
Prince of Wales, and when, a little later, Leicester House was vacated by Lord Gower, a
communication was opened between the two,
the smaller being devoted to the royal children.
It belonged originally to the Aylesbury family,
and came through them to the Saviles, one of
whom was the Sir George Savile who is by
some supposed to have sat for Goldsmith's Mr.
Burchell. Sir George was its tenant in the riots
of '80, when (as Dickens has not failed to remember in " Barnaby Rudge ") it was besieged
by the rioters because he had brought in the
Catholic Bill. " Between Twelve and One

O'clock Yesterday morning [June 6th] " — says the " Public Advertiser " — " a large Body [of rioters] assembled before Sir George Savile's House in Leicester Fields, and after breaking all the Windows, destroyed some of the Furniture." They were finally dispersed by a party of the Horse Grenadier Guards, but not before they had torn up all the iron railings in front of the building, which they afterwards used effectively as weapons of offence. Burke, who had also supported the Bill, was only saved from a like fate by the exertions of sixteen soldiers who garrisoned his house in Charles Street, St. James's Square. With the later use of Savile House, as the home of Miss Linwood's Art Needlework, which belongs to the present century, this paper has nothing to do.

Moreover, we are straying from Leicester House itself. Deserted of royalty, it passed into the hands of Mr., afterwards Sir Ashton Lever (grand uncle of Charles Lever the novelist), who transferred to it in 1771 the miscellaneous collection he had christened the " Holophusikon " — a name which did not escape the gibes of the professional jester. His *omnium gatherum* of natural objects and savage costumes was, nevertheless, a remarkable one, still more remarkable when regarded as the work of a single man. It filled

sixteen of the rooms at Leicester House, besides
overflowing on the staircases, and included, not
only all the curiosities Cook had brought home
from his voyages, but also a valuable assortment
of bows and arrows of all countries contributed
by Mr. Richard Owen Cambridge of Twickenham.[1] Its possessor had been persuaded that his
treasures which, in their first home at Alkrington near Manchester, had enjoyed great popularity, would be equally successful in London.
The result, however, did not justify the expectation (an admittance of 5s. 3d. per person must
have been practically prohibitive), and poor Sir
Ashton was ultimately " obligated " as Tony
Lumpkin would say, to apply to Parliament for
power to dispose of his show, as a whole, by
lottery. He estimated his outlay at £50,000.
Of 36,000 tickets issued at a guinea each, only
8000 were taken up. The lottery was drawn in
March, 1786, and the winner was a Mr. Parkin-
son, who transferred his prize to the Rotunda at

[1] See "Cambridge the Everything," in "Eighteenth
Century Vignettes," Third Series, pp. 178–204. In an out-
house of the "Holophusikon," it may be added, were exhibited (stuffed) Queen Charlotte's elephant and female
zebra — two favourites of royalty, which, during their lifetime, had enjoyed an exceptional, if not always enviable,
notoriety.

the Southern or Surrey end of Blackfriars Bridge, changing its name to the Museum Leverianum. But it was foredoomed to misfortune, and in 1806 was dispersed under the hammer. A few years after it had crossed the river, Leicester House in turn disappeared, being pulled down in 1790.[1] In 1791 Lisle Street was continued across its garden ; and a little later still, Leicester Place traversed its site, running parallel to Leicester Street, which had existed long previously, being described in 1720, " as ordinarily built and inhabited, except the west side, towards the Fields, where there is a very good house."

Leicester Place and Leicester Street, — like Leicester Fields itself, — directly preserve the memory of what Pennant aptly calls the "pouting-place of Princes." But there are other traces of Leicester House in the nomenclature of the neighbourhood which had grown up about it. One of the family titles survives in " Lisle Street " ; another in " Sidney Alley." Bear Street again recalls the Leicester crest, a bear and ragged staff, while Green Street (one side of

---

[1] A house in Lisle Street, looking down Leicester Place, still (1898) perpetuates the name, and bears on its *façade* in addition the words, "New Lisle Street, MDCCXCI." It is occupied by a foreign school or schools ("Écoles de Notre Dame de France ").

which has been recently rebuilt), according to Wheatley and Cunningham, derives its name from the colour of the Leicester Mews, which stood to the south of the Fields. The central inclosure seems to have been first systematically laid out — though it had long been railed round — about 1737. Eleven years later arrived from Canons (Lord Burlington's seat at Edgeware) that famous equestrian statue of George I., which Londoners so well remember. At the time of its erection it was lavishly gilt, and was one of the popular sights of the Town. By some it was attributed to Buchard ; by others to Van Nost of Piccadilly, once a fashionable statuary (in lead) like Cheere of Hyde Park Corner. The horse was modelled upon that by Hubert Le Sœur which carries King Charles I. at Charing Cross.

Considering its prolonged patronage by royalty, Leicester Fields does not seem to have been particularly favoured by distinguished residents. Charles Dibdin, the song-writer, once lived in Leicester Place, where in 1796 (on the east side) he built a little theatre, the Sans Souci ; and Woollett, of whose velvety engravings Mr. Louis Fagan, not many years ago, prepared an exhaustive catalogue, had also his habitat in Green Street (No. 11), from the leads of which he was wont — so runs the story — to discharge a small cannon when he had successfully put the last touches to a " Battle of La Hogue," or a " Death of General Wolfe." Allan Ramsay (in his youth), Barry, and John Opie all once lodged in Orange Court (now Street) ; and here — at No. 13 — was born, of a shoemaker sire and a mother who cried oysters, into a life of many changing fortunes, that strange Thomas Holcroft of the " Road to Ruin." In St. Martin's Street, next door to the Congregational Chapel on the east side, lived Sir Isaac Newton from 1710 until January, 1725, or two years before his death at Kensington. Few traditions, however, connect the abstracted philosopher (he was nearing seventy when he came to the Fields) with the locality, beyond his visits to Princess Caroline at the great house opposite.[1] But

---

[1] A so-called Observatory on the roof, now non-existent, was for many years exhibited as Newton's. Recent authorities, however, contend that this was the fabrication of a later tenant. But it should be noted that Madame D'Arblay, who also lived in the house, and wrote novels in the room in question, seems to have had no doubts of the kind. She says ("Memoirs of Dr. Burney," 1832, i. 290–1) that her father not only reverently repaired the Observatory when he entered upon his tenancy of No. 35 [in 1774], but went to the expense of practically reconstructing it when it was all but destroyed by the hurricane of 1778.

there was one member of his household, a few years later, who must certainly have added to the attractions of the ordinary two-storied building where he superintended the revision of the second and third editions of the " Principia." This was his kinswoman, — the " *jolie nièce* " of Voltaire, — the " famous witty Miss Barton " of the " Gentleman's Magazine." At this date she was " Super-intendant of his domestick Affairs " to Charles, Earl of Halifax, who, dying in 1715, left her £5000 and a house, " as a Token " — so runs the bequest — " of the sincere Love, Affection, and Esteem I have long had for her Person, and as a small Recompence for the Pleasure and Happiness I have had in her Conversation." This, taken in connection with the fact that, since 1706, she had been in receipt of an annuity of £200 a year, purchased in her uncle's name, but for which Halifax was trustee, has led to the conclusion that the relation between the pair was something closer than friendship, and that, following other contemporary precedents, they were privately married.[1]

---

[1] See " Newton : his Friend : and his Niece," 1885, by Professor Augustus de Morgan, which labours, with much digression, but with infinite ingenuity and erudition, to establish this satisfactory solution of a problem in which the good fame of Newton cannot be regarded as entirely unconcerned.

Be this as it may, Catherine Barton is also interesting as one of the group of gifted women to whom Swift extended the privilege of that half-patronising, half-playful, and wholly unconventional intimacy which is at once the attraction and the enigma of his relations with the other sex. He met her often in London, though not as often as he wished. "I love her better than any-one here," he tells Stella in April, 1711, "and see her seldomer." He dines with her "alone at her lodgings"; he goes with her to other houses ; and, Tory though he has become, endures her vivacious Whiggery.

When, at Halifax's death, Catherine Barton, in all probability, returned to her uncle's house, Swift had already gone back to Ireland, and there is no reason for supposing that, although he had lodgings "in Leicester Fields" in 1711, he ever visited his friend in St. Martin's Street. In August, 1717, Mrs. Barton married John Conduitt, M. P., Newton's successor as Master of the Mint, and when in town continued to reside with her husband under Newton's roof. And though Halifax was dead, and Swift in exile, and Prior "in the messenger's hand," there can be little doubt that during her brief widowhood(?) and second wifehood, those friends who had clustered about the former

toast of the Kit Cats must still have continued
to visit her. The chairs of Lady Worsley and
Lady Betty Germaine must often have waited
In the narrow entrance to St. Martin's Street,
while the ladies "disputed Whig and Tory"
with Mrs. Conduitt, or were interrupted in their
tête-à-tête by Gay and his Duchess. After Sir
Isaac — a long while after — the most notable
tenant of the old house was Dr. Charles Burney,
author of the "History of Music," and of
Fanny Burney. Indeed, it was in this very
building — with the unassuming little chapel on
its right where "Rainy Day" Smith had often
heard Toplady preach — that a mere girl in her
teens — no, ungallant Mr. Croker discovered
her to have been actually a young woman of
five-and-twenty — wrote that "Evelina" which,
in 1778, took the Town by storm. There were
panelled rooms and a painted ceiling in the
Newton-Burney house of yore, but it could
scarcely be here that the little person whom in
her graver moments Mrs. Piozzi nicknamed the
"Lady Louisa of Leicester Square" danced
round an unmetaphoric mulberry tree with delight at her success in letters, as there are no
traces of a garden. At present, in this quiet
backwater of street traffic, where Burke and
Johnson and Franklin and Reynolds all came

formerly to visit their favourite authoress, nothing is discoverable but a dingy tenement with
dusty upper windows, with a ground floor that
is used as a day school, and a front of stucco'd
red brick upon which the blue tablet of the
Society of Arts has something of the forlorn effect
of an order of merit upon a chimney-sweep.

Turning out of St. Martin's Street on the
north another tablet is discernible in the angle of
the Fields to the right upon the comparatively
modern red brick *façade* of another school,
known as Archbishop Tenison's.   Here, at one
of the many signs of the "Golden Head," lived
William Hogarth.[1] The golden head in his case
was rudely carved by himself out of pieces of
cork glued together, and represented Van Dyck.
To this, says Nichols, succeeded a head in plas-
ter ; and this again, when Nichols wrote in 1782,
had been replaced by a bust of Newton. About
the interior of the house very little seems to be
known, but, as it was rated to the poor in 1756
at £60, it must have been fairly roomy. In the
later days, when it formed part of the Sablonière

---

[1] There was even another, in Hogarth's day, in the
Fields itself. "At the Golden Head," on the south side
(Hogarth's was on the east), lived Edward Fisher, the
mezzotint engraver, to whom we owe so many brilliant
plates after Reynolds.

Hotel, before the hotel made way for the existing school, there were traditions of a studio, probably far less authentic than those of Sir Isaac's
observatory. Not many years after Hogarth
first took the house, the square was laid out
(it had long been railed in), and he is said to
have been often seen walking in the inclosure,
wrapped in his red roquelaure, with his hat cocked
on one side like Frederick the Great. His
stables, when he set up the fine coach which
Charles Catton decorated for him with the
famous Cyprian crest that figures at the bottom
of " The Bathos," were in the Nag's Head Yard,[1]
Orange Street. He had — as we know — a
country box at Chiswick ; but he was at home
in Leicester Fields. His friends were about
him. Kind old Captain Coram had lodgings
somewhere in the neighbourhood ; Pine, the
" Friar Pine " of " Calais Gate," lived in St.
Martin's Lane ; beyond that, in Covent Garden
and its vicinity, were George Lambert the scene
painter, Saunders Welch the magistrate, Richard
Wilson, Fielding, and a host of intimates. It
was in Leicester Fields that Hogarth died. He
had been driven there from Chiswick on the

---

[1] The site of the Nag's Head — an ancient and wooden-
galleried inn — is now [1898] occupied by the new premises of Messrs. Macmillan and Co.

25th of October, 1764, cheerful, but very weak.
" Receiving an agreeable letter from the *American* Dr. *Franklin*," says Nichols, [he] " drew
up a rough draught of an answer to it ; but going to bed, he was seized with a vomiting, upon
which he rung his bell with such violence that
he broke it, and expired about two hours afterwards in the arms of Mrs. *Mary Lewis*, who
was called up on his being taken suddenly ill."
He is buried in Chiswick churchyard, where
some years subsequently a monument was
erected to his memory, with a well-known
epitaph by Garrick.　After Hogarth's death
his widow continued to keep up the " Golden
Head," and Mary Lewis sold his prints there.
Richard Livesay, the engraver, was one of
Widow Hogarth's lodgers, and the Scotch
painter, Alexander Runciman, was another.　If
the house had any further notable occupants,
they may be forgotten.

Mrs. Hogarth herself died in 1789.　Six years
before her death she had a next-door neighbour
in the Fields, who, in his way, was as illustrious as Hogarth or Reynolds.　This was John
Hunter, who, in 1783, became the tenant of
No. 28,[1] and at once began extending it back-

---

[1] Now rebuilt by the Alhambra Company as part of
their premises.

ward towards Castle Street (now the Charing
Cross Road) to receive his famous museum of
Comparative and Pathological Anatomy. Hogarth had then been dead for nearly twenty
years ; and it is unlikely that the painter knew
much of the young surgeon who was subsequently to become so celebrated ; but he was
probably acquainted with his brother, William
Hunter of Covent Garden, who attended Fielding in 1754. William Hunter had just died
when John Hunter came to Leicester Fields.
John lived there ten years in the height of his
activity and fame, and it was during this period
that Reynolds painted that portrait of him in a
reverie (now in the Council Room of the College of Surgeons), which was engraved by
William Sharp. He survived Sir Joshua but
one year.

The house of Reynolds was at the opposite
side of the Square, at No. 47, now Puttick and
Simpson's auction rooms. He occupied it from
1760 to 1792. We are accustomed to think of
Hogarth and Reynolds as contemporaries. But
Reynolds was in the pride of his prime when he
came to Leicester Fields, while Hogarth was
an old and broken man, whose greatest work
was done. Apart from this, there could never
have been much real sympathy between them.

Hogarth, whose own efforts as a portrait-painter
were little appreciated in his lifetime, must have
chafed at the carriages which blocked up the
doorway of his more fortunate brother ; while
Reynolds, courtly and amiable as he was, capable of indulgence even to such a caricaturist as
Bunbury, could find for his illustrious neighbour,
when he came to deliver his famous Fourteenth
Discourse, no warmer praise than that of " successful attention to the ridicule of life." These
things, alas ! are scarcely novelties in literature
and art.   It is pleasanter to think of No. 47
filled with those well-known figures of whom
we read in Boswell and Madame D'Arblay ; —
with Burke and Johnson and Goldsmith and
Gibbon and Garrick ; — with graceful Angelica,
and majestic Siddons, and azure-stockinged
Montagu ; — with pretty Nelly O'Brien and
charming Fanny Abington ; — with all the
crowd of distinguished soldiers, sailors, lawyers,
and literati who by turns filled the sitters' chair [1]
in the octagonal painting-room, or were ushered
out and in by the silver-laced footmen.   Then
there were those wonderful disorderly dinners,

[1] This, with the carved easel given to him by Gray's
friend Mason, is preserved at the Royal Academy.   His
palette is said to be in the possession of Messrs. Roberson
and Co., of 99, Long Acre.

where the guests were so good and the feast so
indifferent ; where there were always wit and
learning, and seldom enough of knives and forks ;
where it was an honour to have talked and lis-
tened, and no one remembered to have dined.
Last comes that pathetic picture of Sir Joshua,
when his sight had failed him, wandering sadly
in the inclosure with his green shade over his
eyes, and peering wistfully and vainly for the
lost canary which had been wont to perch upon
his finger.

When Reynolds died, Burke wrote his eulogy
in the very house where his body lay. The
manuscript (which still exists) was blotted with
its writer's tears. Those royal periods in which
the great orator spoke of his lost friend are
too familiar to quote. But after Sir Joshua,
the interest seems to fade out of the Fields,
and one willingly draws one's pen through the
few remaining names that are written in its
chronicles.

20

MARTEILHE'S "MEMOIRS."

THE threadbare dictum of Terentianus Maurus touching books and their destinies, was never more exactly verified than by the story of the record which gives its title to the present paper. In the year 1757 was issued at Rotterdam, by J. and D. Beman and Son of that Batavian city, a little thick octavo of 552 pages, on poor paper with worse type, of which the following is the textual title: — " *Mémoires d'un Protestant, Condamné aux Galères de France pour Cause de Religion ; écrits par lui même : Ouvrage, dans lequel, outre le récit, des souffrances de l'Auteur depuis 1700 jusqu'en 1713 ; on trouvera diverses Particularités curieuses, relatives à l'Histoire de ce Temps-là, & une Description exacte des Galères & de leur Service.*" In 1774 a second edition of the book was published at the Hague, to be followed four years later by a third. In the Rotterdam impression the names of some of the personages and localities had been simply indicated by initials; in the third issue of 1778 — the author having died not many

months before — these particulars were inserted
at full. It then appeared that the " Memoirs "
— concerning the authenticity of which, from
internal evidence, there could never have been
any reasonable doubt — were those of a certain
Jean Marteilhe of Bergerac on the Dordogne,
in the Province of Périgord in France, and that
they had been edited and prepared for the press
from Marteilhe's own manuscripts by M. Daniel
de Superville — probably the second of that
name, since Daniel de Superville, the elder, a
notable personage among the leaders of the
Reformed Church, had long been dead when
the work appeared in its first form.

Circulating chiefly among the members of a
proscribed community, and published in a foreign country, these remarkable autobiographical
experiences, notwithstanding their three editions, had been practically lost sight of in France
until some thirty years ago ; and the account of
their revival — as partly recorded in a lengthy
note to the excellent *" Forçats pour la Foi "* of
M. A. Coquerel Fils — is sufficiently curious.
About 1865, according to M. Coquerel, copies
of the volume were so rare as to be practically
unobtainable. There was none in the Bibliothèque Nationale of France ; and the only example known in Paris belonged to a Protestant

banker, M. Félix Vernes, by whom it had been lent occasionally to historical students and connoisseurs. At Amsterdam there was a second copy in the library of M. Van Woortz, and it was believed that other copies existed in Holland. There was also, or at all events there is now, a copy at the British Museum. Meanwhile, the book had greatly impressed the fortunate few into whose hands it had come. Michelet, who makes mention of it both in his " *Louis XIV. et le Duc de Bourgogne*," and his "*Louis XIV. et la Révocation*," spoke of it in terms of the highest enthusiasm. It was written, he said, " *comme entre terre et ciel.*" Why was it not reprinted? he asked. The reply lay no doubt in the difficulty of procuring a copy to print from ; and its eventual reproduction was the result of an accident. In a catalogue of German books, M. François Vidal, pastor of the Reformed Church at Bergerac, came upon the title of a work purporting to relate the history of a fugitive Camisard. Himself a native of the Cevennes, and therefore specially interested in the subject, he sent for the volume, only to discover that, instead of relating to the " fanatics of Languedoc " (as Gibbon calls them), it was really an account of a Perigourdin Protestant who, after the Revocation, more than a century and a half earlier,

of the Edict of Nantes, had fled from that very
Bergerac in which he (M. Vidal) was then
exercising his calling. He had seen some extracts from M. Vernes' copy of Marteilhe's
" Memoirs," as those extracts had been made
public in the Journal of an Historical Society
(the *Bulletin de la Société de l'Histoire du Protes-
tantisme français*), and he felt convinced that,
notwithstanding certain (to him) transparent dis-
guises of personages and localities, he was reading, in German, the story of Jean Marteilhe.
He accordingly wrote, through the publisher
of the German book, to its author, who proved
to be the copious Dr. Christian Gottlob Barth,
the founder of the Calwer Verlags-Verein in
Wurtemburg, and a well-known writer on theo-
logical subjects.   Dr. Barth informed M. Vidal
that the material for the adventures of his sup-
posititious Camisard, whom he had christened
Mantal, had been derived from F. E. Rambach's *" Schicksal der Protestanten in Frankreich,"* a work published at Halle in 1760, and
alleged to be no longer procurable. Thereupon
M. Vidal set about reconstructing the history in
the light of this discovery. He translated Barth's
summary into French, restored to Marteilhe the
name of which Barth, with nothing but initials
in his source of information, had been ignorant,

and then (having by good luck chanced upon a copy of the Rotterdam edition at Le Fleix, not many miles from Bergerac), incorporated with his version some of the more striking passages of the original record. Why he did not at once substitute that original for the summary, is, in all probability, to be explained by difficulties in the way of obtaining prolonged access to the Le Fleix copy. But the revelation of Marteilhe to France, even in mangled form, was still to be deferred. A portion of M. Vidal's book had no sooner made its appearance in *L'Église Réformée*, a journal issued at Nîmes, than that journal was suddenly suppressed. In 1863 he therefore printed on his own account what he had written, in the form of a small 12mo pamphlet. One result of this publication — to which he still somewhat unaccountably gave the title of "*La Fuite du Camisard*" — was to stimulate search for further copies of the original " Memoirs," another of which was found soon after in La Vendée, and was acquired by the Bibliothèque Nationale. Finally, in 1865, the *Société des Écoles du Dimanche* printed the complete text from the copy of M. Vernes with four fancy illustrations by the marine artist, Morel-Fatio,[1]

[1] M. Antoine Léon Morel-Fatio, whose illustrations are not reproduced in the English and American edi-

and a Preface and Appendices by M. Henri
Paumier. Of this, four thousand copies were
sold between 1865 and 1881, in which latter year
a new and revised edition, with a second Preface
by M. Paumier, was put forth. In the interim,
an English version was published under the
auspices of the Religious Tract Society, which,
in addition to a translator's Preface, gave some
further particulars respecting Marteilhe himself,
said to be derived from an article in the *Quarterly
Review* for July, 1866, though they are there
admittedly taken from M. Coquerel. To these
again, some slight supplementary contributions
were made by the French editor in his new and
revised edition of 1881. The translation of the
Religious Tract Society was also issued in New
York in 1867 by Messrs. Leypoldt and Holt
under the title of " The Huguenot Galley-
Slave."

From what has been stated, it will be seen
that, previously to the issue by the *Société des
Écoles du Dimanche*, no edition of the original " Memoirs " had been published in France.

tions, should have been well qualified for his task. He is
described as the " Horace Vernet of the sea-piece," and
was a worthy rival of Isabey and Gudin. He died of
grief at the Louvre in 1871, when the Prussians entered
Paris.

But it will also be observed that, as early as 1760, or only three years after their first appearance in the United Provinces of the Netherlands, those " Memoirs " had been incorporated in abridged form with Rambach's " *Schicksal der Protestanten in Frankreich.*" What is perhaps even more remarkable is that — as M. Coquerel and the English translator of 1866 did not fail to point out — they had been translated earlier still in England, where, indeed, they appear to have attracted immediate attention in their first form, since the *Monthly Review* for May, 1757, includes them in its " Catalogue of Foreign Publications." They must have been " Englished " shortly afterwards, for, in February, 1758, Ralph Griffiths of the " Dunciad " in Paternoster Row, the proprietor of the *Monthly Review*, and Edward Dilly of the " Rose and Crown " in the Poultry, issued conjointly, in two volumes 12mo, a version entitled " The Memoirs of a Protestant, Condemned to the Galleys of France, for His Religion. Written by Himself." To this followed upon the title-page a lengthy description of the contents, differing from that of the French original, in so far as it laid stress upon the fact that the " Protestant " was " at last set free, at the Intercession of the Court of Great Britain " ; — and the work was further

stated to be "Translated from the Original,
just published at the Hague [Rotterdam?],
by James Willington." For this enigmatical
"James Willington," whose name as an author
is otherwise entirely unknown to fame, it has
long been the custom to read "Oliver Goldsmith." Goldsmith, in fact, was actually engaged as a writer of all work upon the *Monthly
Review* when the Rotterdam edition was announced among its foreign books. To the
same May number in which that announcement
appeared, he supplied notices of Home's
"Douglas," of Burke "On the Sublime and
Beautiful," and of the new four-volume issue of
Colman and Thornton's *Connoisseur.* He continued to work for Griffiths' magazine until the
September following, when, for reasons not now
discoverable with certainty, he ceased his contributions to its pages.

What appears to be the earliest ascription to
his pen of the English version of the "Memoirs"
of Marteilhe is to be found in the life prefixed
by Isaac Reed to the "Poems of Goldsmith
and Parnell," 1795. Here he is stated to have
received twenty guineas for the work from Mr.
Edward Dilly. The next mention of it occurs
in the biographical sketch by Dr. John Aikin
in the "Goldsmith's Poetical Works" of 1805.

Dr. Aikin says (p. xvi.) that Goldsmith sold the book to Dilly for twenty guineas. Prior (" Life of Goldsmith," 1837, i. 252) confirms this, upon the authority of Reed ; and he further alleges, though without giving his authority, that Griffiths " acknowledged it [the translation] to be by Goldsmith." Forster follows suit (1848, p. 107 ; and 1877, i. 129) by stating that " the property of the book belonged to Griffiths," and that " the position of the translator appears in the subsequent assignment of the manuscript by the Paternoster Row bookseller to bookseller Dilly of the Poultry, at no small profit to Griffiths, for the sum of twenty guineas." Reed, it will be observed, says that Goldsmith received the twenty guineas ; Aikin, that Goldsmith sold the book ; Prior, as usual, writes so loosely as to be ambiguous, and Forster, although, in his last edition, he cites Reed and Aikin as his authorities, affirms that Griffiths sold it to Dilly. None of these statements would seem to be exactly accurate. The translation of the " Memoirs of a Protestant " was in reality sold by the author — much as, some years since, it was ascertained that the " Vicar of Wakefield " was sold [1] — in three separate shares. By the kindness of the

[1] See the Preface to the *facsimile* Reproduction of the First Edition, Elliot Stock, 1885.

late Mr. Edward Ford of Enfield, a devoted
student of Goldsmith, the present writer was
favoured with a transcript of Goldsmith's receipt
for one of these shares from the hitherto unpublished original in Mr. Ford's possession.[1] It
runs as follows : —

LONDON, Jany 11th, 1758

Rec'd of Mr Edward Dilly six pounds thirteen shillings
and four pence, in full for his third share of my translation of a Book entitled *Memoirs of a Protestant condemned
to the Gallies for Religion,* &c.

OLIVER GOLDSMITH.

£ 6 13*s.* 4*d.*

From this document — the signature only of
which is in the handwriting of the poet — two
things are clear, — first, that Goldsmith himself
sold the book to Dilly and two others, one being
Griffiths, whose name is on the title-page ; and,
secondly, that the translation was by Goldsmith
and not by James Willington.

But why, it may be asked, was the name of
Willington (an old Trinity College acquaintance
of Goldsmith) put forward in this connection ?
The question is one to which it is not easy to give
an entirely satisfactory answer. Mr. Forster,

---

[1] This interesting relic now [1898] belongs to his son
and successor, Mr. J. W. Ford, of Enfield Old Park.

it is true, does not feel any difficulty in replying. " At this point," he says, " there is very mani- fest evidence of despair." But it is a character- istic of Mr. Forster's sympathetic and admira- ble biography that it occasionally appears to be written under the influence of preconceptions, and the evidence he mentions, however manifest, is certainly not produced. Mr. Forster fills the gap with eloquent disquisition on the obstacles in the path of genius, and so conducts his hero back to Dr. Milner's door at Peckham.[1] How Goldsmith subsisted in the interval between his ceasing to write regularly for the *Monthly Review* and his return to his old work as an usher, is no doubt obscure. But it is probable that there was little variation in his manner of living, although his labours were not performed under *surveillance* in the Back Parlour of the " Dun- ciad." It has been discovered that about this time he was contributing portions of a " History

---

[1] " Time's devouring hand," it may be noted here (for the Chronicler of the fugitive must make his record where he can), has now removed all trace of Dr. John Milner's Peckham Academy, which stood in Goldsmith Road (formerly Park Lane), opposite the southern end of Lower Park Road. " Goldsmith House," as it was called latterly, was pulled down in 1891. A sketch of it appeared in the *Daily Graphic* for 24th February in that year.

of Our Own Times " to the *Literary Magazine ;*
and it is also conjectured that these were not
his sole contributions to that and other periodicals. Moreover, the version of Marteilhe's
" Memoirs " must have been made in the last
months of 1757, since the above receipt is dated
January 11, 1758, and the book was published
in the following February. In addition to this,
he was again, by his own account, attending
patients as a doctor. " By a very little practice
as a physician, and a very little reputation as a
poet " — he tells his brother-in-law, Hodson, in
December, 1757, " I make a shift to live."
He was in debt, no doubt ; but he had already,
says the same communication, " discharged his
most threatening and pressing demands." Upon
the whole, — Mr. Forster's " very manifest evidence " not being forthcoming, — it must be
concluded that Goldsmith's position after ceasing to write for the *Monthly Review* (though not
for Griffiths) was much what it had been before
that event, perhaps even better, because he was
more free ; and this being so, we are driven to
the commonplace solution that, even in his Salisbury Square garret, he was too conscious of
those higher things within him to care to identify himself with a mere imitation " out of the
French," executed for bread, and not for repu-

tation ; and that he put Willington's name to the
book in default of a better. He gave evidence
of his genius in his most careless private letter ;
he could not help it ; but the man who subsequently refrained from signing the " Citizen of
the World," may be excused from signing the
translated " Memoirs of a Protestant."

That the translation produced under these
conditions might have been better if the translator had taken more pains, is but to turn Goldsmith's *bon mot* against himself. " *Verbum
verbo reddere* " was scarcely his ambition, and
those who wish for plain-sailing fidelity will do
well, if they cannot compass the French original,
to consult the rendering prepared for the Religious Tract Society.[1] The chief merits of the
version of 1758 are first, that it is a contemporary version, demonstrably from Goldsmith's pen ; and secondly, that it is Goldsmith's
earliest appearance in book-form. It is not
only characterised by its writer's unique and
peculiar charm, but it is as delightful to read as
any of his acknowledged journey-work. Even
Griffiths of the " Dunciad," who reviewed it
himself in the *Monthly Review* for May, 1758,

[1] This rendering, however, is incomplete, inasmuch as
it omits the " Description of the Galleys," etc., about
ninety of the final pages of the original.

cannot deny its merits in this respect. Speaking
of the "ingenious Translator," he remarks that
he " really deserves this epithet, on account of
the spirit of the performance, tho'," he adds,
grudgingly, " we have little to say in commendation of his accuracy. Upon this latter
count, it may be observed that in one instance,
at least, inaccuracy is excusable. In telling,
early in the book, the story of the abjuration by
Marteilhe's mother of her Huguenot faith, Goldsmith makes her add to her declaration that she
was " compelled by Fear." This is manifestly
inexact, seeing that the French original runs :
" *Elle ajouta ces mots :* la Force me le fait faire,
faisant sans doute allusion au nom du Duc " (i. e.
the Duke de la Force). All this, as we know,
must have been Greek to Goldsmith, because
the names in the *editio princeps* of 1757, from
which he was working, were not given at full.
But it must certainly be admitted that he deals
freely with his text, occasionally suppressing
altogether what he regards as redundant, and now
and then inserting supplementary touches of his
own. Speaking of the soup prepared in the
gaol at Lille he says : " Even *Lacedæmonian*
black Broth could not be more nauseous."
There is nothing in the text of this classic die-
tary, and what is more, Marteilhe would scarcely

have used the simile.   Elsewhere the decoration
is in what Matthew Arnold used to call the
" Rule Britannia " vein.   Of the valiant captain
of the *Nightingale* who held his own so long
against the galleys in that memorable engagement
which plays such a moving part in Marteilhe's
record, the writer says : " *Ce capitaine, qui
n'avait plus rien à faire pour mettre sa flotte en
sûreté, rendit son épée.*"   This Goldsmith trans-
lates : " At last the captain gave up his Sword
without further Parley, like a true Englishman,
despising Ceremony, when Ceremony could be
no longer useful."

Dealing in this place rather with the story
of the book than its contents, it would be beyond
the purpose of our paper to linger longer upon
the extraordinary interest and simple candour of
Marteilhe's narrative.   But the mention just
made of the captain of the *Nightingale* reminds
us that some further particulars respecting this
obscure naval hero were not long since brought
to light by Professor J. K. Laughton.[1]   His
name (which Marteilhe had forgotten) was Seth
Jermy, and he had served as a lieutenant at the
battle of Barfleur.   He became captain of the
Spy brigantine in January, 1697, and five years
later was appointed to the command of the

---

[1] *English Historical Review,* January, 1889, pp. 65-80.

Nightingale, a small 24-gun frigate, chiefly employed in convoying corn-ships and colliers
between the Forth, the Tyne, the Humber, and
the Thames. In this duty he was engaged up
to the fight with the French galleys, which took
place, not, as Marteilhe says, in 1708, but in
1707. In August, 1708, Captain Jermy returned from France on parole and was tried by
court-martial for the loss of his ship. The following are the minutes of the trial from documents in the Public Record Office : —

"At a court-martial held on board her Maj-
esty's ship the *Royal Anne* at Spithead, on
Thursday, 23 Sep. 1708; Present : The Hon.
Sir George Byng, Knight, Admiral of the Blue
Squadron of her Majesty's fleet. . . .

" Enquiry was made by the Court into the
occasion of the loss of her Majesty's ship the
Nightingale, of which Captain Seth Jermy was
late commander, which was taken by six sail
of the enemy's galleys off Harwich on 24 Aug.
1707. The court having strictly examined into
the matter, it appeared by evidence upon oath
that the *Nightingale* was for a considerable time
engaged with a much superior force of the
enemy, and did make so good a defence as
thereby to give an opportunity to all the ships
under his convoy to make their escape ; and it

is the opinion of the court that he has not been anyway wanting in his duty on that occasion ; and therefore the Court does acquit the said Captain Jermy and the other officers as to the loss of Her Majesty's said ship *Nightingale*."

Beyond the fact that he was exchanged against a French prisoner a little later, served again, was superannuated, and died in 1724, nothing further seems to be known of Captain Jermy. But of the captain who succeeded him on the *Nightingale* when that ship passed by capture into French hands — the infamous renegade whom Marteilhe calls "—— Smith,—" Professor Laughton supplies data which, since they are included only in one very limited edition of the " Memoirs," may here be briefly set down. After chequered experiences in the service of her Majesty Queen Anne, including a court-martial for irregularities while commanding the *Bonetta* sloop, Thomas Smith, being then, according to his own account, a prisoner at Dunkirk, yielded to solicitations made to him, and entered the service of the King of France. In November, 1707, he was made commander of the captured *Nightingale*. In the December following, being in company with another Dunkirk privateer, the *Squirrel*, he was chased and taken by the English man-of-war *Ludlow Castle*,

Captain Haddock. Smith was brought to London, tried for high treason at the Old Bailey (2nd June, 1708), and found guilty. " On 18th June he was put on a hurdle and conveyed to the place of execution. . . . Being dead he was cut down, his body opened and his heart shown to the people, and afterwards burnt with his bowels, and his body quartered." And thus Marteilhe, when he came to London in 1713 to thank Queen Anne for her part in his release, may well, as he avers, have seen Smith's mangled remains " exposed on Gibbets along the Banks of the *Thames*."

Marteilhe's story, it may be gathered, differs in some respects from the official account disinterred from the Public Records. But the discrepancies are readily explained by the fact that much which he related must have been acquired at second hand. Speaking from his personal experience, he is accurate enough. What is known of him and his book, beyond the date at which it closes, needs but few words. "The author [of the ' Memoirs ']," says Goldsmith in his Preface of 1757, " is still alive, and known to numbers, not only in *Holland* but *London;*" and it is quite possible that in one or other of these places, Goldsmith himself may have seen and conversed with him. An *Aver-*

tissement des Libraires prefixed to the Rotterdam edition, but not reproduced by Goldsmith or M. Paumier, is equally confirmatory of the authenticity of the book : " *Des Personnes de caractère, & dignes de toute créance, nous ont assurés, que cet Ouvrage à été véritablement composé par un de ces Protestans, condamnés aux Galères de France pour cause de Religion, & qui en furent délivrés par l'intercession de la Reine* ANNE *d'Angleterre peu après la paix* d'Utrecht. *Les mêmes Personnes nous ont dit, qu'elles ont eu des liaisons personnelles avec l'Auteur ; qu'elles ne doutent pas de sa bonne foi & de sa probité ; & qu'elles sont persuadées, qu'autant que sa mémoire a pu lui rappeller les faits, cette Relation est exacte.*" Opposite the word " *créance,*" in the British Museum copy, is written in an old hand, " Mrs. Dumont & De Superville." As Daniel de Superville Senior was dead in 1757, the De Superville here mentioned was no doubt his son of the same Christian name, — a doctor, who, as above suggested, was probably the editor of Marteilhe's manuscripts. After this come naturally the details given, from Coquerel and elsewhere, in M. Paumier's second Preface, and already referred to. Marteilhe, we learn, did not reside permanently in the Netherlands — " that Land of Liberty and Happiness," as

Goldsmith renders " *Ces heureuses Provinces* "
— but for some time was in business in London
He died at Cuylenberg, in Guelderland, on tho
4th November, 1777, at the age of ninety-three.
Little is known about his family; but it is
believed that he had a daughter who was married at Amsterdam to an English naval officer
of distinction, Vice-Admiral Douglas.

GENERAL INDEX.

GENERAL INDEX.

A.

Abbaye, the Prison of the, 40.

Abbey, Edwin A., 166.

Abel, 41, 42.

Abington, Mrs. Fanny, 104, 304.

Absolon, 177.

Achilles, Gay's, 270.

Ackermann, 174.

Adam and Eve Gallery, the, 192.

Adams, Parson, 79.

Addington ministry, the, 149.

Addison, Joseph, Goldsmith's admiration for and imitation of, 12, 15; *Letter from Italy to Lord Halifax*, 15; 57, 58, 60, 61, 76, 77, 81, 82, 84, 158, 245; *Cato*, 256; 286.

Addison, Life of, Miss Aiken's, 57.

Admiralty buildings, the new, 234.

Agas, Ralph, 221, 222, 231, 277.

Aguecheek, Sir Andrew, Dodd as, 105.

Aiken, Miss, *Life of Addison*, 57.

Aikin, Dr. John, 313, 314.

Aitken, George A., *Life of Richard Steele*, 57–86; 239.

Aix, 259, 260.

Albano, 154.

Albany, the, 53.

Albemarle, Duke of, 186, 187.

Albemarle Street, 54.

Albinus, 91.

Alembert, D', 55.

Alexander Le Imaginator, 223.

Alhambra, the, 275, 276.

Alhambra Company, the, 302.

Alkrington, 293.

Allen's, of Prior Park, 102, 103

Allworthy, Fielding's, 102.

"Almack's," 205, 210, 212.

Almanac Généalogique, the, 179.

Alvanley, Lord, 204.

Amelia, Fielding's, 115.

America, 7.

Amesbury, 37, 38, 268, 269.

Amiens, the Peace of, 149.

Amorevoli, 289.

Amsterdam, 308, 325.

Anacréon, 157.

Analysis of the Gaelic Language, an, 114.

Anatomy of the Horse, Stubbs', 42.

Anderson, Alexander, 173.

Double Dealer, the, 101.
Double Transformation, The,
  Goldsmith's, 13; Prior the
  model for, 13.
Douglas, Charles, 240.
Douglas, Home's, 313.
Douglas, Vice-Admiral, 325.
Dover, 163.
Dover, the Duke of, 240.
Dragon, the, man-of-war, 36.
Drake, 76.
Drayton, Michael, 278.
Dress, Gay on, 250.
Dromore, Bishop of, 229.
Drummer, the, Addison's, 58.
Drummond's Bank, 237.
Drury Lane, 23, 28, 42, 44, 67.
Drury Lane Theatre, 80, 97, 98,
  250, 255, 261.
Dryden, John, Goldsmith's ad-
  miration for the work of, 12;
  Quack Maurus, 64; 142, 143.
Dublin, 7, 9, 60, 270, 282.
Dublin street-singers, Gold-
  smith's ballads for, 9.
Duchesnois, Mlle., 156, 158.
Dugazon, 158.
Duill, Mrs., 105.
Du Maurier, 166.
Dumont, Mrs., 324.
Duncannon Street, 231.
Dunciad, Griffith's, 312, 313,
  316, 318.
Dunciad, Pope's, 109.
Dunkirk, 78, 322.
Duperrier, François, 194.
Dupont, Gainsborough, 144.
Dutch school, the, 153.
Dyer, 117.
Dyers, the, 80.

E.

EATON SQUARE, 107.
Eclogues, Gay's, 273.
Ecole des Armes, the elder
  Angelo's, 55.
*Écoles de Notre Dame de
  France,* 294.
Edgeware, 295.
Edgware, 27.
Edinburgh, the, 57.
Edward VI., 192.
Edwin and Angelina, Gold-
  smith's, 17.
Egerton, T., 56.
Eginton, 172.
Egleton, Mrs., 265.
Église Réformée, l', 310.
Egmont's MSS., Lord, 77.
Eighteenth Century Vignettes,
  Dobson's First Series, 269;
  Second Series, 233; Third
  Series, 237, 288, 293.
Eleanor, Queen, 220, 221, 222.
Election Entertainment, the,
  238.
Election of Gotham, the, 67.
Elegy, Gray's, 12; Goldsmith's
  criticism of, 12.
*Elegy on the Death of a Mad
  Dog,* Goldsmith's, 14, 15, 181,
  182.
Elizabeth of Bohemia, 279.
Elizabeth, Queen, 150, 185, 221.
Elliot's Light Horse, 34.
Ellis, Dr. Welbore, 61.
Elphinston, Mr., 114.
Elwin, Mr., 250.
Embankment, the, 191.
Empire, the, 276.

360